The Scholarship of Academic Development

SRHE and Open University Press Imprint
General Editor: Heather Eggins

Current titles include:

Catherine Bargh *et al.*: *University Leadership*
Ronald Barnett: *Beyond All Reason*
Ronald Barnett: *The Idea of Higher Education*
Ronald Barnett: *The Limits of Competence*
Ronald Barnett: *Higher Education*
Ronald Barnett: *Realizing the University in an age of supercomplexity*
Tony Becher and Paul R Trowler: *Academic Tribes and Territories (second edition)*
John Biggs: *Teaching for Quality Learning at University*
David Boud *et al.* (eds): *Using Experience for Learning*
David Boud and Nicky Solomon (eds): *Work-based Learning*
Tom Bourner *et al.* (eds): *New Directions in Professional Higher Education*
Anne Brockbank and Ian McGill: *Facilitating Reflective Learning in Higher Education*
Ann Brooks and Alison Mackinnon (eds): *Gender and the Restructured University*
Sally Brown and Angela Glasner (eds): *Assessment Matters in Higher Education*
James Cornford and Neil Pollock: *Putting the University Online*
John Cowan: *On Becoming an Innovative University Teacher*
Gerard Delanty: *Challenging Knowledge*
Chris Duke: *Managing the Learning University*
Heather Eggins and Ranald Macdonald (eds): *The Scholarship of Academic Development*
Gillian Evans: *Academics and the Real World*
Andrew Hannan and Harold Silver: *Innovating in Higher Education*
Norman Jackson and Helen Lund (eds): *Benchmarking for Higher Education*
David Istance *et al.* (eds): *International Perspectives on Lifelong Learning*
Merle Jacob and Tomas Hellström (eds): *The Future of Knowledge Production in the Academy*
Peter Knight: *Being a Teacher in Higher Education*
Peter Knight and Paul Trowler: *Departmental Leadership in Higher Education*
Ian McNay (ed.): *Higher Education and its Communities*
Moira Peelo and Terry Wareham (eds): *Failing Students in Higher Education*
Craig Prichard: *Making Managers in Universities and Colleges*
Michael Prosser and Keith Trigwell: *Understanding Learning and Teaching*
John Richardson: *Researching Student Learning*
Stephen Rowland: *The Enquiring University Teacher*
Maggi Savin-Baden: *Problem-based Learning in Higher Education*
Peter Scott (ed.): *The Globalization of Higher Education*
Peter Scott: *The Meanings of Mass Higher Education*
Anthony Smith and Frank Webster (eds): *The Postmodern University?*
Colin Symes and John McIntyre (eds): *Working Knowledge*
Richard Taylor *et al.*: *For a Radical Higher Education*
Susan Toohey: *Designing Courses for Higher Education*
Paul R. Trowler (ed.): *Higher Education Policy and Institutional Change*
Melanie Walker (ed.): *Reconstructing Professionalism in University Teaching*
David Warner and David Palfreyman (eds): *The State of UK Higher Education*
Gareth Williams (ed.): *The Enterprising University*

The Scholarship of Academic Development

Edited by
Heather Eggins
and Ranald Macdonald

The Society for Research into Higher Education
& Open University Press

Published by SRHE and
Open University Press
Celtic Court
22 Ballmoor
Buckingham
MK18 1XW

email: enquiries@openup.co.uk
world wide web: www.openup.co.uk

and
325 Chestnut Street
Philadelphia, PA 19106, USA

First Published 2003

A catalogue record of this book is available from the British Library

ISBN 0 335 21103 8 (pb)   0 335 21104 6 (hb)

Library of Congress Cataloging-in-Publication Data
The scholarship of academic development / edited by Heather Eggins and Ranald Macdonald.
p. cm.
Includes bibliographical references (p.) and index.
ISBN 0-335-21104-6 – ISBN 0-335-21103-8 (pbk.)
1. College teachers–In-service training. 2. Curriculum planning. 3. Learning and scholarship. I. Eggins, Heather. II. Macdonald, Ranald, 1952–

LB1738 .S39 2003
378.1′2′00715–dc21   2002074958

Typeset by Graphicraft Limited, Hong Kong
Printed by St Edmundsbury Press, Bury St Edmunds, Suffolk

This book is dedicated to
Viv Macdonald
and
Rosanne Eggins

Contents

Contributors

Peter D. Ashworth is Professor of Educational Research and Director of the Learning and Teaching Research Institute at Sheffield Hallam University, UK.

Liz Beaty is Director of the Centre for Higher Education Development at Coventry University, UK.

Tom Bourner is Co-Director of the University of Brighton's Management Development Research Unit, UK.

Angela Brew works in the Institute for Teaching and Learning at the University of Sydney, Australia.

Glynis Cousin is Senior Research Fellow in the Centre for Higher Education Development at Coventry University, UK.

Heather Eggins is Director of the Society for Research into Higher Education, UK.

Graham Gibbs is Director of the Centre for Higher Education Practice at the Open University, UK.

David Gosling is Co-Director, National Coordination Team, Centre for Higher Education Practice, Open University, UK.

Mick Healey is Professor of Geography at the University of Gloucestershire and Director of the Geography Discipline Network, UK.

Alan Jenkins is an educational developer in the Oxford Centre for Staff and Learning Development at Oxford Brookes University, UK.

Ray Land is Director of the Centre for Teaching, Learning and Assessment at the University of Edinburgh, UK.

Gregory Light is the Director of the Searle Center for Teaching Excellence at Northwestern University, Chicago, USA.

Ranald Macdonald is Head of Academic Development in the Learning and Teaching Institute at Sheffield Hallam University, UK.

Sarah J. Mann is a lecturer in the Teaching and Learning Service at the University of Glasgow, UK.

Roger Murphy is Director of the Institute for Research into Learning and Teaching in Higher Education at the University of Nottingham, UK.

Suzanne O'Hara is Co-Director of the University of Brighton's Management Development Research Unit, UK.

Stephen Rowland is Professor of Higher Education in the Department of Education and Professional Development at University College London, UK.

Keith Trigwell is Principal Research Fellow in the Institute for the Advancement of University Learning at the University of Oxford, UK.

Trix Webber is MBA Programme Leader in Brighton Business School at the University of Brighton, UK.

Mantz Yorke is Professor of Higher Education in the Centre for Higher Education Development at Liverpool John Moores University, UK.

Preface

This book is published at a time when the academic community is re-evaluating and reconceptualizing the role of academic developers within higher education institutions. Its history relates back to a 1999 Conference jointly organized by the Staff and Educational Development Association and the Society for Research into Higher Education whose theme was 'Research and Practice in Educational Development(s): Exploring the links'. Collaboration between the two bodies has brought positive advantages to both groups. The Society, founded in the early 1960s, had developed a strong Staff Development Group which, in 1992, merged with the Standing Conference on Educational Development in order to form the SEDA whose remit was specifically concerned with staff and educational development.

The Society, meanwhile, continued to publish influential books on all aspects of staff and academic development, as part of its mission 'to stimulate and publish research into all aspects of higher education'. It is noteworthy that virtually every chapter in this volume contains references to books published by SRHE/Open University Press, and the work of its authors is frequently cited in the text.

The 1999 joint Conference, however, came at a key moment when the academic community was beginning to recognize that there was a need for rigorous research studies on academic development itself. The world was changing: the Quality Assurance Agency in the UK and other similar bodies elsewhere had a remit to assess the quality of teaching and learning, and make recommendations which impinged on academic development. The Higher Education Funding Council for England, and its counterpart in Scotland, were recognizing that teaching and learning, learning and teaching, were moving up the agenda. Questions were beginning to be asked concerning research findings into academic development and into all aspects of learning and teaching.

At that point, 1999, the area was a thinly researched field. There were some thoughtful, thorough studies available, but their significance had not been teased out. There was little funding to support the area. Tony Becher's seminal book, *Academic Tribes and Territories* had come out in 1989, and Ernest Boyer's *Scholarship Reconsidered: priorities of the professoriate* in 1990. Graham Webb had published *Understanding Staff Development* in 1996. It is a mark of the modern world that one of these titles came out of the UK, one from the US and one from the Antipodes.

Following the 1999 Conference the editors decided that a book which would draw together the work being done on the topic of the 'scholarship of academic development' would be timely. Several of those who had made presentations at that conference are included in this volume, for example Sarah Mann and Mantz Yorke. New perspectives were opening up and the pace of research and publishing in this area has undergone noticeable development since that decision was taken.

We present this volume, therefore, as a contribution to a specific research area, that of academic development. The place of the academic developer in our community is now attracting serious attention. Major funding will be available within the next year to strengthen the research base.

Angela Brew writes in the concluding chapter of this book 'Academic developers need to be at the forefront of encouraging academics to be open to new problems and new questions and finding new ways of searching for new solutions.' We hope that the volume will enable this group of scholars to be recognized for their value to the whole of the academic community and for their ongoing contribution to the complex society of the twenty-first century.

The editors also wish to acknowledge the support of their families, and helpful discussions with colleagues, in enabling the book to be finalized. Thanks are particularly due to Rosanne Eggins who contributed much time and effort to putting the editorial changes into the text.

Heather Eggins
London
June 2002

1

Developing a Scholarship of Academic Development: Setting the Context

Ranald Macdonald

Introduction

The title of the book and of this chapter are immediately problematic in that they involve two terms – scholarship and academic development – which are neither well understood nor have unambiguous and widely-shared meanings. The chapters in the book also reflect a variety of approaches and definitions from the extremely broad to the very narrow. What many have in common is a reference to the pioneering work of Ernest Boyer (1990a). Further, in common with most of the chapters in this book, this chapter draws primarily on writings from the English-speaking world and, even more specifically, on those from the US, Australia and the UK.

It may be overly dramatic to suggest that academic development is at a crossroads, but it is certainly at a point where a serious evaluation of what it is, who the academic developers are and what they do, is timely, not least in the context of the debate about professionalization of roles within higher education. Further, in times of pressure on financial resources, the search for savings often focuses on those elements which do not contribute directly to the core business of the institution – research and teaching. As a result, the case needs to be made for academic development to be recognized as a legitimate area, with its own traditions of research, scholarship and practice. Or, to draw on Becher and Trowler (2001), is it time for academic development to receive recognition as an academic tribe with its own territory?

A number of writers (Fraser 2001; Gosling 2001) have recently carried out surveys of what academic developers do and what they conceive as their role. Here we are more concerned with conceptualizing academic development and examining the nature of scholarship within it. As a result the book is divided into two main sections; first, on the nature or conceptualization of academic development and, second, on the nature of research in academic development. However, as will be argued later in this chapter, it is not the research *per se* which makes academic development scholarly but rather its role within the approach to the practice of academic development.

A contrasting picture of academic development will be found by reading both this introductory chapter and the concluding one by Angela Brew. At first sight they would appear to be covering the same ground, but the outcomes are significantly different. It is interesting to note that Angela is a British, Australia-based academic developer, who works in a country where interest in the modern notions of scholarship as developed by Boyer and others took root far earlier than in the UK. In a sense this book represents a 'catching up' whilst in another it is a unique collection representative of the growing scholarly outputs of the academic development profession.

What is 'academic development'?

The definition of 'academic' development itself proves problematic. However, the decision to include it in the title follows a meeting of a number of the authors who felt that this was becoming a widely used and understood term. Following on from Boyer's (1990a) notions of the scholarship of research, application, integration and teaching, a scholarship of academic development was also thought to fit well within the current discourse of practice in higher education.

There is some debate as to whether academic development is what people 'know' or what they 'do' and whether it is a profession or an activity. The following two quotes, whilst not necessarily fully inclusive of those engaged in the field or the activities in which they engage, may prove a useful starting point:

> . . . academic development is taken to mean practices designed to enhance the academic performance of an institution of higher education. For purposes of convenience, this is assumed to subdivide into staff (often in North America, faculty) development, where the focus is on enhancing the professional competence of academic faculty members; and educational development, which includes curriculum development and instructional design, as well as input to policies governing the design, delivery, evaluation and recognition of teaching.
>
> (Candy 1996: 17)

> . . . an academic developer is any person who has a role in which they are explicitly expected to work with academics to assist them to reflect upon their academic role in relation to teaching, research, scholarship, leadership, funding applications and supervision of students. An academic developer may also work at a departmental/institutional level in a developmental role.
>
> (Fraser 2001: 55)

Rowland (2001) defines academic development as currently practised as 'the field of teaching and learning in higher education' and hence sees it operating primarily at a generic level as a support service, with little contact with educationists in their institutions. Others also adopt this narrower definition, which fails to identify or acknowledge the wider range of activities in which academic developers engage, particularly in policy, strategy and more developmental areas.

Whilst it might be going too far to say that the area is contested, it is true to say that there is no one dominant approach, not least because of the different traditions within institutions and between countries. It has even proved too much to find agreement on a commonly understood term to describe the area of practice. The term 'educational development' is widely used in the UK, partly to distinguish it from staff ('faculty' in the US) development but also variously encompassing terms such as 'academic' or 'professional' development (Macdonald 2002). Webb (1996a: 1) chooses to use the term 'staff development', whilst acknowledging that 'in tertiary institutions such as universities staff and/or professional development has mostly been concerned with educational development – the development of teaching and learning'.

The term 'academic development' is becoming more widely used, not least in Australia and increasingly in the UK, though as Fraser (2001: 57) notes in her report of a survey of Australian academics 'educational development was conceptualised by some to be a subset of academic development while others believed the reverse'. She goes on to conclude that 'I conceive of academic development as sitting within staff development and educational development as overlapping with academic development' (p. 61).

Fraser attributes the term 'staff development' to work with academic and non-academic staff, whilst academic development relates to developmental work specific to academics and includes the development of research and teaching roles. She describes educational development as focusing on teaching and notes that it can occur at individual, departmental, faculty and institutional level. Similarly, Hounsell (1994) sees educational development as being concerned with 'sustaining and enhancing the quality of learning and teaching within the institution.'

Baume and Baume (1994: 9) distinguish between staff development for pedagogy – 'a matter of training teachers in certain reasonably well-defined skills, attitudes and approaches' – and educational development – 'working with people to solve their educational problems, to meet their educational challenges'. Whilst acknowledging that they may be oversimplifying the situation in the process, they summarize the difference as that 'staff development implies workshops and trainer-led content and, sometimes, client boredom or, hopefully, storage of ideas and techniques for future use. Educational development implies consultancy and client-led content and, usually, client active participation and immediate use of what is learnt'.

So, with some minor areas of disagreement, we are probably closer to a definition of academic development, which encompasses those activities concerned with developing learning and teaching at individual, departmental, faculty, institutional and even at national/international level (as evidenced by the activities of the International Consortium for Educational Development). However, Webb (1996c: 65) argues that 'there should be no model for educational and staff development; we should be looking for edification (enlightenment, knowledge, learning) – which are always in process – rather than closure upon a particular foundational position.' Further, in a paper on the pragmatic scholarship of academic development, Badley (2000) also concludes that 'I espouse an eclectic model of academic development that encourages inquiry into, and continuous conversation (indeed contestations) about, our problems and our practices with the objective of producing nothing more than useful, though perhaps tentative, suggestions for action.'

There is perhaps the first sign with Webb and Badley of the tension some see between the academic developer as an 'expert' as against them being a partner or colleague working towards the understanding of a situation or resolution of a problem.

What do academic developers do and how do they do it?

One of the problems for academic developers is knowing what impact our practice has. Our role is often described as being to improve the quality of teaching and learning in our institutions but we often have little direct contact with students to be able to evaluate the effectiveness of what we are doing. Ours is an indirect effect through staff, who will take the credit or blame for the impact of the changes they implement. Similarly, where we are engaged in organizational development activities, we may be unable to measure the impact of our activities separate from the other players with whom we work.

In itself this is not a problem, except to the extent that we all value recognition for what we do and need feedback on the effectiveness of how well we are doing it. Additionally, the roles, responsibilities and even location of academic developers have changed over time. Boud (1999: 4) identifies a number of qualitatively different phases in the development of academic development with key theoretical ideas associated with each phase. Firstly, development can be seen as being 'embedded and invisible in academic life', followed by 'development as a moral imperative', 'development as corporate policy' and, finally, 'development as multidimensional and distributed'. In describing the recent phase of academic development as 'reciprocal peer learning' or 'localized practice', Boud sees the need for the bringing together of central and local activities to counter the criticisms and enhance the strengths of both. In particular, whilst local development activities 'are often limited by a tendency to parochialism, a lack of awareness of research on higher education and the reinforcement of bad habits which occurs when existing cultural practices are taken for granted' (p. 5) they are more likely to ensure that new initiatives become embedded in changing work patterns of departments.

In analyzing how academic development officers go about their work, Gosling (1997) conceptualized five broad approaches: the 'reflective practitioner' approach, the 'educational researcher' approach; the 'professional competency' approach; the 'human resources' or 'managerial' approach; and the educational developer as a consultant or expert with the role of disseminating best practice. Contrast these with Land (2001, and in this text) who identifies twelve orientations to academic development, or 'variations in practice'. The orientation(s) – 'which include the attitudes, knowledge, aims and action tendencies of academic developers in relation to the contexts and challenges of their practice' – to be effective, will need to be congruent with the organizational culture in which the developer finds him or herself.

Recognizing that academic development has, in recent years, moved for the margins to the mainstream in many institutions, Candy (1996) contrasts the role of staff and educational development in industrial organizations – 'fundamentally deficit-oriented, designed to remedy shortcomings in people's current level of skill' (p. 8) – with knowledge-based organizations, where the nature of the work is non-repetitive, non-standardized, and involves problem-solving (p. 9). In the latter case, where it is those who are able to develop non-standardized solutions to non-recurrent problems who are valued most, it is investment in this expertise that gives the organization its competitive advantage. Arguing that staff development in higher education should meet the needs of a learning organization, Candy develops what he terms the CAREER model of staff development: 'Comprehensive, Anticipatory, Research-based, Exemplary, Embedded, Reflective and Geared towards the notion of lifelong personal and professional development' (p. 11).

In his follow-up survey of the activities of educational development units in the UK, Gosling (2001) summarizes other writers as identifying aspects such as improvements of teaching and assessment practices, curriculum design and learning support; professional development of academic staff; organizational and policy development; and learning development of students. Quoting the work of Badley and Webb who note, respectively, that much of the writing on educational development offered no place for research or scholarship and that 'development' itself is a contested term, Gosling (2001: 75) adds two further elements to the definition of higher educational development: 'Informed debate about learning, teaching, assessment, curriculum design, and the goals of higher education; and promotion of the scholarship of teaching and learning and research into higher education goals and practices.'

Candy (1996: 16) contends that academic developers should be identified, not as para-professionals, but as meta-professionals, who are academics par excellence. He argues that their effectiveness in changing individual attitudes and institutional culture 'is dependent on being, and on being seen to be, reputable academics whose area of research and teaching happens to be higher education itself'. Which leads us nicely on to the notion of scholarship and academic development.

The scholarly dimension of academic development

Whilst 'scholarship' obviously has a long tradition of being used often, but not always, as a substitute for research, in recent times it is the work of Ernest Boyer (1990a) at the Carnegie Foundation for the Advancement of Teaching in the US which opened a whole new debate about what it is and what it means to be 'scholarly'. Boyer's ideas are widely quoted but it is to the writings of such as Rice (1992), Glassick *et al.* (1997) and Hutchings and Shulman (1999) that many look for interpretations or adaptations.

Whilst many writers continue to use the categorizations of scholarship outlined by Boyer – discovery, application, integration and teaching – many feel that Boyer did not go far enough in drawing a clear distinction between excellent teaching and the scholarship of teaching (research, application or integration). Hutchings and Shulman (1999: 13) contend that all teachers have an obligation to teach well but that the scholarship of teaching involves four additional attributes – being public or 'community property', open to critique and evaluation, in a form that others can build on and involving question-asking, inquiry and investigation, particularly around issues of student learning. The same attributes should perhaps equally apply to 'scholarly' academic developers.

In noting that Boyer argues that each discipline or professional area has to define scholarship for itself, Brew (2001: 32) contends that in some disciplines 'scholarship is less relevant than others, for example professional areas which do not have a tradition of scholarship'. However, there would seem to be no reason why a professional area, including academic development, cannot work within established scholarly conventions to establish its own traditions. For example, Brew, in reporting her earlier work, identifies five conceptions of scholarship: preparation; adding new knowledge to the existing literature; dissemination through, for example, publication and teaching; scholarship and research being the same thing; and *the way* in which academics work, referring to 'the qualities of meticulousness and rigour associated with academic inquiry and reporting'. This latter category Brew refers to as the 'quality variation'. It would seem to be quite appropriate to start defining the scholarship of academic development using the last conception identified by Brew.

So, what does it take to make academic developers scholarly?

Andresen (1996: 44) argues that academic developers are professional because 'we are academics: we do academic work by pursuing and advancing scholarship within our own field in (and sometimes outside of) higher education institutions'. 'Our own field' may be our original discipline, a transdisciplinary notion, or Higher Education Studies – an area also identified by Candy (1996) and Rowland (2001).

In a report based on the findings of the Carnegie Foundation's 'National Survey on the Re-examination of Faculty Roles and Rewards', Glassick *et al.* (1997: 25) found that all works of scholarship go through a series of unfolding stages. These stages – having clear goals, adequate preparation, appropriate methods, significant results, effective presentation and reflective critique – subsequently 'provide a powerful conceptual framework to guide evaluation'. This categorization of the standards for scholarly work provides a challenge for academic developers. To take one element of the process, reflective critique, Glassick *et al.* (1997: 36) define the standard as: 'Does the scholar critically evaluate his or her own work? Does the scholar bring an appropriate breadth of evidence to his or her critique? Does the scholar use evaluation to improve the quality of future work?'.

We might ask similar questions of our activities as academic developers.

In arguing that 'for the health of their profession and the enhancement of its contribution to the whole academic enterprise', Andresen (1996: 47) suggests that 'academic developers must continue to participate in relevant discourse about their theory and practice. They should develop their capacity to hand on their practices and discourse, learning from and contributing to appropriate academic disciplines (e.g., the study of Higher Education) and engaging in pragmatic self-criticism'. However, in his more recent writing Andresen (2000a: 139) warns against 'scholarship' becoming a meaningless buzzword, 'progressively less useable for conveying the distinctions or specificities they were originally coined for, they finally deserve the philosophers' ultimate put-down of empty concepts'.

Research as part of academic development

Whilst many academic developers have come from disciplines where they established their academic credentials through research, teaching and other scholarly activities, the growth of research into educational development activities is a relatively recent phenomenon. Increasing use has been made of the research into, for example, student learning, but research into the support for teaching which makes use of the earlier findings or of institutional initiatives to improve both the quality of teaching and the learner's experience are relatively new within higher education.

In support of a more research-focused approach to our work, the launch of *The International Journal for Academic Development* in 1996 sought to 'enable staff and educational developers around the world to debate and extend the theory and practice of academic development, in support of the quality of higher education' (front page). In the journal's first editorial, Baume (1996) wrote that the journal's distinctive focus 'will thus be the processes of helping institutions, departments, course teams and individual staff to research into, reflect on and develop policy and practice into teaching, learning and other activities in support of learning'.

Much of the research is thus focused on educational practice and policy within higher education as either part of the process of change or in evaluating the effectiveness of that change (Macdonald 2002). The methods used are wide and well-represented by the contributions in this book, though there has been an emphasis on qualitative research methods, drawing extensively from social science research traditions.

However, in seeking to work collaboratively with colleagues, there has been extensive use made of action research as a way of researching developing or changing practices in learning and teaching (Zuber-Skerritt 1992b). Beaty *et al.* (1997) advocate action research for use by academic developers 'because it involves an experiential learning cycle that fuses research, development and evaluation into a dynamic process'. They go on to articulate their own approach – 'consultancy style action research' – as an appropriate variant because it is based on a triangular partnership involving 'the knowledge of the educational developer, the skills and time of the social researcher and the concerns and expertise of staff'. In fact it provides a good example of a collaborative, collegial approach to development which contrasts with some of the more managerial tendencies (Rowland *et al.* 1998). However, Webb (1996a) warns us to exercise caution as there may be real or perceived power imbalances within an action research relationship. Action research by groups may lead to conformity where the individual may have been more radical and challenging of the *status quo.*

One area that has impacted significantly on academic development has been the use of phenomenography (Prosser and Trigwell 1999). Arguing that it is not a method in itself nor a theory of experience, Marton and Booth (1997: 111) describe phenomenography as 'a way of – an approach to – identifying, formulating, and tackling certain sorts of research questions, a specialization that is particularly aimed at questions of relevance to learning and understanding in an educational setting'. The approach is used as a way of seeing the qualitatively different ways in which people are capable of experiencing various phenomena, particularly learning or, in the context of this book, scholarship (Brew 2001). It has been used as such by researchers and academic developers as a way of better understanding the context in which they are working.

Another distinction to be made is that between research and evaluation (Macdonald 2002), which may or may not use the same methodologies, but may differ in the intentions and outcomes expected. Scott and Usher (1999) note that 'evaluators are more concerned with assessing the effectiveness, or describing the impact, of a deliberately engineered social intervention'. By contrast, 'researchers do not operate with such a close relationship between themselves and the initiators of those interventions, though they may still be dealing with the effects of policy interventions, since these are an abiding feature of educational systems.' However, the use made by academic developers of action research obviously draws this into question and perhaps exemplifies the blurring of the boundaries between research and evaluation.

The changing environment of academic development

Much of the literature makes assumptions about an homogeneous higher education sector. However, the reality is that there is considerable variation and variety, making it inappropriate to assume that all academics treat research as their primary activity and teaching as secondary. The US, in particular, exhibits much greater heterogeneity from community colleges to the research-intensive universities. Similarly, with the growth in higher education student numbers in further education colleges in the UK and greater selectivity in the allocation of research funds, this diversity between institutions is likely to increase further.

The roles of academic developers have also widened recently as, for example, in the UK where the Higher Education Funding Council for England launched its Teaching Quality Enhancement Fund, which has three strands – individual, institutional and subject-based. The institutional strand has involved institutions in developing and implementing learning and teaching strategies, providing an opportunity for academic developers to be at the centre of institutional policy making. Each institution receives entitlement funds, based on student numbers, rather than having to bid for them. The subject strand has involved the establishment of the Learning and Teaching Support Network, incorporating 24 subject centres and a generic centre. In addition, the funding council has supported a fourth round of projects under the Fund for the Development of Teaching and Learning.

These initiatives, together with various others, have provided a growing cadre of staff engaged in educational development activities, though not all of them would necessarily describe themselves as academic developers. Similarly, all countries have, to varying extents, experienced the growth of 'quality' initiatives such as that of the Quality Assurance Agency in the UK with its subject and academic review processes, codes of practice and other frameworks. In the UK, though perhaps less so in other countries, many academic developers have also been involved in developing accredited courses for teachers in higher education, often through programmes originally recognized by the Staff and Educational Development Association and now also by the Institute for Learning and Teaching.

However, the obvious tensions between supporting managerial 'top-down' initiatives and the needs or wishes of 'ordinary' staff mean that academic developers can sometimes feel like either the filling in a sandwich or as a cushion between conflicting interests. This does not, however, remove the need for us to work both vertically and horizontally across organizational structures (D'Andrea and Gosling 2001). In the context of this book there is also the need to be aware of the lack of consistency between much academic development practice – which is often experiential and technique-oriented and not explicitly based on research or evidence – and our espousal to others to be more scholarly.

Professional associations have no small part to play in this. Through the national networks associated with the International Consortium for Educational Development – including the Staff and Educational Development Association in the UK, the Higher Education Research and Development Society of Australasia and The Professional and Organizational Development Network in Higher Education (POD) in the US – academic developers are able to look to their own professional development as scholars and practitioners within the field. Annual conferences, networks and publications all form part of the scholarly activity necessary to support both individuals and the profession in developing a credible academic profile within higher education.

Conclusion

The contributions to this book thus reflect the characteristics of scholarship identified by Andresen (2000a) and others: critical reflectivity as a sensibility, a habit of mind; scrutiny by peers as permitted, for example, by publication; and inquiry as a motivation and drive. However, even within this broad definition the writers here represent a broad church of experience, roles and approaches to academic development. The spectrum represented is from those working at a subject or departmental level through a central educational development unit to an institutional or even national role. They range from hands-on practitioners to those in mainly research roles; from mainstream academic developers to managers; and from a variety of higher education institutions.

What they all have in common is that they both recognize and practice the scholarship of academic development. Through critical inquiry, continually exposing their ideas and findings to peer scrutiny at conferences and through publication, and by both challenging and supporting developments in learning and teaching in higher education – at whatever level of the institution they occur – the contributors have helped the profession move from the purely pragmatic to a central role in shaping both policy and practice.

As with establishing the credibility of any new profession, the emergence of academic development as a legitimate and credible academic field has not been without controversy, as evidenced by Rowland's (1998 *et al.*: 135) reference to educational development and similarly-named units as 'non-academic' and their inhabitants as 'Professors who have nothing to profess'. However, perhaps the strength of the profession is that this 'attack' came from one within it and that a equally robust reply from Andresen (2000b: 23) challenges us all to look to the scholarship of our practice, which is not alone in being a 'second-order practice in the same family as literary and artistic criticism and similar fields'.

Part 1

Conceptualizing Academic Development

2

Academic Development: A Practical or Theoretical Business?

Stephen Rowland

Academic development as a critical practice

The most fundamental oppositional, or rather *dualistic*, relationship that underlies much thinking about teaching and learning, and hence about academic development, is the relationship between theory and practice. The view that teaching is a practical activity which is (or rather, should be) based upon theory derived from specialist educational research is a view which comes from a particular conception about the relationship between theory and practice. According to this conception, theory provides us with a pure, idealized and abstract model, and practice is what actually happens. Good practice – in, say, teaching – is what takes place when what actually happens – our teaching – is as close as possible to the theory. Now this view of theory and practice might make sense as an everyday way of thinking about, say, Copernicus's theory about the planets revolving around the sun: the practice nicely fits the theory. But its value is extremely limited when it comes to thinking about teaching, academic practice or academic development.

Before I go any further, however, I need to say just a little about how I shall use the terms 'teaching', 'learning', 'academic practice' and 'academic development' in this chapter. Teaching describes what teachers typically do when working with students to support their learning. Learning I use to describe what students and lecturers sometimes, but not always, do as a consequence of being taught or doing research. (There are also, of course, many other things that may lead to learning.) Academic practice includes research as well as teaching, and the learning which results from both. Academic development is then the development of academic practice. It depends largely upon learning about academic practice: learning, that is, about research as well as learning about teaching and learning about learning.

It follows that central to the practice, and any theory, of academic development, then, must be the process of engagement between those who are to learn about their practice in order to develop it. This engagement is concerned with learning about academic practices including, but not restricted to, teaching. It is therefore academic in two different ways. First, it is a process of learning and so is an academic process. Second, its subject matter concerns academic practice. Academic development is thus a doubly academic practice: it is an academic practice about an academic practice.

The most characteristic feature of an 'academic', as opposed to any other kind of, practice is that it is critical. As teachers in higher education, we aim for our students to be critical, to think critically, or engage critically with the subject matter of their studies. What is meant by 'critical' in this context varies widely. For some it is a propensity for 'deep' (as opposed to 'surface') learning (as in, for example, Marton *et al.* 1993, 1997). Others focus on critical thought, and critical thinking (e.g. Browne and Freeman 2000). For others the idea is that students should develop powers of critical self-reflection and critical action (Barnett 1997). Whatever view we take about this, however, if academics are to expect a critical engagement on the part of their students, one must expect no less of them as they struggle to understand their own professional practices. If higher education is a critical business for students, so must it be for their teachers and for all the processes of academic development.

How, then, are academics to develop critical ways of engaging with one another? This presents our first problem. How can we speak to each other, and learn from each other, across the divides between the disciplines and roles which we take on? At a practical level, what (and how) can a dentist learn from a historian about learning (learning that may be a consequence of research or teaching)? At a more theoretical or philosophical level, what assumptions about what it means to 'know' something underlie dentistry and history and how do they differ?

Over more than 45 years in UK there has been an increase in the opportunities for students to cooperate with specialists from other disciplines than their own (Beard and Hartley 1984: 4). Current policy documents reflect a similar concern for multidisciplinary work (NCIHE 1997). In spite of this, however, academics work in an increasingly fragmented environment.

This fragmentation relates, however, not only to the differentiation between disciplines themselves, but between teaching and research, academics and managers, teachers and students, and between academics and academic developers. Indeed, the idea of *uno voce* (one voice) or universality, which the etymology of the word 'university' might seem to suggest, is far removed from the experience of many of us who work in these institutions. It is an old cliché that the only thing which academics share is a joint concern to find a car parking space.

It is against this experience of a fragmented work setting that we should understand the institutional demands for standardization, mission statements, quality audit, and the rest of the paraphernalia which is aimed at creating an appearance of order and control in the face of chaotic and disconnected experience. The challenge for those concerned to develop teaching in higher education, or academic development more widely, is to engage academics in a discourse of learning which is critical in a context which is fragmented. The danger is that in a culture of audit and surveillance, academic development is seen, by academics in departments, as yet another imposition.

Is academic development generic?

In attempting to engage questions about learning with an audience from such widely different ways of thinking, with different ways of expressing their ideas, and with different interests, it is tempting to view teaching and learning (and increasingly research skills) as being *generic*. This is the common assumption that although university teachers are scholars of a particular subject, questions about the development of learning, and thus academic development, are of a different order. From this generic viewpoint, the academic dentist and the historian have much to learn about the nature of learning (and how to do it and support it) which is independent of their subject. Starting from this premise, one of two different conclusions is often drawn.

The first is that teaching and learning (and hence academic development) is primarily a practical, rather than theoretical, activity. It is a set of crafts or skills and interventions that can be learnt through familiarity without undue intellectual effort. According to this view, the academic's *intellectual* efforts should be directed towards research. Teaching is a practical, rather than theoretical, activity which they have to take part in which may, or may not, be of interest. It follows from this that the development of university teaching is largely a matter of academics taking part in programmes of training to ensure they gain the necessary familiarity and practice. I shall call this perspective the 'atheoretical perspective'.

In the context of higher education teaching development the job of the academic development worker, according to this atheoretical perspective, is to provide training in the craft of teaching. Such a role is not an academic or theoretically based one. In a university culture which traditionally values its intellectual contribution to society, it is not surprising that, from this atheoretical perspective, teaching is viewed as a somewhat menial and amateurish task compared to the real intellectual work of research (Booth 1998: 1), and those concerned to develop it are 'merely' trainers. Compulsory teacher training for university staff, conducted by non-academic development workers, is likely to reinforce this narrow view unless teaching is also seen to be intellectually challenging.

An alternative conclusion, to be drawn from the assumption that teaching is largely generic across different subject matters, is that questions of teaching and learning and their development are the special concern of *educationists* and educational researchers who develop educational theory. According to this way of thinking, it seems unrealistic to expect an academic who is a historian or dentist also to be an educationist, for the study of education is a different discipline, which requires a different way of thinking. It follows from this that the development of university teaching should be guided by specialists who theorize, conduct research and produce 'findings' about teaching and learning. These findings would then be applied by the non-educationist academics in their discipline. It is an activity which, although directed towards the development of academic practices, is theoretically based. The theories involved are educational theories.

In the UK, following recent initiatives that have been aimed at raising the status of teaching, academic developers have increasingly been appointed on academic (rather than academic related or administrative) grades, up to the level of professor. This would appear to reflect a growing trend towards viewing them as researchers and experts in education, whose activity is more academic and who have a more theoretical understanding. This may increase the credibility of academic developers in the eyes of their colleagues in the disciplines. (We should bear in mind, however, that the field of education as a discipline, even when practised within an academic department, is still viewed by many university colleagues as being a somewhat low status field.)

An interdisciplinary perspective

I am somewhat sceptical, however, of both the 'atheoretical' and the 'educational theory' models of academic development. I would question the premise upon which both are based: that teaching and learning are largely generic. While learning (and therefore teaching about and researching into) how to fill a tooth, or interpret a historical text, or investigate subatomic particles might have some interesting things in common, the *differences* between them might be even more revealing as we explore ways of developing our own teaching and learning. Indeed, dentists and historians are likely to think differently by virtue of their different academic backgrounds. These differences will shape the ways they think about their teaching and learning.

Valuing the insights, concerns and epistemological assumptions that are particular to the different disciplines, rather than generic, Jenkins (1996) argues that an effective context for academic development is with colleagues working from their disciplinary perspectives. He goes on to suggest that 'even with workshops drawing on staff from a range of disciplines, it may be appropriate *initially* to centre the course on disciplinary concerns . . . but to do so at a meta-level' (pp. 54–5, my *italics*). But why is this only an *initial* part of the process?

Like staff at Stanford University, referred to by Jenkins (1996: 54), our experience of working with mixed groups of lecturers at Sheffield (Rowland

2000) suggested that they learn much from each other by drawing upon these differences, rather than by submerging them within the generic aspects of teaching. But more than this, such encounters in a mixed setting provide an opportunity for these disciplinary epistemologies, assumptions, concerns, or just plain customary practices, to be challenged by others from different backgrounds.

This perspective is interdisciplinary. It is at the point of such challenges that *critique* can emerge. A historian, for example, is likely to have a different understanding of the status of data and its interpretation than a specialist in information studies. This will influence how they evaluate the nature of educational evidence. In such a climate of critique, academic development can become a *critical* interdisciplinary field. It is important to distinguish interdisciplinarity from multidisciplinarity here. The latter is merely an addition of the knowledge, insights and practices of different disciplines. Interdisciplinarity – or at least, 'critical interdisciplinarity', as Barnett (1997) develops the concept – involves the learner in confronting the critique which emerges as different disciplines contest each other's theoretical frameworks, perspectives and practices.

But what exactly are the boundaries of this field? What is the subject matter of the academic developer? If they are not trainers in the craft of teaching, nor educationists, what exactly are they? Unless they can be clear about that, it is difficult to see what they have to offer academics in the disciplines and in what field their theoretical understanding is employed.

What is the field of academic development?

One way of describing an academic field is in terms of its dominant discourses. We might therefore be able to describe the field concerned with the development of teaching and learning in higher education (or academic development) by considering the texts in the field. But this, of course, begs the question, for where do we look for these texts? In order to illustrate the problem here I want to draw upon just two books. Although both are by widely respected researchers, and concern learning in higher education, familiarity with them is not important for my argument. I draw upon them merely to make a point.

The first book is titled *The Impact of Teaching on Learning Outcomes in Higher Education: A Literature Review* (Entwistle 1992). Although the title is not very recent nor quite contemporaneous with the second book I shall draw upon, it is a fairly wide ranging review of the literature which the author believes relates to the subject of how teaching affects what students learn.

The second book, *Higher Education: A Critical Business* (Barnett 1997), is concerned to develop the idea that higher education should have the outcome of helping students to 'reflect critically on knowledge but (they) also develop their powers of critical self-reflection and critical action' (back cover).

Both books are concerned, then, with the outcomes of higher education teaching: the first in general terms, and the second in relation to its critical purpose. One might expect, therefore, that these texts draw upon a similar field of literature.

In fact, this is very far from the case. Entwistle's book refers to texts from 132 primary authors and editors; Barnett's refers to 126. Apart from one writer (David Boud) who appears as an editor in one of the bibliographies and an author in the other, there is no other author or editor who is referred to by both Barnett and Entwistle.

The only reasonable conclusion we can draw from this is that in spite of a surface appearance that both books might relate to the same field, in fact they have very different concerns. Indeed, each author may well claim to be addressing different fields of investigation. Such a conclusion must be pretty confusing to anyone who wants to study, or develop, the field of teaching and learning in higher education. How can it be that two important texts both about the outcomes of learning in higher education, and both of whom value critical abilities amongst students, should have so little in common?

The answer, I believe, is that when Barnett and Entwistle think about learning, they think about very different things. Barnett has described himself as a social philosopher (Barnett 1994: 1). He is therefore interested in how learning relates to the wider context of society (as a sociologist) and in analyzing in some depth the concepts involved (as a philosopher). Entwistle, on the other hand, has a more psychological orientation and is interested in learning and teaching processes and how they influence each other.

Now I do not wish to discuss the relative merits of these works. I could easily have chosen other pairs of writers to make the same point. I do, however, want to make just two salient observations.

First, the field of 'teaching and learning in higher education' is itself fragmented. There are major writers in the field who appear not to be speaking to one another. Earlier I mentioned the fragmentation that characterizes academic work. What I have illustrated here is that this fragmentation occurs *within* the field of teaching and learning, and therefore academic development, in higher education as well as between the disciplines. Such fragmentation occurs within the social sciences and humanities generally and increasingly in the natural sciences too. We can no longer assume to be able (or interested) to carry out a dialogue about our work, even with colleagues who share our discipline. Indeed, inasmuch as this is the case, the very concept of a 'discipline' is brought into question. As knowledge has rapidly expanded, so the multitude of voices, discourses or special languages has increased with the result that communication becomes more problematic and confined to increasingly narrow communities. In order to develop a critical discourse of academic development we must learn to speak across the divides *within* the field of education, as well as between the different disciplines. The need to move across such 'sub-disciplinary' boundaries is not, however, a problem peculiar to academic developers.

Second, any discourse, which is critical, must be concerned to consider broader questions. These concern, for example, the purpose of teaching, the values which might underlie it, the kind of academic community and the kind of society we are involved in creating, as well as the immediate questions of what to do with a group of students. To concentrate only on the former broader questions may amount to little more than armchair philosophy. To concentrate only on the latter may lead to technical competence but not professionalism. In order to be *professional* teachers, which must be a concern for academic development, academics need to understand how practice relates to wider social values and purposes. Without this, academic development may well promote teaching that serves purposes which are beyond the teacher's ken, which may be quite at odds with his/her own moral values, and which may merely reflect current fads and fashions about teaching. Such an approach to academic development – and to teaching and learning generally – would be uncritical: learning about it would be only a surface learning, like that of the undergraduate student who learns how to perform experiments without understanding their wider significance. Academic development, from this point of view, is no more than a technical or practical activity. It is a critical one.

Much that is written and understood about academic development reflects this lack of connection between questions about teaching and learning and wider social, moral and political questions. The challenge for academic developers, I am suggesting, is to stimulate a questioning approach amongst academic staff not only to learning, but to the very purposes of higher education itself, how it is managed and the wider social context in which research (staff learning) and student learning takes place.

What are the implications of this for staff who are generally understood to provide a service to the institution? Should they be questioning the very purposes and management of their institutions? Might this not be seen as subverting their service function in the institution? Indeed Gosling has suggested that, for this very reason, such a critical stance is unlikely to be supported by management (Gosling 1997: 214). My own experience, however, is at odds with this (Rowland 2000: 39). HEIs are often complex and contradictory, valuing genuinely critical practice, while at the same time managing this in ways which minimize risk, maintain conformity and thereby inhibit critique. A truly *educational,* rather than technical, service, however, is one that *must* raise difficult questions concerning purposes. How can academic developers do this while maintaining a primarily service role?

How institutional structures reflect uncritical discourses

Higher education institutions (HEIs) in the UK and in most other countries have evolved structures that reflect the dominant discourses of teaching and learning. A cursory consideration of these structures would indicate that the development of higher education teaching (as opposed to school teaching) and academic development is in general viewed as a generic, atheoretical and non-academic activity. This conforms to the stereotype which academics in the disciplines have of academic developers.

While HEIs in the UK are not all the same in their structures or the same as those in Australia or the USA, the similarities are more striking than the differences. I shall therefore present the situation in an 'old' university in the UK.

Often (but by no means always) there will be a Department of Educational Studies (and/or School or Faculty of Education). It will be concerned with schoolteacher education and possibly continuing, further and professional education but by and large it is unlikely to be involved in the study of higher education. There are very few academic departments that have the primary function of studying or developing the kind of institution in which we work, or the professional practices of its staff. Academic development is therefore not seen to be an academic, theoretical or intellectual pursuit, judging by the structures that support it. While staff in education departments typically have a background in educational theory and educational practices outside of higher education, they are unlikely to know much about the educational practices across their own institution.

Units concerned with academic development are normally organized as a subset of staff development, personnel or, in the USA, administration. Such units usually have a university-wide brief (although increasingly this brief is related to a particular faculty). They often contain academic developers who have an academic background in a discipline, a research record, and experience of teaching and research in HE. They are often, indeed, the '*rather superior academics*' that Andresen (1996: 43) describes in a fictional dialogue in which an academic developer attempts to describe his work. But because their work in academic development is 'positioned' as a support activity, it is not given academic credibility.

Social workers, nurses, lawyers, doctors, architects and schoolteachers are all professional groups whose professional development is the business of academics. It is recognized as being intellectually demanding. On the other hand, judging by the structures that support the professional development of higher education teachers, this is not considered to be an academic business or to require an intellectual involvement of the same order as these other professional groups.

In this extraordinary situation it is hardly surprising that academic development is plagued by a perceived lack of academic respectability and a presumption that its work is atheoretical. It remains to be seen whether the recent increase in academic appointments amongst academic development workers in the UK leads to an increase in the 'respectability' of academic development work. Several HEIs have recently developed new structures, as well as new appointments in order to emphasize the academic nature of academic development. How will these new structures effect the academic developer's identity? Can they – and should they – escape from their role as people who 'service' the needs of disciplinary departments?

Where 'research' is given a place in academic development, it often finds expression through methodologies that have developed quite unaware of the developments in educational research practised in education departments. The question here is not just whether research findings concerning teaching and learning methods might be transferred from school settings to university settings. Academics from these education departments are used to a wider variety of research methodologies than their colleagues in academic development units. They draw upon sociological and philosophical as well as psychological approaches to investigation. Their contact with, familiarity and understanding of the university, however, are often minimal. Their professional identity is typically more closely aligned with the school than with the HEI.

Conclusion

In this situation, we have communities of academic educationists and communities of support staff. The former know about education, but are largely blind to the concerns of higher education. The latter know about higher education, but are largely blind to the broader and deeper concerns and insights of educationists. Both groups often feel they have little to learn from each other: academic developers do not want to know about schools, and educationists have little interest in HEIs. Given this general reluctance to believe that they *have* got something to learn from each other, how can they be persuaded? How are they to learn from each other? What structures might enable this to happen?

The solution might be to develop new units that draw educational understanding from educational departments, and understanding of the HE context from the support units. Such units, it might be envisaged, would be the appropriate sites for developing professional practice in HE teaching. Some universities have attempted to pursue this strategy, but it has been fraught with problems. Academics from education departments may be understandably reluctant to take on the service role of academic developers, or to redirect their attention to the concerns of their own institution. At the same time, academic developers from service units may be largely ignorant of the potential of the educational work done in academic education departments, and are rarely given the opportunity to collaborate across these boundaries.

If the Institute for Learning and Teaching in Higher Education in the UK is to succeed in its aim of raising the status of teaching in higher education, we might expect more institutions to restructure academic development. Boundaries between educational and support units may be redrawn in ways which reflect the greater academic significance attached to teaching. What will these new structures be and how will they reflect the growing status of teaching and its development as academic work?

The struggle to do this will be at both a level of institutional politics and also an ideological level in which the very purposes of higher education are thrown into debate. Such a debate is needed if academics in education departments and academic developers in service roles are to construct more critical conversations about teaching and learning in higher education, to the benefit of staff and students across the institution. Out of such critical conversations might emerge an appropriate theoretical basis for academic development.

3

A Relational Approach Model for Academic Development

Keith Trigwell

Introduction

The extensive research studies conducted on university students' experience of learning and university teachers' experience of teaching have provided considerable insight into the processes of teaching and learning, including ways of improving those practices. For example, the studies of students' experience of learning showing relations between their conceptions of learning and their approaches to and outcomes of learning (Marton and Säljö 1976; van Rossum and Schenk 1984) helped teachers become aware of those conceptions of learning, and of changing them when it appeared that they might be barriers to learning (Millar, Prosser and Sefton 1989). This chapter draws on the ideas that have evolved from those studies, and presents an analysis of how, in the context of academic development, they might help inform the 'teaching' aspects of that practice.

Relational models developed from this relational research into teaching and learning have been used to help explain variation in individual acts of teaching and learning (Prosser and Trigwell 1999). The research and philosophical bases of these models are summarized and, to the extent that there are parallels between ways of experiencing teaching/learning and academic development, used as a tool in an analysis of variation in ways of experiencing academic development. In this chapter I also introduce and make use of the theory of variation in which it is argued that for learning to occur, there must be an awareness of variation (Marton and Trigwell 2000).

Any analysis of academic development can do no more than touch on a small part of this huge and growing enterprise. In this chapter the focus is limited not only to the role of the individual academic developer, but also within that role to those aspects of the practice that resemble teaching, or are thought by the developer to be teaching (Fraser 2001). This means that some components of academia known to be crucial in successful development schemes, such as the role of leadership (Ramsden 1998), and the influence of time and money (Camblin and Steger 2000) and departments and colleagues (Ramsden 1998; Ballantyne *et al.* 1999; Quinlan and Åkerlind 2000) are not addressed. It also means that many of the other roles described by Andresen (reproduced in Brew 1995: 11) for academic developers, even those closely allied to teaching such as leaders, consultants, change agents, evaluators, advisers and subversives are treated, at best, peripherally. These and other aspects of the role of academic developers are described in more detail in other chapters in this book.

Restricting the focus to academic development as teaching, is, in practice, still something of a challenge for one chapter. There are many ways of conceiving of academic development teaching. Gilbert and Gibbs (1999) present a summary of models used in action directed at teachers to improve teaching and learning. This chapter addresses just three of them – student learning (how students approach learning, what they learn and what aspects of teaching influence learning), conceptual change (personal conceptions of teaching and learning and how they change), and reflective practice (ability to reflect on practice and articulate personal theory of learning). All three are seen here as parts of a whole – awareness of variation in ways of experiencing academic development.

Elsewhere, I have argued that there are two elements of good teaching which have either been overlooked, or about which we are mostly unaware (Prosser and Trigwell 1999). The first is that good teaching is about teachers becoming aware of their own conceptions of learning and teaching, their approaches to teaching, and their teaching outcomes. The second is that in good teaching a major task is to ascertain the perceptions students' have of their learning situation, and to work towards developing learning and teaching contexts which students experience in similar ways to that intended by the teacher. This involves putting the focus on the individual students and their experience – a student-focused approach.

In this chapter I will use these ideas, and how they might apply to academic development. I will also re-introduce, in a new form, that aspect of good teaching that has largely been taken for granted – an understanding of the subject matter being taught and how that content is selected and structured for learning.

Awareness of variation in the experience of university teaching

In attempts to understand variation in individual acts of teaching, Prosser and Trigwell (1999) used the research on teaching and learning to produce a relational model of ways of experiencing university teaching. The model, reproduced in Figure 3.1 describes how the experience of two university teachers in the same teaching context or the same teacher in two different contexts may differ. It has been used to explain the variation in outcomes of teaching, in teacher's approaches to teaching, their perceptions of their teaching situation, and their prior conceptions of teaching.

Figure 3.1 A relational model of ways of experiencing teaching

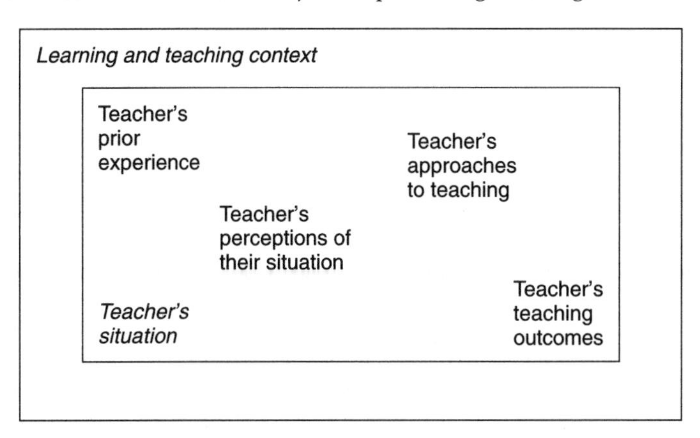

Behind the model is the idea that in any act of teaching, prior experiences, perceptions, approaches and outcomes are simultaneously present, although in some contexts, one or more of these aspects may be more to the foreground of awareness, while other aspects may be more to the background. The inner box in Figure 3.1 represents an individual teacher's experience of teaching. It describes the *situation* of an individual teacher in a teaching/learning context. When a teacher enters a teaching/learning context (the 'world' outside the inner box) the interaction between the teacher and this context constitutes a unique teaching situation for this teacher (represented by the inner box and its contents). The situation will be different for each teacher even though they may be in the same context. The reason for this is that the situation is constituted as the interaction between the teacher and the teaching/learning context – including the individual students and the milieu. The model explains variation in ways of experiencing teaching.

Research studies on the variation in ways of experiencing teaching have been summarized by Prosser and Trigwell (1998, 1999). Conceptions of teaching range from those where teaching is seen as helping students change their conceptions of the subject matter, through to conceptions focused on teaching as transmission of the subject information and/or the teacher's view or understanding of that information (see Kember 1997, for an overview). The former conceptions are thought to be related to an awareness of more aspects of teaching. For example, teachers working with this conception may see the purposes of teaching as increasing knowledge through the transmission of information, helping students acquire the concepts of the discipline, developing their conceptions and changing their conceptions. Those who work with the transmission-based conceptions may not see the purpose of teaching as being any more than increasing student knowledge through the transmission of information.

Lecturers' approaches to teaching were also found to vary qualitatively and to be closely related to these conceptions (Trigwell and Prosser 1996b).

For teachers who see teaching as helping students develop and change conceptions, the approach they adopt is student-focused and involves action designed to develop or change the student's conceptions of the material being learned. These approaches are found to be related to an awareness of more methods of teaching (Gibbs and Coffey, in press). The approaches of teachers who see teaching as essentially about transmission are focused on activities of the teacher (such as how the information is transmitted) rather than on the students.

Variation has also been found in the outcome of teaching. From the perspective of the model described here, teaching outcomes are a part of the teacher's experience of teaching. Outcomes include any teacher-learning that may have resulted from the teaching experience and affective elements, such as increased interest in their subject and enjoyment of teaching. Variation in these three dimensions has recently been found to be related to variation in approaches to teaching (Trigwell 2002). Student learning is also an outcome of teaching. At least three studies have been conducted which show relations between teaching and learning. Two have been reported (Trigwell, Prosser and Waterhouse 1999; Trigwell, Prosser, Ramsden and Martin 1999). They both show that higher deep approach to study scores are associated with higher scores on the student-focused approach to teaching variable, and higher surface approach to study scores are associated with higher scores on the teacher-focused approach to teaching variable. Ingerslev (personal communication) in a small-scale Danish study has observed relations of the same form as those described above.

The research described here strongly suggests that there is qualitative variation in how teaching is conceived and approached, and in the products of those approaches. Some ways of conceiving of, and approaching teaching are more likely to be associated with more desirable student learning outcomes than others. So, good teaching can be seen as being about teachers becoming aware of their own conceptions of learning and teaching, and their approaches to teaching. But how are teaching staff to become aware of their conceptions? To be able to do so means being able to discern one conception from others or one approach from others, and discernment requires the experience of variation.

People see and experience phenomena in the world in relation to other phenomena. We see things as they vary from, and are similar to, other things. If we are not aware of the variation in the way that teaching can be conceived, then we cannot become aware of our own way of conceiving them. Becoming aware of the variation in the way our colleagues and others conceive of teaching and approach teaching is a key step in developing our own awareness of our own way of conceiving of, and approaching teaching. It is also the key step in understanding academic development, as we will see in the next section.

These ideas are derived from the theory of variation – that there is no learning without discernment and there is no discernment without variation (Runesson and Marton, in press). They apply equally well to the process of teachers learning about their own conceptions, or to the establishment by teachers of an object of learning for students. Good teachers constitute a space of learning: a context in which critical aspects of the object of learning are presented as simultaneously variant, while less critical aspects are held invariant. Good teachers, using pedagogic content knowledge (Shulman 1993), are able to identify the likely learning areas for which the experience of variation is critical.

From the perspective of the analysis used here, the final element of good teaching is an awareness of the students' learning experience, particularly their perceptions of their environment and their conceptions of learning. Both have been shown to be related to the quality of student learning (van Rossum and Schenk 1984; Ramsden 1991). Action by teachers to change conceptions of learning and perceptions of context is as much a part of teaching as organizing and/or presenting content.

To summarize: use of the relation model of ways of experiencing teaching and learning, and the ideas from the theory of variation suggest that there are five aspects of the experience of teaching that are fundamental to good teaching practice. They are an awareness of:

(a) conceptions of teaching evoked;
(b) approaches to teaching being adopted;
(c) the learners' conceptions of learning;
(d) the learner's perception of his or her learning environment; and
(e) what constitutes the space of learning for any particular topic.

As noted earlier, this analysis of the experience of teaching will have relevance for those developers who see themselves (at least for a part of their work) as teachers. But even for those who work with teachers, but do not see themselves as teachers, the outcomes (a)–(d) constitute elements, for developers, of the pedagogic content knowledge of academic development. An awareness of, and use by (non-teaching) developers of this knowledge is discussed in the next section.

Awareness of variation in ways of experiencing academic development

A relational model for academic development similar to that described above for teaching could be constructed. The research identifying relations between elements of the experience of academic development has not been reported, so at this stage such a model is without empirical support. However, there are parallels between teaching and academic development, and in this section they are used to gain further insight into ways of experiencing academic development.

Based on the summary presented at the end of the last section, good academic development, by analogy, could be considered to involve five similar elements – an awareness of:

(a) conceptions of academic development evoked;
(b) approaches to academic development being adopted;
(c) the teacher's conceptions of change in teaching;
(d) the teacher's perception of his or her teaching environment; and
(e) what constitutes the space of learning in academic development.

Reported research associated with qualitative variation in each of these elements, and an analysis of the extent to which the variation contributes to an understanding of academic development practice is presented in more detail in the remainder of this section.

Awareness of conceptions of academic development

From time to time, academic developers are asked (or they ask themselves) to articulate the values or conceptions that inform their practice. For some, this has proved to be a difficult task. Is academic development fundamentally about creating contexts which make learning possible, or is it limited to the development of teachers and teaching? And if it is the latter, is it based on changes in ways of thinking and doing or on simplistic theories that say that if we add extra skills to each lecturer's repertoire, then we will get better teachers? And finally, in any of these qualitatively different conceptions, is it the ideas from the literature informed by relations between learning and teaching, or the expressed development wishes of the 'client' that is the focus?

Fraser (2001), as far as I am aware, has conducted the only empirical study of academic developers' conceptions of academic development. She notes that virtually all respondents conceptualized having a role in changing the teaching of academics in their institutions. Supportive quotes, the first two of which are reproduced below, are included.

> It's traditionally, at our place, been helping people to be better teachers.
>
> . . . working alongside academic staff members in whatever way seems to be appropriate in developing their teaching. (p. 57)

What is apparent in these and all the other quotes is that there is no mention of student learning in any of them. This conception, where teaching rather than student learning is at the fore of awareness, is confirmed by the number of quotes from developers who consider that they do not teach. It is based, as Fraser notes (p. 59), on a narrow conception of teaching itself, and is in contrast to more inclusive conceptions where teaching development (as with teaching) is seen as the means to student learning ends.

Academic development conducted from a conception that includes both a narrow conception of teaching and the improvement in teaching as the focus, is less likely to result in the improvement of student learning, than development conducted from more inclusive conceptions.

Awareness of approaches to academic development

Much use is made in academic development of the 'teaching tips literature' (for example Gibbs, Habeshaw and Habeshaw 1984–1988). This approach includes presentation of, discussion and reflection on strategies, and on adopting or experiencing the strategies. The outcomes of this approach are likely to meet the lecturers' desires to add extra skills to their repertoire, but without other changes the effects on the quality of student learning are going to be minimal. In describing his (successful) approach to academic development, Gibbs (2001) illustrated how it is qualitatively different to the approach described in the opening sentences of this paragraph. Using his extensive collections of materials illustrating variation in teaching strategies in contexts that make sense to the teachers, he helps them to *know teaching differently*. Variation in tips, strategies and tactics are used to illustrate and derive principles, and these become routes to changes in conceptions of teaching. It is the focus on achieving conceptual change through the experience of variation that differentiates his approach from most others using his materials.

Other approaches to academic development focus directly on challenging and changing conceptions of teaching. Ho (2000) describes how she has used the conceptual change literature, and knowledge of the variation in teachers' conceptions of teaching to bring about change. When confronted with (student learning) inadequacies in their current conceptions, some teachers in her programme adopted more elaborate or more inclusive conceptions. Not only did the programme yield detectable conceptual change in two-thirds of participants, but in the classes of half the teachers who adopted more inclusive conceptions, students reported adopting more desired approaches to learning (Ho, Watkins and Kelly 2001).

Awareness of teachers' conceptions of changing teaching

In her study of university teachers' conceptions of changing their teaching, McKenzie (2001) describes four qualitatively different categories of experience. In the first (Category A) change in teaching is seen as a change in the content being taught. The second (Category B) focuses on a change in teaching strategies. The third and fourth categories contain a shift in focus from the teacher to the implications of teaching (i.e. learning). In Category C experiencing change in teaching is seen as relating teaching more effectively to student learning. This may also involve change in content and strategy, but the purpose is to improve learning rather than, for example, to make things more comfortable for the teacher. Categories A–C are seen as involving development within existing paradigms or conceptions of teaching. In Category D, change is seen as experiencing teaching differently, as a shift in the teachers' ways of conceiving of teaching, rather than as confirmation or development of existing understanding.

The implications for developers of this variation are clear. If the aim of development is to improve the quality of student learning, and the lecturers' view of development is limited to changes in content and/or teaching strategy without a focus on student learning, the chances of success are low. This is similar to the situation where teachers aim to foster deep approaches to learning with students who conceive of learning as nothing more than a quantitative increase in knowledge, or as memorizing and regurgitating. For progress to be made, these students need to be aware of other ways of seeing learning.

Awareness of teachers' perceptions of the teaching environment

An awareness, by developers, of the teachers' perceptions of the environment they work in is fundamental to good academic development practice. If good teaching is about taking a student's perspective, then good academic development is about taking the teacher's perspective (in contrast to the developers' own perspective).

Lecturers' describe five aspects of their environment that relate to their approaches to teaching (Prosser and Trigwell 1997a). When they perceive that they have some control over what is taught and how it is taught, they are more likely to adopt more of a student-focused approach to teaching. The same approach is also related to their perceptions that the workload is not too great, that student diversity is not too great, and that class size is not too large. A teacher-focused approach is related to perceptions that the teaching unit does not have a strong commitment to student learning, and to perceptions that the teacher has little control over what is to be taught. More recently, perceptions of the quality of teaching leadership have also been shown to relate to approaches to teaching (Trigwell *et al.* 2000).

If an aim of academic development is to improve student learning through the development of teaching, an awareness of the factors listed above that may inhibit desired approaches to teaching would appear to be an important component.

Awareness of what constitutes the space of learning in academic development

It has been said of good teaching that knowledge of the subject matter being taught is a necessary but not sufficient condition. Most university lecturers do have the necessary subject matter knowledge, but the variation in the nature of their understanding of that subject matter has recently been shown to relate to variation in their approaches to teaching (Martin *et al.* 2000). Teachers who constitute objects of study that are more relational adopt more student-focused approaches to teaching. Where approaches are more teacher-focused, objects of study that are more multistructural are constituted.

Academic developers work in a disciplinary area that is considerably less well developed than most other subject areas taught in universities. Many academic developers have entered their discipline from other disciplines, and very few have engaged in research in the discipline of academic development before becoming a developer. As a result there is likely to be greater variation in the nature of the understanding of the academic development subject matter than in other disciplines. This variation may account for the differences in the confidence that developers have in working with that knowledge, and for the reasons why some programmes are based more on the development of teaching by adding strategies to existing strategies (multistructurally) than on more relational approaches.

How do good developers use their knowledge of academic development? The theory of variation introduced earlier may offer an answer. Good developers help teachers experience variation. They establish a space of learning which contains those aspects of the object of learning that are subject to variation simultaneously. For learning to occur there must necessarily be a certain pattern of variation present to experience, and this pattern must be experienced. It is the task of the developer to establish this space of learning, and there is research indicating that this is happening.

In McKenzie's (2001) study of ways of experiencing change in teaching, she describes how teachers experiencing different patterns of variation describe different degrees of conceptual change. For example, Lecturer B in her study experienced change as acquiring and applying teaching strategies with the focus on teaching. Lecturer C experienced change in teaching as relating teaching more effectively to student learning. Both experiences arose from acts of reflection on teaching in the context of their practice. The differences were found to be associated with the aspects of the teaching/learning system that were the focus of that reflection. For Lecturer B, the experience was of variation in teaching strategies, whereas for Lecturer C the critical aspect of the variation was not strategies (though this was discerned) but in ways of experiencing teaching in terms of the nature of the student learning that might result from that strategy.

> I'm strongly influenced by the problem-based learning approach . . . sitting in that seminar [I got] very strong confirmation that this is the right track. . . . I've had this real sense that the students get so much out of the fuzzy edge stuff that they've had to solve. It draws a lot more out of them. And if they can identify with the problem and they want to solve it, they can learn a lot more.
>
> (Lecturer C)

Both teachers experience variation in the environment of their practice, both teachers experience variation in ways of teaching, but only Lecturer C experiences variation in what has been described throughout this chapter as a critical aspect: the dimension associated with what the focus of the teaching is on – teacher or student.

In terms of academic development, the outcomes achieved by both lecturers are desirable, but the changes achieved by Lecturer C are more likely than those of Lecturer B to lead to improved student learning.

In a section above, I described how Gibbs established a space of learning by helping lecturers experience variation in teaching strategy and linking this to principles (Gibbs 2001). I have also described elsewhere (Trigwell 1995; Prosser and Trigwell 1997b) how we have established a space of learning for conceptual development of teaching. Using extracts from transcripts of interviews with teachers who expressed contrasting conceptions, participants are helped to experience variation in the critical aspects (teacher-focus or student-focus) being varied. This provides a context for teachers to examine their own experience and change their way of seeing teaching. It is set in a context where teachers can see the connections between teaching and learning such that the goal of changing teaching to improve student learning appears to the teacher as relevant.

Examples such as these are hard to find in the academic development literature. Even where these principles may be being applied, they are rarely made explicit. Research is needed to articulate critical aspects of variation in key academic development areas.

Existing research into the practice of academic development and descriptions of that practice confirm that there are indeed qualitatively different ways of experiencing academic development. I have argued here that an awareness of that variation is necessary if learning about effective academic development is to happen. But this argument is based on parallels with a relational model of the experience of teaching, not on the empirical research exploring internal relations between elements of the experience of academic development. This research has yet to be attempted.

Summary

The arguments presented in this chapter are based on a model of ways of experiencing teaching. Using this perspective, I have presented good academic development as being about three things. First, it is about developers arriving at a coherent, well-articulated and inclusive view of what they are trying to achieve and how they are planning to achieve that outcome. This is derived from an understanding of their own conceptions of, and approaches to academic development and, in turn, these are developed from an awareness of variation in ways of experiencing academic development. If reflection on practice is a part of good practice, then it is on these aspects of awareness that reflection should be focused. Second, it is about developers discovering the variation in the ways university teachers conceive of development and perceive that planned learning environment. Teachers' limiting conceptions of development may be barriers to desired developmental outcomes, as well as offering an explanation for why so few academic teaching staff voluntarily embrace academic development. And third, it is about working towards creating contexts where teachers experience variation in those aspects critical to learning about that development activity. The essence of these contexts are the constituted spaces of learning, because without them meaningful learning is less likely. But this is an area about which we still know little, and one that would benefit from more research.

There is no doubt that what I have presented here is an incomplete account of the practice of academic development. It is an account that is derived from one perspective. It focuses on the key aspects of the structure of the variation in experiences of academic development, and does not include accounts where there is no known qualitative variation. It is not intended to be a full and rich description even of the narrow view of academic development chosen for this analysis. But, as is the case for the experience of teaching, the aspects of the experiences that I focus on are likely to be powerful aspects in the sense that they are ones that are most likely to relate to variation in the quality of teaching and in the students' learning outcomes – the improvements of both being key aims of academic development.

4

Orientations to Academic Development

Ray Land

Introduction: practice and meaning

The practice of academic development engages its practitioners in considerable 'negotiation of meaning', to use Wenger's phrase (Wenger 1998). In reading, interpreting and acting within complex organizational, cultural and often discipline-specific contexts they find themselves operating within challenging 'economies of meaning'. In such settings their analysis, planning and subsequent collaborative or programmatic initiatives are negotiated against competing meanings arising from multiple factors – managerial imperatives, disciplinary cultures, the priorities of colleagues, resource constraints and wider environmental influences. 'Meaning is not pre-existing' suggests Wenger, 'but neither is it simply made up'. It is, he argues, 'at once both historical and dynamic, contextual and unique'.

> The negotiation of meaning is a process that is shaped by multiple elements and that affects these elements. As a result this negotiation constantly changes the situations to which it gives meaning and affects all participants. In this process, negotiating meaning entails both interpretation and action.
>
> (Wenger 1998: 55)

The degree of 'negotiability', or their capacity to negotiate meanings, that academic developers might exercise within the specific settings that they find themselves, varies considerably. It is inevitably a part of the relations of power in these situations. Their own academic and professional biographies will undoubtedly to some extent inform their agency in these contexts. However, their identities as academic developers will also be constructed and reconstructed through this process of participation and negotiation, a process Weick refers to as 'sense-making' (Weick 1995).

It is the variation in this process of sense-making that this chapter attempts to identify. It seeks to provide insights into the way academic developers perceive priorities and make strategic choices within the cultural and political constraints of their local organizational environments and against the backcloth of national policy initiatives. It will present findings from an ethnographic study of academic developers as a community of practice across UK higher education. The study drew upon a sequence of 33 semi-structured interviews with key informants in a range of types of British universities and colleges. From these interviews the following orientations to practice were identified.

Orientations to academic development

Managerial

Within this orientation practitioners are concerned with developing staff towards the achievement of the institutional goals and mission. The primary operational focus and level is the institution itself.

> I think institutions can become good at institutional signalling. They can do this through contractual requirements, performance review, putting appropriate policies in place, applying resource constraints. These are all levers for change that can be used but all the levers must be pointing in the same direction, and this leads us back to the need for clear strategic direction and management.
>
> (Respondent 28)

The metaphor of levers assumes both a centralized agency – the signal box – and that change can be managed in some directive fashion. Some developers of a managerial orientation ally themselves firmly with aspects of the institutional mission, almost to the point of devising institutional systems that will render the educational process teacher-proof.

> Teachers have an obligation to teach well. Institutions have an obligation to make it possible for teachers to teach well. They actually have an obligation to make it difficult or impossible in the medium term for teachers to teach badly. And staff developers have the role of helping all this good stuff happen. And that's where I locate myself in the grand scheme of things.
>
> (Respondent 27)

Political strategist (investor)

These developers are principally aware of shifting power relations within the organization and wider HE environment. They align development with the agencies most likely to yield dividends. From this perspective, as academic development is perceived by some colleagues as marginal, vulnerable and, because of its centralized 'top-sliced' funding, a somewhat 'parasitic' operation, it behoves academic developers to keep a wary weather-eye on shifts in organizational power relations, and to seek strategic alliances or support from wherever they may be gained. The need for optimal positioning of the educational development unit within the organization becomes paramount. Effort is invested judiciously to maximize return:

> You can talk about change in an individual . . . well an individual changing themselves because of your interventions. But in strategic terms if that individual is a lowly unimportant person it doesn't really matter. It's not going to change your department. So what you really need to ensure is that a change occurs in the minds of people who can influence more people than just themselves.
>
> (Respondent 1)

Identification of champions becomes a key factor in assisting development units to instigate and sustain initiatives.

> What supports it is the converts in influential positions – heads of school or deans or individual course directors. What hinders it is other prevailing attitudes.
>
> (Respondent 5)

Politically-oriented developers readily exploit senior managerial 'muscle' when necessary in order to achieve aspects of their own change agenda with less tractable colleagues.

> So unfortunately – and this is where educational development needs the support of champions in order at some point or other maybe to say to some of the diehards 'You gotta do this guys'. So I think that's overtly political and I think that educational development has always been a political process and some of us I suppose have continually delayed the day in which we have least knowingly been accomplices in a kind of manipulative strategy of change.
>
> (Respondent 2)

Entrepreneurial

This orientation tends to foster innovative practice related to the needs of employment and other external stakeholders. Developers are often involved in income-generating, partnership approaches. The development orientation they exemplify is characterized by a number of related qualities including a strong focus on incorporating graduate employability factors within the higher education curriculum, such as transferable skills and involvement in the development of partnerships with external agencies both locally and internationally. They show a concern with access and equity issues, particularly in relation to the needs of mature students and involvement in community development.

> Its culture is really geared towards employability in all shapes and forms and goes beyond the idea that we're going to produce business studies graduates. So even with the media, arts, communication type approaches there is still an eye on graduate employment. There's a culture that is geared towards friendliness and high quality teaching provision. There isn't so much of a research culture.
>
> (Respondent 11)

The preferred operational approaches of these developers appear to be strongly project-driven, both internally and externally. They actively pursue opportunities to acquire funding for policy-related projects.

> We've been fairly successful over the years in utilising externally funded projects to initiate change by bringing money and support from elsewhere but very rarely doing it to do something that we wouldn't want to do anyway.
>
> (Respondent 11)

This exemplifies the high-energy, high-achievement determination of entrepreneurial developers to instigate new initiatives, establish them, then pass their steady-state operational maintenance to other agencies within the organization whilst they pursue the next opportunity. Freedom to initiate is highly valued. The risk-taking approach seeks forgiveness rather than permission.

> . . . we are constantly carving out our own niche, because, whatever the set agenda is, we're actually fairly free agents, and that is something that I am sort of keeping as my ace. So, you know, although there is a spelt agenda and there is a framework, because of the way the university has been managed that is exploitable. And, although I've tried strategic methods to get things done, it's possible just to go ahead and do things and present them as innovations.
>
> (Respondent 5)

One Head of Unit described her own approach as essentially one of 'creative disobedience' (Respondent 1).

Romantic

This is an outreach approach concerned with the personal development, growth and well-being of individual practitioners within the organization. The operational focus tends to be the individual practitioner.

> I think staff development is about supporting staff to grow and develop as professionals and I am delighted when I see someone say 'Gosh, I write so much better now' as a result of having been through this programme. 'Gosh, you know I never thought I'd be here six months ago!' That gives me the biggest thrill to actually see the face and feel I made a contribution.
>
> (Respondent 30)

The open-ended, client-focused characteristics of this conception of development are clearly not congruent with the strategically-driven, mission-directed approaches favoured by managerialists. In this orientation the emphasis, in quasi-counselling fashion, is on the individual's development and on the importance of trust, integrity and personal 'growth'. Organic metaphors prevail.

> If I work with an individual I never represent myself as an expert; it is always the *enabling*. If you like, the counselling, rapport, enablement of other people, to find within themselves. It's heavily influenced ultimately by Carl Rogers . . . to provide freedom in structures and, in the case of counselling theory, freedom of space for individuals to explore their concerns and their resources in their own way.
>
> (Respondent 18)

There is often a moral dimension attributed to the notion of development:

> Similarly, for staff, I don't believe that you can be a good teacher without being in some sense a good human being. The two things are kind of congruent? One encloses the other. In order to be a better teacher I believe you have to become a better person.
>
> (Respondent 17)

The orientation is located strongly within a humanist framework focusing upon the individual:

> There's 'development' on a number of planes. I'm very concerned myself about the person's development. An individual's development.
>
> (Respondent 17)

It is also an orientation that privileges the practitioner's own subjectivity and self-esteem.

> It really is important to go home at night with that feeling inside that you have been effective, and the most important way that I know that I get that feeling is when I work effectively and see an individual, see change or enabling change with someone, in a context which is concrete, and where someone is going to try something that you have hoped to lead them towards or support. Or even better, when you get feedback from it and someone has been successful. I think that is just *rich*. It is terribly important.
>
> (Respondent 18)

Vigilant opportunist

This orientation exploits topical developments and opportunities in strategic ways as they arise within the institution or environment. One academic developer uses a metaphor of predation to describe this tendency:

> I think it's like most things in educational development. You alight on some shiny substance, raven-like, and if it's really nice you kind of fly off with it and show it to as many people as you think might be interested or something.
>
> (Respondent 2)

A Head of Academic Development talks of hitching the Unit's activities to promising passing juggernauts, such as Quality Reviews, but emphasizes the importance of timing in such opportunistic incursions.

> One of the things I have learned in doing the job over the years is that timing is everything. . . . if your timing is wrong and people don't *see* the need to do it there and then, even though you might be right and you've diagnosed it absolutely 100%, it'll not happen. They're busy, they've got a lot to do, and if they don't think it needs to happen tomorrow, basically they're not going to do it. You'll get enthusiasts doing it but you'll not get widespread change. You can get them to address it when they all kind of recognise it's now becoming an imperative.
>
> (Respondent 14)

The orientation recognizes the fashionable appeal of certain topical developments (again drawing attention implicitly to the appropriacy of timing). One experienced developer uses the metaphor of flotsam to describe this tendency.

> Well you focus, you focus on the issues of the day, don't you? You kind of float (if we're using the watery metaphor) you hang on to the bit of old door that you can and try not to get too swept away and actually what surfaces is what you work with. And that's not to say the other stuff isn't all there underneath and isn't going to pop up any minute, but we can't do the whole thing all the time.
>
> (Respondent 3)

Not all opportunistic investments, however, yield rich returns.

> In this line of business you have to cast an awful lot of bread on an awful lot of water, and sometimes what you end up with is just a lot of soggy bread.
>
> (Respondent 15)

Researcher

These developers see the most effective way of influencing colleagues' practice as being through the presentation of compelling educational research evidence. Operational emphasis tends to be on the discipline or community of practice and it assumes a rational–empirical notion of change.

> . . . if you can really marshal together a compelling idea then people will find it hard to . . . and some of them may still resist it but people will come on board because they will see the logic of it.
>
> (Respondent 12)

Involvement in research is seen as adding credibility to the academic development function, despite the often difficult operational climate in higher education in which the privileged status of research often serves to undermine the status of teaching. A well-established researcher in a prestigious English traditional university sees the value of a research approach as follows:

> There was a piece of evidence that was very telling but people don't know about it. In Australian universities educational development some fifteen years ago had a very high profile and it was very accepted. And then as money became scarce they cut back on their research work, they became more 'service', and down it went. More recently they've come up again with research and up in prestige. The fact that academics don't respect you if you don't do research I think is being demonstrated very clearly.
>
> (Respondent 7)

However, the distinction between theory and practice is not necessarily seen as helpful. It is a question of both encouraging and enabling colleagues in other research disciplines to have ownership of educational research.

> I see my role really has a lot to do with the interface between theory and practice and trying to apply the research to pragmatic problems, but then using that application and going back and looking at theoretical models. I can't see these as being separate. They are just so intimately related together. I go into a department like Marketing and they have their set of problems but I'm looking at the research and I'm coming back with some solutions but I'm trying to push the boundaries of what they're doing outwards and I'm trying to make the research something that they have ownership of in some way. And I try to make them realise that there is research out there all the time.
>
> (Respondent 12)

Professional competence

Other practitioners see development as bringing academic staff up to a baseline level of skill competence in aspects of teaching and learning. The primary focus here is service to the student body, and ensuring that students are not 'short-changed' (Respondent 21). Unlike the Romantic orientation with its holistic conception of the academic client and its concern for his or her well-being, in this orientation developers seek to build the confidence of academics by enabling them to demonstrate achievement of a prescribed set of professional learning outcomes. 'Classroom' expertise and the more technical aspects of practice prevail.

> We are the route whereby they can gain a qualification. We show them the materials and talk to them about the course and talk to them about how it works, and talk to them about how it's 100% rooted in their *practice,* and they don't have to write essays on educational theory – all they get to do is teach, think about teaching, use the literature to develop ideas for teaching better.
>
> (Respondent 27)

Nonetheless development retains 'a moral dimension' which 'all comes down to students' entitlement to be well taught'.

> In many places they're being very badly taught. And I hate that. It's wrong, to use an old-fashioned word. They are entitled to be well taught. It's the only degree they'll do, probably. It's a huge personal commitment and now financial commitment as well. And they deserve it.
>
> (Respondent 27)

In this perspective theory is clearly the handmaiden of practice.

> Practice first. It provides a way in which they can make useful sense of theory. It provides a way in which they can see it as tools for thinking and doing, rather than as boring old stuff to be learned, and I'd rather be getting on with my teaching thank you very much.
>
> (Respondent 27)

Reflective practitioner

In line with Schön's (1983a) conceptual approach, this orientation seeks to foster a culture of self- or peer-evaluative, critical reflection amongst colleagues, to help them cope with uncertain and ambivalent organizational environments where the process of development tends to be less logically coherent and more conflicted than rational accounts would indicate. There is a degree of complexity within professional practice that is not easily susceptible to a direct technical–rational treatment. However meticulously they might seek to design and implement their projects they find them influenced by unpredictable and often unique factors.

> I suppose you could say the skill, the *expertise* of academic developers rests very much on their capacity to analyse the situation, make judgements about it and come to a decision concerning what will be the most appropriate action. We rarely have any firm and agreed guidelines. We're usually in uncertain situations (every situation's more or less new, a one-off), sometimes scared stiff, and I suppose we test the

> validity of our decisions by thorough critical reflection, you know, Schön and company, Kolb, the old reflective practice bit, and by reference to and consultation with our peers. And it's in this way, I suppose, that we become self-evaluating practitioners and learn to have confidence in our own professional judgements and values.
>
> (Respondent 21)

Developers adopting this orientation can come to feel that their practice itself is developmental for them personally.

> My work in itself is profoundly developmental of me. I will discover something about the questions, hopes and fears of those who are just starting on it. And I'll discover something about the concerns of those who are helping other people through it, the mentors and so on. I will learn about my practice through my act of practice.
>
> (Respondent 27)

However, one critique of this orientation from other perspectives is that it can be construed as a form of self-regulation in the Foucauldian sense (Foucault 1979), a reactive response to strongly managerialist or surveillance cultures.

Internal consultant

Some developers prefer to work more like internal consultants in their organizations. They operate in an observational, advisory and sometimes evaluative capacity, often on a longer-term basis, with specific departments or course teams. Developers working in this way talk of 'holding up a mirror' to the practice of their colleagues, of not being judgmental but of 'reflecting back what's happening' from their point of view.

> . . . it's all about situated cognition so you go in and you listen and you watch and you say very little at first. And you talk to people and you say 'Mmmh . . .' And sometimes you get a chance and you say 'Well, why don't you try that or why don't you try this?'
>
> (Respondent 12)

They emphasize the need for credibility and for offering practical solutions but point out that a proactive approach can be a useful means of infiltrating departments.

> Effective consultancy usually comes about through the contacts, the networking you do. You've got to put yourself about a bit, get known, seed some interesting ideas around the place to get others interested. You have to let them know who you are, of course, and what you can do, what you can offer. Got to drum up a bit of business. You have to be a bit *promiscuous* I suppose [*laughs*].
>
> (Respondent 21)

The consultancy-oriented developer will often incorporate a research approach, either in the form of helping establish and sustain an action research project, or in the form of evaluation research, working with students to ascertain their experience of a programme.

Modeller–broker

Certain developers adopt a 'Trojan horse' approach of working alongside colleagues to demonstrate good practice or innovation. 'Do as I do' rather than 'do as I say' informs an approach that exploits exemplars, and models their own practice directly to colleagues. This is seen as ultimately a more effective operational approach than the patient development and implementation of policy.

> I think we actually are the 'brown knees brigade', i.e. we put our shorts on and we get out there and we go in and we do things. That's obviously limited by how few we are, and what we can do, but we do actually go in and support and encourage and work with people. I adore actually doing it. I love getting into a workshop environment with people and helping them to think about how they might develop their practice.
>
> (Respondent 3)

A variant of this approach is to disseminate the good practice of others, to act as broker.

> I regarded what we were doing in EDS as being a brokerage. And what I did was I tried to run and manage events – we had people who were put in touch with each other and actually I could step back to some extent. I was proud of that because I have a belief that you can't change the way people behave in teaching and learning if you're the only driver. You've got to be working with people.
>
> (Respondent 3)

The use of one's own practice as exemplar does of course bring a sense of obligation to ensure that one's current practice remains sufficiently professional and of an appropriate standard. This inevitably raises the issue of what it is that qualifies the educational developer to assume the role of development with his or her colleagues, and of the possible need for an effective scheme of accreditation.

> It would be bloody hypocritical of us to be telling teachers they ought to become professionals if we carry on as bumbling amateurs in the worst sense of that term ourselves. We have to practise what we preach. We have to model good behaviour. That's where the SEDA Fellowships came from historically.
>
> (Respondent 27)

Interpretive–Hermeneutic

This can be characterized as a dialectic or dialogic approach with colleagues in which the balancing of different views, relation of local to wider perspectives, part to whole, can lead to critical synthesis and production of new shared insights and practice. This is characterized by Webb (1996b: 66), in its simplest form, as 'a conversational kind of process in which the interpreter learns by adjusting his or her perspective. It necessitates entry to the inner world of the thing or person to be understood – the "other"'. Developers in this tradition turn away from the 'bipolar', 'hierarchical, linear and causal' nature of much educational theorizing in favour of the 'somewhat different view' afforded by the insights gained from the moving back and forth between part and whole that are characteristic of the hermeneutical circle'. Webb sees this approach as 'being more open to the experiences of others, and to re-evaluating and reinterpreting our own experiences' (ibid). This means reconceptualization on both sides, for developer and 'developed', though use of these latter terms would probably be anathema for Webb. In an earlier work he pointed out the challenge that a hermeneutic approach raises for academic developers:

> If you are a staff developer, try thinking about your dealings with the people you 'develop'. How do you attempt to privilege your own view of the world? What developmental notion are you pushing and is the high point of development someone just like yourself? What stages do you see people going through to become like you and how do you go about creating the recapitulation of your own progression in others? Then think that your message is wrong.
>
> (Webb 1993: 104)

Better, perhaps, to think of development, as in chess, as an 'opening up'.

> Development is strange. Do you play chess? You know that 'development' in chess involves arranging your pieces so that the big pieces can use their resources to the maximum. So your bishop isn't blocked on this diagonal. So you open things up really. So I see development as 'opening up' so that people's potential could be fully realised. You haven't got this powerful queen . . . you don't want to move really. Open spaces really. Of course the point is when you've opened it up the queen can go straight, left, all sorts of places. It just doesn't open up one single channel which is pre-determined as the queen's route. It means that the queen is able then to go in five different directions, backwards even. It's an unblocking. Yes, well not a bad analogy. . . . A lot of people are actually just blocked really, and for various reasons, and if you can open it up, open the spaces. . . .
>
> (Respondent 8)

Discipline-specific

In the last few years within the UK an approach to academic development has gained ground, predicated on the notion that colleagues identify primarily with their subject-specific 'guild' culture, and hence development tends to be more effective when going with the grain of disciplinary needs, when one is 'thinking like an economist' or a musician or mathematician. Development, from this perspective, can be seen as 'situated learning' within a disciplinary community of practice (Lave and Wenger 1991).

> I have 26 half-time seconded people. They're seconded for two or three years so they're a big substantial project. They are change agents inside the subject area. They are the spokes. I manage that project. My job really is to make more out of that than just a series of projects. They've all got individual projects which are subject-based. I'm increasingly trying to push them towards staff development inside the subject area and working together on thematic issues. They are quite a powerful group.
>
> (Respondent 17)

Jenkins (1996: 50–60) recommends a strategy that recognizes and values staff's disciplinary concerns, trusts discipline-based staff to 'develop wider concerns', helps them locate 'relevant discipline-based pedagogic literature, organisations and contacts' and encourages them to research the teaching and learning of their discipline. He also stresses the importance of helping academic colleagues to build careers in the teaching of their discipline, and warns that this transformation will be a long and difficult process. The institutionalization of this approach is now becoming apparent with the establishment of the Learning and Teaching Support Network (LTSN) Subject Centres across the UK and the subsequent emergence of specialist conferences and discipline-specific pedagogic journals. This activity is attracting colleagues who might describe themselves as 'in' academic development but not necessarily as 'academic developers'.

Conclusion

We might perceive the context and 'strategic terrain' of academic developers (Stones 1991, 1996) as the organizational forms, academic and professional cultures and subcultures within which they have to practise. Their strategic conduct within these settings can be characterized by what I have called here their *orientation* to academic development. These orientations are analytic categories that include the attitudes, knowledge, aspirations, action tendencies and processes of identification of academic developers in relation to the contexts and challenges of their practice. They are not fixed attributes but an enabling means of sense-making. A developer may (and indeed often does from the data available in this study) adopt differing orientations in different strategic contexts. The differing orientations may be viewed as *variations* on practice, in line with Marton's (1999) emphasis on variation as a crucial dimension of understanding the nature of skill and expertise. Each of these orientations reflects and is informed by different conceptions of change. They can, similarly, be mapped against organizational cultures and the needs and expectations of differing stakeholder groups (Land 2001).

As developers negotiate these dynamic, complex and unique settings, both deriving meaning from them and attributing meanings to them, the notion of development itself becomes problematized.

> 'Development' may be viewed as a site for contest: *it is not a unitary concept* for which, one day, we will provide a model. The very meaning of the word 'development', how it is constituted, the kind of activities it implies, are all discursive, and can be interpreted according to various ontological and epistemological standpoints.
>
> (Webb 1996b: 65)

Webb rules out the possibility of any 'super-standard' from which we can determine these positions, considering our notions of development as 'of necessity a site for encounter and dispute' (ibid). The orientations that have been presented here can be seen as one manifestation of such contestation.

5

Discipline-based Educational Development

Mick Healey and Alan Jenkins

The way that educational developers should seek to work with the vast majority of academic staff is to recognize, value and build upon staff's concern for their discipline

(Jenkins 1996: 51)

. . . for most academics, developing the scholarship of teaching will only bring about change in their priorities if it is embedded in disciplines and departments

(Healey 2000: 172–3)

Introduction

Our argument can be simply put: working within and with disciplinary communities is central to developing academic, or rather educational, development as a scholarly activity.

In critically appraising our argument, you need to recognize that we come from a particular, possibly 'foreign', disciplinary tribe and seek to challenge and perhaps transgress the boundaries and scholarly beliefs of some educational developers. One of us (Jenkins) worked for a long time as a geographer and then moved into educational research and development within his institution, but has remained actively involved in national and international development projects in the discipline (Jenkins 1997). The other (Healey) continues to practice geography, but over the last dozen years has shifted his main research area from economic geography to geography in higher education and pedagogic research.

For most academic staff *academic* development is primarily about staff being scholars (and perhaps 'active' researchers) in a discipline *per se.* Thus for us the book's focus and that of this chapter is on the scholarship and research which underpins teaching. Or building on the language of the Higher Education Funding Council for England (HEFCE) we are clearly differentiating between the scholarship (academic development) *of* teaching and the scholarship (academic development) *for* teaching (HEFCE 2000b). Our focus is firmly on the scholarship (and research) *of* teaching in the disciplines (Healey 2000; Huber 2001; Donald 2002; Huber and Moreale 2002).

While recognizing that there are different views about the nature of the scholarship of teaching, there is evidence of a general consensus around the definition offered by Martin *et al.* (1999) (Healey 2002). They say that it involves three essential and integrated elements: engagement with the scholarly contributions of others on teaching and learning; reflection on one's own teaching practice and the learning of students within the context of a particular discipline; and communication and dissemination of aspects of practice and theoretical ideas about teaching and learning in general and teaching and learning within the discipline. It is significant that two of the elements in their definition refer explicitly to developing scholarship within the context of one's discipline.

This account, while drawing on the wider literature, is based on our experience of working in geography and related disciplines to promote *discipline-based* educational development, curriculum development and pedagogic research in a range of national/international projects and activities. These include a long involvement with the *Journal of Geography in Higher Education* (JGHE) (Jenkins 1997); producing guide books for geographers and linked workshops on a range of aspects of teaching in higher education (Gravestock and Healey 1998, 2000, 2001); and working with geographers, earth and environmental scientists and specialist researchers in higher education to raise the capacity to undertake pedagogic research through a series of linked projects into the effectiveness of fieldwork. Nevertheless, while geography has its own distinct 'community of practice', its position in the academy, bridging the natural and social sciences and including elements of the humanities, means that our experience is relevant to staff in a wide range of disciplines.

The focus on the generic

Certainly in the UK, much of the focus of educational development practice and scholarship has been generic. That which has been proselytized and indeed required by this emerging profession has focused on practices and scholarship that could be applied to any discipline; and often appears to ignore the disciplines. Thus the requirements of SEDA (the UK-based, Staff and Educational Development Association) to gain professional standing of its members through its Fellowship scheme or to gain 'trained teacher' status through its academic programmes in institutions, do not specifically mention disciplines or subjects. Staff are 'trained' to teach and demonstrate knowledge of the generic literature on teaching. Any explicit connection to the discipline the academic is teaching (and probably researching) has been generally notable for its absence; or is there at the initiative of individual academic staff and/or developers. It has not been seen as central to the professional training and public scholarship by educational developers. Indeed at times, staff allegiance to their discipline has been seen as an obstacle to improving their students' learning.

In David Baume's (1996: 4) editorial in the first issue of the *International Journal for Academic Development*, he argued that:

> There remains great resistance, passive and active to the notions that teaching and assessment are in any ways problematic activities, worthy of much attention in a university. *Many academics derive most of their professional identity from their discipline* (emphasis added).

Schulman (1993, cited by Neumann 2001) takes this argument in a more positive direction by suggesting that one of the reasons for the isolation of teaching in universities is that it has become disconnected from the disciplines and thus from its intellectual community. The view that teaching is generic reduces it to the technical matter of performance. Consequently, teaching is something you lay on top of your real work, unconnected with the disciplinary community at the heart of being an academic.

The rise of discipline-based pedagogy: recognizing the territories of academic disciplines

This generic focus has been challenged in the last few years through the development of organizations for, or explicitly valuing, discipline-based academic development, and the emergence of scholarship and research about and for discipline-based pedagogy.

The organizational focus on disciplines is now apparent in the UK, Australasia and North America. In the UK, the requirements for accreditation for programmes for postgraduate certificate courses for teachers through the Institute for Learning (ILT) has moved beyond the purely generic approach of SEDA. The ILT requires its members to know about 'the *subject material* they are teaching . . . appropriate methods for teaching and learning in their *subject area* . . . models of how students learn both generically and in their *subject*' (emphasis added) (ILT 2001). In Australia many projects funded by The Committee for the Advancement of University Teaching, and its subsequent replacements, have been discipline-based. Similarly the Carnegie Foundation for the Advancement of Teaching in the United States has been guided by the principle that the scholarship of teaching is intimately linked to the concerns of the discipline being taught (Huber 2000). For example, their Pew National Fellowships Program selects Carnegie Scholars in disciplinary groups to provide collegial interactions within the discipline (Cambridge 1999).

The UK has gone a stage further and in 2000 established a Learning and Teaching Support Network (LTSN) consisting of a Generic Centre, a Technologies Centre and 24 National Subject Centres (http://www.ltsn.ac.uk). The latter build on twenty years experience of running discipline-based programmes (Healey 1998).

Such then is the evidence of a more discipline-based organizational focus for educational development. But that is supported by, and itself promotes, a scholarly and research focus on discipline-based pedagogy. Becher's (1989) pioneering work on how research is distinctly conceived and developed in the disciplines is now paralleled by a growing research literature on the particular pedagogies of the disciplines (Hativa and Marincovich 1995; Rust 2000b; Neumann 2001). Smart, Feldman and Ethington (2000), for example, show that different clusters of academic disciplines and their respective degree programmes have distinctive norms and values; and academics in different disciplinary clusters show wide difference in their teaching practices and their expectations of the relative importance of alternative student competencies.

Why a discipline-based approach to academic development

In our view there are at least five central reasons why educational development in its practice and scholarship needs to take a discipline-based approach (see also Jenkins 1996; Healey 2001).

1. For most academic staff their primary allegiance is to their subject or profession, and their sense of themselves as staff at a given institution is secondary or but one of their professional identities.
2. Some disciplines are characterized by distinctive forms of teaching, such as: laboratory practicals in the sciences; studio critiques in art; work-based learning in teaching, social work and nursing; and fieldwork in geography and the earth sciences. Staff teaching in those disciplines need support in developing good practice, and scholarship and research to inform that practice. Yet too often, as in many of the Fund for the Development of Teaching and Learning (FDTL) projects in the UK, the focus of public scholarship and educational development has been on generic issues, such as assessment.
3. All disciplines, by definition, have particular conceptions of knowledge and concerns with particular areas of 'content' and epistemology, which are ever changing through research in the disciplines. Thus all academics confront what are for them the challenge of designing curricula that attempt to 'explore' the complexity of current discipline-based research and scholarship. Thus geographers are continually working in their everyday pedagogic worlds with how to analyze and explain the interconnections between the physical and social worlds, and the

research methodologies that attempt to understand them (Healey, Jenkins and Kneale 2000). Yet in the literature on curriculum design the main focus is on generic issues such as aligning assessment to learning outcomes. Stark and Lattuca (1996) and Jenkins (1998) are two of the few texts that explore the scholarship of discipline-based curriculum design.

4. Most forms of teaching need to be 'translated' into the culture and concerns of different disciplines. Thus in geography much of the student experience of group work and its assessment is through learning off campus through fieldwork. While the generic advice and scholarship/research on group work offers insights into this world, that scholarship needs 'translating' into those contexts, and we also need primary research that explores these particular group work pedagogies.
5. For most university staff, teaching is but one of their concerns and institutional requirements. Research in the discipline *per se* and its border territories is a major professional concern. Yet the scholarly literature on educational development generally ignores how research by staff in the disciplines can best be integrated into courses. Yet that is where many staff 'are'. It is little wonder that they do not want people who do not value their territory coming into that world.

Strategies for effective discipline-based scholarly educational development

Such then are our arguments for discipline-based educational development. We now set out our views as to how this form of educational development may best be promoted by discipline-based colleagues and supported by generic educational developers.

Expect hostility, and work for rewards from your disciplinary tribe

You have to expect confrontation and/or being sidelined and ignored – at least initially. Depending upon where you and your discipline are 'starting' from, you have to recognize that the processes of developing discipline-based pedagogic scholarship are slow and difficult. For example we have 'scars', including vitriolic rejection letters when we have submitted what we see as scholarly pedagogic work to mainline geography journals. Yet we also have to acknowledge that we have obtained 'prizes' and recognition from *within* the discipline for our work in pedagogy that we would never have got if we had only focused on geography *per se.* Both of us were promoted to full professors in large measure because of the work that we had undertaken on geography in higher education. There are ecological niches in such border territories.

Recognize the limitations of a (purely) discipline-based approach

To capitalize on the strengths of a discipline-based approach we have to recognize its limitations. Many discipline-based staff, as we noted previously, treat teaching as 'unproblematic'; or perhaps rather do not look to the scholarship and research on teaching and learning for 'solutions' to their pedagogic concerns and passions. This came out in Weimer's (1993) review of discipline-based pedagogic journals, such as *Teaching Sociology* and *Journal of Geological Education.* She found that most of the journals exist in a sort of 'splendid isolation' with respect to any writing or research done outside the discipline, even to cognate discipline-based journals, while reference to the scholarship of generic educational development literature was also generally absent. Certainly most of the articles submitted in the early years of *Journal of Geography in Higher Education* (*JGHE*) were accounts of innovations that lacked any grounding in the wider pedagogic literature, or awareness of how to carry out basic action research to evaluate the effectiveness of their practice. However, if at that stage we had rejected those articles on those grounds, we would have mainly published blank paper. It has to be recognized that the processes of developing a scholarship of discipline-based pedagogy take time.

On the other hand, depending on one's discipline and personal epistemological stance, one needs to recognize the view that higher education is moving towards 'Mode 2' (Gibbons 1999), in which 'both research and teaching are increasingly issue and problem based; they go beyond discipline boundaries' (Martin and Ramsden 2000: 135). Interdisciplinary concerns are perhaps growing in importance both in research and in terms of undergraduate and postgraduate curricula – particularly in the context of the development of professional courses such as nursing and tourism. However, that also means that generic scholarship and courses on, for example, course design and assessment have to support staff in meeting those challenges.

Recognize and seek to work with other discipline-based educational developers

In working effectively within a discipline one thus has to reach out to other disciplines – and in particular to that disciplinary group of educational developers and their scholarship and research. There are no magic recipes for doing this though our experience may serve as a guide. Initially on *JGHE* we looked to that group of specialists on discipline-based pedagogy at school level. They did play a key supportive role in educating the rest of the editorial board as to how to encourage a more scholarly approach in those writing for the journal. But their involvement also reinforced the public impression in our disciplinary community that a concern for teaching was effectively largely a concern for those teaching in schools. Eventually we reached out to a number of specialists in *higher* education who were willing to work with *our* concerns, and we think that did support the gaining of academic credibility in our discipline. Hopefully we were open to 'their' concerns and being changed by working with 'them'. Eventually we felt confident when developing materials for a major curriculum development project, that involved producing ten guide books on aspects of teaching geography in higher education, to invite into the project a team of educational developers to work with 'us' (Gravestock and Healey 1998). However, we also recognized that we thought that such a strategy would help to lever money out of the funders (i.e. we were sensitive to the values that we perceived that 'tribe' held). So there were 'machiavellian' reasons in adopting this strategy.

Use, extend and perhaps challenge your discipline's research methodologies

In developing scholarly and research frameworks and practices to your disciplinary pedagogy, you need to recognize and value your discipline's research methodologies and how it would evidence 'effective practice'. Some disciplines, such as psychology and sociology, have methodologies that are part of the research methods in scholarship and research in higher education. Indeed many of these staff will be far more competent at them than the educational development community. They will have little difficulty in analyzing the scholarly and research literature on pedagogy and developing discipline pedagogic research. Staff in healthcare, for example, can readily analyze their discipline-based pedagogy according to their disciplinary expertise with respect to evidence-based medicine. With some disciplinary communities, the connections are harder to draw with their own scholarly practices. Some of the problems of 'translation' and 'adaption' may be largely cultural; a resistance in some of the hard sciences to softer qualitative research methodologies and a cultural, and in their terms principled, objection to the validity and reliability of action research. One approach here is to work with the disciplinary traditions and work with those methodologies and practices with which discipline-based staff are comfortable and to which they will listen. A superbly executed study, which fails to connect with the disciplinary community, has limited or even no 'value' in changing practice and policy.

Mary Huber (2000: 24, 27), reflecting on working with the disciplinary Carnegie Scholars, comments that:

> Disciplinary styles empower the scholarship of teaching not only by giving scholars a ready-made way to imagine and present their work, but also by giving shape to the problems they choose and the methods they use . . . [Later she recounts a new class of scholars] debating whether they would accept as the scholarship of teaching a project that examined a single student's engagement with the material for a course. Most of the humanists said 'yes', but the past editor of the journal *Teaching Sociology* said that a report on research with a sample of one would simply not be acceptable in his field. To which a historian replied: 'But do we all have to be social scientists?'

For Huber the answer is clearly 'no'. We agree that one starts with and should continue to value and even prioritize the research methodologies in the discipline *per se.* However, we need also to recognize that studies of pedagogy are by definition areas of the social sciences, 'because it is an aspect of human behaviour that they are engaged in and are studying' (Gibbs 2000: 50). Thus to really understand and improve the pedagogies of the disciplines, means adopting and, certainly as a 'baseline', understanding and recognizing the value of these social science disciplinary research methodologies. The logical and practical consequences of this are probably that in the harder science communities, first, the goal for most staff has to be a baseline understanding of the insights from these 'alien' methodologies; and that, secondly, those few in these disciplines who go across into these different methodologies have much to learn, including how to take these insights back to their tribe.

Cultivate the disciplinary ecological niche

You need to see this process as similar to developing any other scholarly/research specialism in your discipline. As with those who seek to ensure that issues of gender or understanding the role of information technology are taken onboard, you may see your role in developing discipline-based educational development as integral to the whole discipline. However, to achieve that you need to develop a critical mass of those who are sympathetic and a critical mass of those who see this as central to their professional identity. The strategies to do this are probably those that can be used for any disciplinary specialism. They include projects that bring together and develop the specialists; and conferences and presentations at mainstream discipline-based professional organizations to influence the many – and hopefully bring some of them into your section of the disciplinary tribe. These kinds of initiative are essential aspects of developing a discipline-based network (Healey 1998, 2001). To express that differently, developing the specialist discipline-based pedagogic journal, the *Journal of Geography in Higher Education* (*JGHE*), has been central to the development of pedagogic scholarship in our discipline. It has significantly educated and supported those on the editorial board in seeing themselves as specialists in this area, and helped them act as 'change agents' in their departments and beyond; *JGHE* has given discipline-based scholarship 'visibility' in geography; also there is now a corpus of some 25 years of articles that provide a scholarly basis to our work. Yet at some point those publishing in *JGHE* need to move out of this protective 'ghetto' and publish in mainstream geography journals and in the generic higher education literature. Our experience is that persistence, flexibility and a thick skin are necessary prerequisites in persuading the 'gatekeepers' of the mainline disciplinary journals of the relevance of discipline-based pedagogic research.

Use the national and international disciplinary networks

Two of the great strengths of disciplines is that generally there are strong national and international organizations, and in effect 'communities of practice' (Wenger 1998) through which ideas and practices are communicated. In developing this ecological niche one needs to work with and to shape the national and international frameworks in your discipline. For example, though *JGHE* started in the UK, we immediately sought to ensure that it had an international 'element' through editorial board advisers and soliciting articles from outside the UK. Over time we have ensured that this initial international 'element' is now a strong feature of the journal and we have appointed separate editors for North America and Australasia. Clearly there are commercial factors that support this approach for it can increase sales, but what it is also doing is giving higher prestige and visibility to this work and drawing on a wider community of practice to improve student learning in the discipline.

Work with staff's concern for discipline-based research

Earlier we commented that many staff see themselves as researchers in their discipline and are concerned with current research directions in the field. However, these concerns are not generally reflected in most of the texts on curriculum design, or from our experience in most of the courses for new or established staff organized by educational developers. For example, in the UK linking teaching and research is not mentioned in the outcomes or values of the ILT – though it is, of course, potentially there in the explicit valuing of a discipline-based approach. We recognize that a preoccupation with research may be a factor shaping some staff's unwillingness to enter into serious scholarly discussion of pedagogy. However, that is not the same as seeing staff concern for research in the discipline as something that cannot be 'harnessed' to shape course design and improve student learning. Thus while Boyer's (1990) classic *Scholarship Reconsidered* is rightly seen as a critique of the dominance of 'discovery research', much of the powerful reform movement that stems from Boyer's work is to bring research or student enquiry guided by (research-based) staff into the undergraduate curriculum. So a major opportunity is potentially there for a scholarly educational development: to forge effective links between discipline based research (staff) and student learning (Jenkins, Breen and Lindsay 2002).

Support staff in their initial training

In many state systems, there are schemes and even requirements for initial training and accreditation. In North America this applies particularly for graduate students and in the UK is reflected in the concern for new academic teaching staff. In our view the main focus of these should be generic – except for specialist courses, such as those aimed at laboratory assistants in the sciences. Probably most of the issues 'new staff' face are generic and certainly from our experience staff learn a lot in such courses from the experience of working with staff in contrasting disciplines – including breaking down the isolation of the disciplinary cultures. However, such initial courses should include a significant disciplinary element, as for example, suggested by the ILT requirements. Institutional programmes need to experiment to find ways to do this effectively. For example the SEDA/ILT accredited course at Oxford Brookes requires participants to carry out a piece of action research on a particular issue regarding the teaching of their discipline, and reflect on their experience of teaching that discipline. But such institutional or course strategies need to be complemented, supported and developed further by the disciplinary communities – and supported by generic educational developers.

Already in the UK various LTSN subject centres are experimenting with different approaches from which we can all learn. Our approach, in the Geography, Earth and Environmental Sciences National Subject Centre (GEES), has been to develop a specialist two-day residential course for new staff in these disciplines, many of whom were already taking a generic accredited course in their own institution. Held towards the end of that 'initial' year the course concentrates on particular aspects of discipline-based pedagogy, for example, fieldwork and the application of generic issues, such as information technology, to the particular disciplinary contexts (Healey 2001; Clark *et al.* 2002). However, that is but one potential strategy. The general point is that disciplinary communities should seek to support staff in their initial years of employment; and the development of web-based resources means that this support can be readily developed at national and international levels. The challenge is to ensure effective links between discipline-based and institutional provision of largely generic educational development.

Support discipline-based continuing professional development

Continuing professional development (CPD) is a more common form of discipline-based educational development than are initial training courses. Many disciplines run sessions as part of their professional association meetings concerned with educational issues facing their higher education members. These meetings can form the basis for developing a discipline-based network of people interested in educational development. Many of the people now running the LTSN National Subject Centres obtained their first experience of organizing educational development sessions through activities of this kind. The twin challenges for discipline-based educational developers are to find ways, first, to move beyond limited-life project funding, and secondly, to extend involvement beyond the converted few in the disciplines.

Conclusion

We believe that discipline-based educational development is an important and necessary form of educational development which complements other generic forms. It is an area which is growing in significance and is receiving increased international attention. However, there is a long way to go before educational development will be fully embedded within the disciplines. This process will be speeded up and more effective the more that discipline specialists and educational developers gain experience of working together. For this to happen both sides need to value the contribution of the other and work together to raise the status of teaching within the academy.

6

The Use of Research and Development Projects in Higher Education

Roger Murphy

Patterns of change with higher education

Higher education in the UK and in other parts of the world is currently acknowledged as an important arena for educational change. The numerous factors contributing to this include an interest in offering higher education opportunities to a wider array of individuals, the explosion of knowledge, the search for ways to increase economic competitiveness and new approaches to promoting student learning, for example through the use of information and communication technology (ICT). Another significant factor is that, compared with other established educational settings such as schools, educational practice in higher education has remained relatively unchanged for quite long periods of time. Anyone who has spent any time dipping into the 'managing change' literature (McDonald and Walker 1976; Fullan 1993) will be aware of some of the complex issues that arise when people set out to bring change within large and diverse systems, such as higher education in the UK. In some ways higher education is much better at resisting change than it is in participating in it.

Thus we have an exciting but challenging cocktail, which combines a system as yet little changed and resistant to change with some very strong forces for change.

Clearly there are many different approaches to bringing about change within higher education. System-wide changes, for example, can be levered through funding mechanisms. Thus a government wanting to 'widen participation' in higher education, can persuade universities to play their part by offering financial incentives to institutions to recruit students from backgrounds which do not generally lead to participation in university education. In this chapter, however, I am wanting to focus upon the use of research development projects as a way of promoting change. The logic of the project approach has been to earmark funds where innovation and change is thought to be required, and make them available to university-based teams who are then charged with the responsibility of innovating and disseminating the outcomes of their innovation.

The 1990s saw a raft of different tranches of nationally funded development work. The most significant schemes included Enterprise in Higher Education (EHE), the Teaching and Learning Technology Projects (TLTP), the Fund for Development of Teaching and Learning (FDTL), and several phases of employment-focused development projects funded by the higher education and employment division of DfEE (now DfES) at Moorfoot in Sheffield. The arrival of such 'development funding' within higher education is still a relatively recent phenomenon and the extent to which it has been successful in levering national changes is a matter of some conjecture. Successive evaluations of HEFCE and DfES development projects have often applauded the quality of innovative work carried out by project teams, whilst casting considerable doubt about the likelihood that their work would be influential outside the immediate context within which it had occurred. That phenomenon is not limited to the UK as the following quote from the US indicates:

> Serious responses to complaints about undergraduate teaching have generated original and creative pedagogical and curricular experiments. But too often bold and promising efforts have vanished after external grant support disappeared, have withered on the fringes of the curriculum or have been so compromised that their originality has been lost.
>
> (Boyer Commission 1998)

Alongside the increase in the number of HE-focused development projects there is also a gradual move towards more educational research studies, which focus upon HE (Murphy 1996). This is reflected in a recent partnership arrangement between HEFCE and the ESRC which has helped to fund Phase 3 of the ESRC's 'Teaching and Learning Research Programme' (TLRP), which has a focus upon post-compulsory education, and is likely to include a number of HE-focused projects.

The failure of dissemination models to deliver lasting change

Most research and development work which has addressed specific higher education issues has included an emphasis on the importance of disseminating findings and new knowledge to those working in higher education. Thus a good research and development project as well as carrying out creative and successful research/development work would often be expected to disseminate its work throughout the HE system. This rather naive model of dissemination has led to a preponderance of rather ineffective one day conferences, and growing recognition that getting change to occur within the mass system of higher education is likely to involve something much more considered and long term.

The very word 'disseminate' can itself project the wrong type of message. For many dissemination focuses upon the activity of passing on project reports or other kinds of outcome, either through distributing papers, downloading materials onto websites, or face-to-face conferences and meetings. This contrasts markedly with the very different emphasis created by a focus upon 'impact'. A concern with the impact of new thinking on others relates more to what change it makes to them and their practices, rather than just on how information is passed or made available to them.

Hawkins and Winter (1997) were asked to write a report for the DfEE reflecting upon what had been learned about impact from the diverse activities that occurred as a result of the Enterprise in Higher Education initiatives. In their report, *Mastering Change*, they set out an organic model for fostering change within HE institutions. Likening this process to that of growing an oak tree they focused on an ACORN model, which is made up of Action, Communication, Reflection, Ownership and Nurture. Whilst noting that such a process of change 'depends upon a number of external factors which are not in the control of any one individual' they point to the important role of change agents 'who can make a difference even with moderate resources by following the ACORN principles'. Their report concludes by proposing 'seven winning characteristics of the successful agent of change'. Such a person:

1. has a sense of purpose;
2. has the capability to act;
3. sells success;
4. is strategically connected;
5. is critically reflective;
6. builds supportive structures;
7. is opportunistic.

The change model proposed by Hawkins and Winter (1997) does assume a much more complicated model of change within higher education, than the rather simplistic models of linear change that have been put forward in the past. Authors such as Nisbet and Broadfoot (1980) have repeatedly attacked the dangers of dissemination models that imply that research and development projects should transmit their findings to users, who will then go ahead and apply them. However, the process by which new ideas and research evidence percolates through to practitioners is very difficult to chart in a precise way. Nisbet and Broadfoot capture the mysteries of the impact of research through the following illustration:

> The impact of research findings is not like a parcel being delivered to the post-room, neatly done up and which finds its way upstairs so that different people can take the wrappings off. It is more like somebody releasing a canister of gas somewhere – it blows about and at any one moment, if you were walking down the corridors you could sniff it but you wouldn't quite know where it had got to – you might find somebody

> coughing and spluttering in a corner who'd actually taken an enormous dose of it!
>
> (Fiske – as quoted in Nisbet and Broadfoot 1980)

All of this gives us a clearer focus upon the dilemmas that face those engaged in research and development projects related to higher education. Naturally the hope is that it will influence practices in higher education. And certainly those funding such projects within higher education are often primarily interested in projects as a mechanism for producing change. Nevertheless the motivation to produce widespread changes on the back of individual research and development projects can often lead to activities that are doomed to have little impact. It is entirely reasonable for those funding such projects to insist that the projects have strategies for publicizing the work, but it is less than helpful for them to impose unrealistic demands on them to ensure national, or even widespread change.

Thus distinctions need to be made between publicizing, disseminating and making an impact on practice on the basis of the findings of research and development projects. Each aim on its own does not necessarily lead to the others. This is an area that has been addressed by many organizing funded projects, for example the National Coordination Team, based at the Open University, who in their advice on project dissemination state that:

> Dissemination is thus a primary purpose of Innovations, but it means much more than simply telling academic colleagues about excellent practice. Dissemination has been successful when educational practice has changed in response to the disseminated excellent practice.
>
> (Innovations Fund Project Briefing 2000)

Behind that guidance lie many issues. Firstly not all development projects are successful in identifying 'excellent practice'. Such projects are often testing untried ideas, experimenting with approaches that are unusual and novel. Thus the first responsibility of such projects has to be to take stock of what has been discovered through the work and report that to others. Too often the simplistic view of project dissemination leads projects to assume that they are required to get others to adopt the innovations that they have been involved in. This is in itself one of the biggest dangers of such work, as it denies the need to collect evidence and assess that evidence to see what has been learned. Development projects will frequently list unanticipated problems, the clever ideas they start out with may not work out as expected, and others need to be able to know that and to learn from the failures as well as the successes. Good research and development projects rely upon an impartial collection and analysis of evidence, which is designed to contribute to conclusions about the success of the experiment that is being conducted. Thus the FDTL advice is most appropriate when 'excellent practice' has been demonstrated and that conclusion is supported by adequate evidence. Where project findings are less clear cut then those involved need to be much more cautious in what they report to others, and how they report their 'key messages'.

Should impact be a major objective for development projects?

In the previous section I have considered some of the problems that surround the translation of research and development work into changes in policy and practice in higher education. Before going any further with that analysis, it is important to stand back from that discussion and consider what type of impact is likely to be appropriate, because if no impact is desirable then the fact that it has not occurred could in some cases be a very good thing.

Mollas-Gullart *et al.* (2000) in a wider consideration of the impact of social science on 'non-academic audiences' include a helpful discussion of the status of new knowledge, which can emerge from research and development projects and raise pertinent questions about the desirability of 'knowledge transfer' depending upon the status and quality of claims to have produced 'new knowledge' as a result of individual projects.

> Although impact may at first appear a straightforward enough notion, the extent to which likely research impact should count as a consideration in the selection and conduct of research agendas is also controversial. The debate on the nature of social and economic research applications is as old as the disciplines themselves. Most would agree that, wherever social and economic research can help to address societal problems, this potential should be exploited; yet to make the pursuit of impact an explicit goal of academic research is a much more controversial issue. There are several reasons why this is the case, including the following:
>
> - The results of social sciences research may be used without being properly understood (Lévy-Levoyer 1986)
> - There are many social research disciplines that make a desirable contribution to knowledge but, because of their nature, are unlikely to be the subject of direct utilisation (for instance ancient history, philosophy, literary criticism, sociology of knowledge, archaeology) (Heller 1986b)
> - Superficial, low quality research has often had a very substantial impact, particularly when conclusions are not threatening to their potential audiences and have been presented in a simple manner (Heller 1986a)
> - Social and economic research can be used to justify political or other decisions, and hence to confirm the prejudices of policymakers (Caplan 1974).
>
> (Mollas-Gullart *et al.* 2000: 7–8)

Those warnings, about the dangers of pressing too hard for research findings to be applied and used, were written in the context of a review of ESRC funded research and its impact on 'non-academic users'. It is possible to argue that in the context of research and development projects in HE, the dangers of inappropriate dissemination that leads to impact and change are even greater. HE development projects are by their very nature not designed along the lines of rigorous research studies, intended to uncover new knowledge and bring forward convincing evidence to support new claims. The recent history of HE development projects through UK initiatives such as TLTP, FDTL and the DfES/DfEE's various rounds of employment-related work in HE, has yielded quite a range of work, much of which has been somewhat speculative. Furthermore, the rigorous testing of ideas through robust research designs has not been a priority. Typical development projects may have some of the characteristics of 'action research' (Carr and Kemmis 1983; Elliott 1987) as those engaging in them are combining their development work with their normal work as higher education practitioners. However, many of those involved in such development work have no training in educational research, and often look for evidence to support their claims from small-scale evaluation activities that often run alongside their projects. All in all this reminds us to treat the claims of HE development projects with some care. Such claims may be based upon small-scale studies often conducted within a local context (say a single HE institution or a consortium arrangement within a geographical location). Those running such projects are often enthusiasts for the ideas they are trialling and as such may not be in the best position to form an impartial view of the status of their findings, and in turn their relevance to the HE system as a whole.

This question of the nature of the knowledge that may or may not emerge from HE development projects makes the discussion of the twin notions of 'dissemination' and 'impact' even more complicated. What is undoubtedly important is that any consideration of disseminating findings and trying to bring about change as a result of them must be preceded by a careful consideration of what has been learned from any specific development project. Those running such projects need to be encouraged to lay out their findings in such a way as to allow others to form judgements about the nature of their claims, and the evidence upon which they are based. In most senses the same rules that are applied in judging research need to be applied to development projects.

Key questions to ask in every case are:

- What did the study attempt to find out?
- What did the study claim to have found out?
- What evidence exists upon which any claims can be judged?
- Are the claims to new knowledge supported by a critical appraisal of that evidence?
- If there are any uncertainties associated with particular claims, what is the degree of uncertainty?
- Does further work need to be conducted to test the robustness of any emerging claims – either in different settings or involving different individuals, etc?

In raising these issues, I do not want to be seen as undermining the usefulness of HE development projects, nor those who have put time into running them. It is, however, necessary to question the dual pressures put on projects to be seen to have succeeded with whatever idea/scheme/initiative they are trialling and to rush out and disseminate the good news to policy makers and practitioners around the UK (and elsewhere), who can then be expected to revise their ideas and practices forthwith. Development projects will not all succeed with the good ideas and intentions that they set out with, and findings that are apparently less promising can be just as valuable as those that report success. The least desirable option is for those running development projects, that are far from successful, to then go ahead under some sense of duty or obligation to disseminate their ideas (as opposed to findings) to others, who may adapt them 'because they come from an apparently high status funded project or experienced developer'.

We need to accept that the existing evidence base in higher education, in relation, for example, to some key questions about student learning, is fairly limited as compared to other areas of educational research (Murphy 1996). So one of the fundamental reasons why research and development projects have not made an obvious widespread impact upon policy and practice is because the nature of the evidence emerging from them has often been equivocal, pointing the way to further enquiry rather than immediate dramatic changes in policy and practice. Higher education in the UK, and elsewhere, is still seriously under-researched, and although the rise in the amount of funding which has been made available to support several tranches of development projects is welcome, there is a long, long way to go if we are to raise the quality of knowledge transfer in this particular area.

I do not want to go into a great deal of detail about the shortcomings of recent development projects in higher education, but will illustrate some of the types of common deficiencies by referring to a list that I developed (Murphy 1998) as a result of a review of over 50 HE development projects for the DfEE in 1998. Clearly not every project reviewed suffered from every problem listed below, but they were all concerns that were widespread across the set of projects as a whole. They can be summarized as follows (Murphy 1998: 9):

- Poor project management.
- Inexperienced staff drafted in to run projects, which had been devised by others.
- Individual projects going over ground, which had already been well covered by other projects in the past.
- Low levels of institutional/organizational commitment to projects leading to poor support and marginality even within the host organization.
- Disproportionate relationship between project aims and funding awarded.
- Poor communication and networking skills, resulting in isolation and lack of effectiveness of individual projects.
- Limited support available for project staff when facing difficulties.

- Neglect of systematic evaluation at the level of individual projects.
- Limited view of how to disseminate development work either within own organization or beyond.
- Variable roles and quality of project steering groups.

Achieving impact where it is appropriate and desirable

Having noted the warnings of the previous section, about weighing the evidence as part of a process of deciding what to disseminate, how to disseminate it and what actions are desirable in response to that dissemination, we can now turn again to considering what mechanisms might work best within higher education. One of the themes of recent years has been to acknowledge that making individual project teams responsible for their own dissemination is one of the least productive ways forward.

Many phases of HE development project work have multiple projects working on interrelated themes. The current phase of DfES/HEFCE Innovations Fund projects includes 48 projects all working within three thematic areas and within the same two-year period of funding. The fact that each project might produce its own report, set up its own website and hold its own end of project conference is highly alarming. Such projects are under pressure to show that they are communicating their findings to others, and such actions are at one level understandable. However, from the point of view of busy academics who may have things to learn from such projects, what is needed are overviews of emerging issues across groups of projects, hopefully presented in such a way that individual users can find their way to the particular specialist knowledge that they are interested in. Sadly that is not always available, and even though the meta-analysis and synthesis of research findings is so important (Chelimsky 1995) it often receives far less attention than it deserves.

In many professions in recent years there have been attempts to promote moves towards 'evidence-based practice', alongside a strengthening of both initial and post-experience professional education and training (Ilott and Murphy 1999). Most prominent among these have been the work in medicine and health areas, but now there is a greater realization in education as well that we ignore research evidence at our peril. The concept of 'evidence-based practice' is, I suppose, quite simple and seductive, what is more difficult is working out how to operationalize it. In medicine the 'Cochrane Collaboration', for reviewing evidence in relation to particular topics, has been fraught with controversy in recent years. In education, and in higher education in particular, we have got a long way to go to establish any substantial central facility for sifting and synthesizing research evidence. The nearest we have come to that is the newly established DfES Evidence for Policy and Practice Information (EPPI) Coordination Centre in London. Such centres by themselves do not, of course, solve the problem of how to translate research evidence into changed practice. They do, however, have an important part to play, as they gather the outputs from numerous research studies, aggregate findings and similar data to build the bigger picture.

In higher education in the UK, the Learning and Teaching Support Network (LTSN) is trying to perform a brokerage role in 24 subject areas. The LTSN centres, it is hoped, will overview existing research and development work and produce easily digested overviews to those working in their particular specialisms. The concept is apparently very simple, but the practical realities are, as we all know, much more complicated. An early flyer produced by the LTSN programme director began as follows:

> There is no shortage of good ideas, good practices and innovations in learning, teaching and assessment in HE in the UK. One of the challenges now facing us is the need to transfer the experience more widely and support the take-up of good practices by individuals, departments and whole institutions.
>
> (Cliff Allan, LTSN programme director 2000)

It is clear how LTSN centres can start to play a role in supporting 'knowledge transfer', say between HE development projects and busy academics working within specific subject areas. The LTSN centres have the job of collecting, summarizing and weighing the evidence and ideas emerging from relevant research and development work, and then, operating as 'educational brokers', they can attempt to distribute the 'distilled wisdom' to their subject communities. As with all such things one can get carried away by the apparent simplicity of such a process, but it is not nearly as simple as it seems. The LTSN centre, assuming that it is in touch with relevant projects, has to face considerable challenges in knowing how to weigh the evidence from development projects, and may wish not to be a broker at all, but just offer 'website space' so that individual projects can send messages via the LTSN centre to the subject specialists. This 'postbox' model is still useful but falls a long way short of the clear, focused implementation of good practice model advocated above by Cliff Allan.

As a former director of a LTSN centre, I can see an important role for the centres in relation to disseminating development work in HE. The idea of a central hub which can collect, synthesize and distribute relevant information is of course a very attractive one, but it is also a role which needs proper resourcing. If the function of a LTSN centre is going to be more than just a 'postbox', then evidence needs to be reviewed and overviewed, and evidence-based judgements need to be made about what is passed on to the subject community. Where this works well, large volumes of research and development work can be distilled, synthesized and passed on in a form that is easy to use, authentic and reflecting the certainties/uncertainties implied by the analysis of available evidence.

So one encouraging feature now available to HE development projects is the network of 24 LTSN subject centres. This network will be a considerable focus for disseminating ideas/outcomes that emerge from HE development projects. It will not, however, immediately solve all of the problems, many of which are related to the difficulty, both of summarizing complex information and of finding creative ways of engaging academics with ideas that could be relevant to their future practice.

The principles of effective dissemination

Fuller *et al.* (1994) along with many others have tried to break down the constituent elements of an effective dissemination strategy. In a report for the Employment Department Learning Methods Branch, they highlighted the following elements as being crucial to such a strategy.

Purpose Is the purpose to distribute information about new approaches . . . or to bring about changes such that new approaches are incorporated . . . ?

The message Establishing the purposes of the dissemination highlights the need to clarify what the intended message is. . . . Alternative intentions could be simply to make the audience aware; to provide detailed awareness, mediated information, or access to in depth information. It would be appropriate to provide different degrees of awareness and support to various target groups.

The audience Asking who the audience is acts as a first step in analysing individual organisational and external factors likely to impinge upon the dissemination process. If, in addition, the question of who the related and relevant intermediaries might be is addressed, the beginnings of an action plan begin to emerge.

The messenger Answers to questions concerning the identification of the 'end users' and the intermediaries with whom they interact should lead to decisions about who would be the appropriate messenger(s). Issues related to the credibility of intermediaries are crucial here.

Action plans Having clarified the 'why' 'what' and 'who' of the dissemination process, we turn to the more detailed consideration of **how**, in practical terms, effective dissemination can be achieved. . . . It is suggested that when formulating a dissemination strategy, consideration should be given to a variety of media. Where the scope of the dissemination is ambitious (i.e. altering the practice of a diverse target group), then it is likely that a rich repertoire of methods and media should be adopted. In addition the findings indicated the potential benefit of 'piggy-backing' the dissemination on related initiatives.

Evaluation As part of the systems approach to dissemination which is being advocated it is important to identify criteria for the success of the dissemination. Such indicators should be derived from the combination of diagnosis and prescription on which the strategy has been formulated.

Conclusion If practitioners' practice is to be influenced . . . then steps will have to be taken to change their behaviour. Whilst dissemination is seen as an important component of the change process, we have stressed that for sustainable changes to happen . . . a broader analysis of the operational and environmental context needs to be conducted. . . . If the aim extends to changing practice within organisations . . . (we) strongly suggest that the dissemination should be accompanied by an organisational development plan. . . . In addition, process and outcome indicators can be developed to focus attention on criteria which provide evidence that the intended changes are occurring.

(All extracts from Fuller, Jones, Maguire and Pugh 1994)

Trying to improve the science of disseminating from research and development projects has been a major concern for grant-awarding and policy-making bodies in recent years. The Fuller *et al.* (1994) work was conducted for DfEE, and is paralleled by the Mollas-Gullart *et al.* (2000) which was conducted more recently for the ESRC and which looked, in particular, at methods for assessing whether dissemination can be shown to effect change. Meanwhile the Learning and Skills Development Agency (LSDA) and the Qualifications and Curriculum Authority (QCA) have ongoing work being conducted in reports and commissioning exercises. The ESRC experience is particularly interesting, as they are now trying systematically to evaluate the impact of the dissemination activities of their major programmes as part of the post-programme evaluation strategy, that they apply after the end of all of their major research programmes.

For reasons that we have explored within this chapter the tracing of direct evidence of impact is an elusive process. Even in situations where everyone is convinced that a major programme of project work has made a big impact, it is often difficult to trace simple linear routes along which information has flowed. That takes us back to Fiske's canister of gas analogy in Nisbet and Broadfoot (1980: 3), or in more sophisticated terms to a way of understanding impact that allows for the process to be less specific and more organic in nature. Nisbet and Broadfoot (1980) and many others have worked with the idea that good research changes things through raising awareness of issues, and brings things onto the agenda that were not there before. Like all human learning it is at times a mysterious process, but no less valuable for that. To illustrate the enduring nature of some of these debates, I would like to quote Powell (1980) who presents a picture which is both realistic and optimistic about how research can, over time, contribute to profound lasting changes.

> It is through its contribution to this *climate of opinion* that educational research probably has its most profound effect. Thus, though an individual piece of research may have little effect, research cumulatively may have a great deal.
>
> (Powell 1980: p. 2)

Conclusions

Higher education currently faces many important dilemmas and those working on policy and practice in changing areas need all available guidance from good educational research and development studies. However, the model of 'knowledge transfer' used needs to be more sophisticated than some used in the past. Educational researchers and educational developers can make their impact as their studies change 'climates of opinion' and their ideas are disseminated through the wide variety of mechanisms, which now contribute to the professional experience of those working in higher education. The greatest need is for the best new ideas to be reflected in the initial and post-experience training and staff development opportunities, which are now happily seen as a much more normal part of the professional experience of academics than they were some years ago.

7

Philosophical Approaches to Academic Development

David Gosling

Academic development is not one thing, but many things. It is constituted by a large variety of processes and activities which may be described in different ways. In a recent article Wright and Miller (2000) show that the range of verbs used to describe these activities and processes of academic development include 'to support, promote, enhance, improve, research' teaching and learning, or sometimes, more specifically, innovations in teaching and learning.

In this chapter I will be exploring ways in which a philosophical approach to academic development can assist in clarifying the goals and values of academic development and why it is important that we should seek such clarity. I also hope to demystify what might otherwise appear to be a daunting and intellectually challenging process by describing some ways in which philosophical approaches can be incorporated into academic development. This entails that we should clarify what we understand by a philosophical approach and philosophical methods. Since there is only limited agreement about these things among philosophers, it is impossible to do this without taking sides on a number of issues.

Let me illustrate my claim that philosophical approaches are needed by reference to two key phrases commonly heard in the field of academic development – one is 'scholarship of teaching and learning', (SOTL) and the other is 'evidence-based practice'.

The first approach, that of the 'scholarship of teaching and learning' is characterized by critical reflection on professional practice, systematic investigation and evaluation of teaching and learning, exploration of theory which informs our practice, accumulating knowledge about teaching and learning (in higher education) and communicating that knowledge to practitioners (Hutchings and Shulman 1999). Higher education has suffered from a polarization between academic development, which has tended to be pragmatic and practitioner based, and pedagogical research, which has, by and large, remained disassociated from actual practice. The wedge that has been driven between teaching and research – for example in the recent

Fundamental Review of Research (HEFCE 2000b) – further exacerbates this polarization. The assumption seems to be that teaching is not a proper subject of scholarly research and can exist in a social world almost entirely devoid of intellectual enquiry.

The scholarship of teaching and learning challenges these bifurcations and brings together what are sometimes treated as polar opposites within a single field of endeavour. In doing so it will clearly consider the phenomenographic and psychological theories which have formed the dominant discourse in learning and teaching in recent times (Webb 1996a; Gosling 2000a). These have focused on students' experience of learning through a categorization of qualitatively different 'approaches to learning' and have emphasized the need to encourage 'deep learning' by treating students as participants in the learning process (see, for example, Ramsden 1992; Marton and Booth 1997; Biggs 1999; Prosser and Trigwell 1999). But this body of theory is weak on explaining the broader social goals of higher education and has little to say about what kind of learning is of value (Webb 1996a). Unless this approach also includes an analysis of the key concepts in the discourses within it, assumptions remain unchallenged or unjustified. Reflection on teaching which does not also subject to critical analysis the under-pinning theories of knowledge and evidence will take for granted what it means to learn something in the sense of coming to know (Barnett and Griffin 1997). The values which teaching supports and the values which are embedded in curriculum choices need to be made explicit and examined. Similarly the social relations between lecturer and student(s) need to be examined in the context of a theory about the place of the individual in society, and the function of institutions of higher education within a state system (Barnett 2000).

A second example relates to the idea of 'evidence-based practice'. Much of national policy on research into higher education (see, for example, NERF 2002) seems to make the assumption that only research which is empirical has value. Indeed it sometimes appears to be the case that unless an activity in some sense provides data upon which others can determine 'best practice' then it doesn't count as research. The assumption that practice is improved by its being informed by systematic collection of data might indeed seem to be a reasonable one. After all, who would want a professional practice that was not based in some sense on evidence?

The concern is that an exclusive concentration on the systematic collection of data using accepted methodologies adopted from the sciences and social sciences leaves enormous gaps in any consideration of educational practice. What are these gaps? What is left out by a thorough going empirically based inquiry? The answer to this question will lead us into an exploration of those areas of conceptual inquiry which traditionally have been regarded as philosophical. What sorts of questions are these? They are questions such as what do we most value in our society? How do we prioritize our values? How do we decide between values when they conflict – for example between liberty and justice, equality and rights, the individual and the social? What is the nature of knowledge and can knowledge be divided into different types or fields? What counts as learning? Is learning always a good or are some forms of learning preferable to others?

Any research into education inevitably raises questions such as these for two reasons. First, because one of the fundamental goals of education is about taking people on a journey from their pre-existing states of understanding, knowledge, skills, and values to what is intended to be a better set of understandings and capacities for action. This, therefore, requires us to have a view about what is 'better' for people – is it being able to act in certain ways or to have better understandings, and what is the relationship between actions and understandings?

Second, because education is a social enterprise it necessarily raises questions of the relationship between education and society, the relationship between teachers and learners, the relationship between the goals of education and our views about what constitutes a good or well-functioning society. The recent debate about graduateness, about the place of key skills in higher education and about vocationalism, competencies and recording achievements takes us very quickly into these questions. Academic development which focused entirely on the technical aspects of how to embed key skills in the curriculum, or to implement progress files across the institution, without facing up to these fundamental questions will be impoverished and naive. Furthermore without that critical, questioning function, academic development becomes merely a tool for the implementation of decisions made by others whether these are by government policy, institutional managers, or teaching departments.

Learning

The literature on approaches to learning is vast but most of it assumes that the terms such as 'effective learning' are uncontentious, but a philosophical approach would soon show that this is far from the case (Gosling 2000a; Rowland 2000). Is effective learning simply a matter of having internalized *any* set of beliefs? Or is effective learning based on more secure knowledge than ineffective learning? How is the effectiveness of learning related to the nature of the knowledge acquired? If learning is defined as coming to know something, then the relationship between learning and knowledge becomes a critical issue.

Learning effectively is not just a psychological process. It is also about the relationship between the learner and the subject of the learning (the knowledge). It is about the evidence for knowledge (what counts as appropriate evidence, how secure the evidence needs to be, and the understanding of the learner about the status of the evidence.

The importance of considering the nature of evidence, and the methods for acquiring and recognizing evidence, is critical for the teaching of a discipline. As Rowland has pointed out 'our commitment to our subject infuses us with the values embodied in it' (Rowland 2000: 113). An important part of the value-set embodied in a discipline is the way in which the discourse of the subject values or denies value to certain sorts of knowledge claims and certain sorts of argument. The extent to which the teacher should make explicit these value commitments is a contentious matter. Foundation science courses vary enormously in the extent to which they encourage students to think about how they are arriving at what counts as knowledge. The teaching method of a tutor who wishes to forefront questions of scientific methodology and the provisionality of scientific knowledge will be very different from one who takes the view that students need to learn, as facts, what is currently the consensus in the discipline about what is reality. There is the additional question about when the engagement with the provisionality of knowledge is appropriate. As Rorty has said 'Education has to start from acculturation'. We can afford to question reality as a given 'only after having passed through stages of implicit and then explicit and self-conscious conformity to the norms of the discourses going on around us' (Rorty 1980: 365). An important question for both curriculum design and for teaching method is how to introduce discussion, and therefore questioning, of the norms of the discipline discourse whilst also reinforcing the value of those norms.

The same issues arise in more acute forms in a multi- or interdisciplinary area of study, or in problem-based learning and experiential learning, where negotiating disciplinary boundaries becomes a key difficulty. The matter is further complicated by the debate in postmodernism about whether such ways of dividing knowledge are legitimate (Barnett and Griffin 1997), the extent to which these 'forms of knowledge' are culturally specific to European conceptions of knowledge (Scott 2000) and the discussion about whether there are new modes of knowledge, mode two knowledge, which break out of the traditional mould (Gibbons *et al.* 1994). Globalization, it is also said, challenges traditional concepts of the 'subject' (Castells 2001) and new technologies may also be creating new ways of thinking (Brown 2000) which are not bounded by existing ways of dividing knowledge into 'subjects' or 'disciplines'. . . . In the light of this complexity (or 'supercomplexity' as Barnett has described the situation for universities in the postmodern world) we must be cautious about talking about learning or 'effective learning' as if it were a simple and uncontentious matter.

I have been arguing so far that philosophical questions are unavoidable in academic development. It is time now to think about how philosophical approaches to these issues can begin to answer these questions, or help others to answer them. What are the distinctive characteristics of philosophical approaches and how can they be incorporated into academic development? In order to simplify a complex issue, I am going to divide the discussion into three types of philosophical approach, which I will call a methodological approach, a content approach and a schools of thought approach. In doing so I do not wish to imply that these are entirely separate and distinct, only that they have different emphases and different foci.

Clearly there is no single way of doing philosophy, and yet without some organizing principles there could be nothing that is recognizably 'philosophical'. In what follows I try to avoid any essentialist assumptions about what constitutes philosophy whilst also trying to prevent what Bishop Berkeley once famously accused philosophers of doing – 'We have first raised a dust and then complain we cannot see' (Berkeley, *Principles of Human Knowledge*, (introduction) p. 3).

Methodological approach

On this view the distinctiveness of a philosophical approach to academic development lies in the adoption of certain methods of enquiry which have been utilized in philosophical discourses. Philosophy is concerned with the concepts and the arguments we use to establish truths, or to engage in discussion, to persuade others or to think for ourselves. Concepts are necessarily related to the language in which they are expressed, and so, as a consequence, philosophy has always had a strong interest in the language we use, or as we might prefer to say today, post-Foucauld, the discourses we use. The relationship between concepts and language is itself a difficult philosophical issue, but any use of a philosophical approach will encourage us to be critical of the key terms we use, and to question their origins, their relationship and the assumptions which are hidden in them. This process was once called analysis, but is sometimes today called 'deconstruction', although these terms carry quite different connotations.

An important point is to recognize that most of the concepts that are relevant to academic development are what has been called 'essentially contested concepts' – that is, different meanings will be attached to them by different people who espouse different belief systems – political, ideological, psychological, cultural. Sometimes when particular meanings are attached to a word like 'development' it is because someone is either trying to give a 'prescriptive' definition – that is to say how the word ought to be used – or a 'persuasive' definition – that is taking up a partisan position about the use of the word – or both.

A good example of an extended attempt to engage in conceptual analysis is Barnett's *The Idea of Higher Education* (1990). He says in his introduction that he needs to analyze key concepts such as 'culture, rationality, research, and academic freedom' as well as that of higher education itself, in order to build what he calls a 'justificatory framework'. What Barnett tries to do is what he calls 'conceptual archaeology' – the examination of ideas that are 'embedded in our shared ideas and our public discourse about higher education' (Barnett 1990: 9). He approaches this by making explicit what he perceives as some underlying trends in the history of discussion about the nature of higher education and exposes these trends so that they can be discussed.

But analysis is not the end of the philosophical method, it is only a key element within it. Even more important is the place of argument. The philosophical method is centrally about developing arguments and being critical of arguments. Key ideas here are about the validity of argument, consistency and contradiction, expanding on taken-for-granted assumptions and testing their implications. A specialist branch of philosophy, logic, has focused on our understanding of the relationship between propositions and what can or cannot be logically deduced from them, but a detailed knowledge of logic is not necessary to engage in an examination of whether a position is consistent or contains fatal inconsistencies. The essential requirement is a willingness to engage in a more or less systematic and critical, rational process of argument. What this rules out is as important as what it includes. It rules out beliefs that cannot be supported by argument; expressions of feeling without any logical support; beliefs supported only by an authority (religious, parental, political leader), expression which cannot be put in propositional form (like much of art). For some, these exclusions strengthen philosophy, as a rationalist would claim; for others they impoverish it, as a religious believer or an artist might claim.

A third element of the philosophical method concerns justification. In traditional empirical philosophy a distinction was drawn between 'facts' and 'values' (Hume 1739). On this view value positions cannot be entirely derived from empirical enquiry. Nor can prescriptions about what we 'ought' to do follow directly from any set of facts. For any set of data to entail an action, Hume argued that there must always be an intervening value statement. Some modern philosophers have argued that the traditional 'is/ought' or 'fact/value' distinction is not as clear-cut as early empiricist philosophers thought. Rorty, for example, argues against the idea that factual or objective statements somehow hold a mirror up to nature, while value statements come from our inner personal commitments. He argues that our only useable notion of 'objectivity' is 'agreement' and that the only difference between value and factual statements is the extent to which they command agreement within communities of language users. There are no unquestionable or privileged representations of reality, because they all exist within frameworks of contingent local conversations which are value laden. That applies to science as much as it does to other areas of discourse (Rorty 1980).

The philosophical method is, as Rorty says, to 'continue the conversation' rather than 'find the truth' (Rorty 1980: 373). Thinking there is a truth, or a matter of fact, to be 'discovered' is a false goal, because it is a way of ending conversations. Equally, the philosophical method resists another way of ending conversations, namely by ideological dictat, by the unassailable value statement which cannot be challenged. The academic development literature appears to be relatively undogmatic and apolitical, but if we scratch the surface we soon find values, ethics and political commitments. The partisanship is only hidden because it is rarely discussed or challenged in a 'community of practice' in which there are strongly held and shared value systems (Lave and Wenger 1991). It is often the case that it is only when the assumptions of a community of practice are challenged that they are made more explicit (Malcolm and Zukas 2000).

Content approach

Another, and overlapping, approach would be to use the traditional philosophical questions and areas of inquiry and then apply them to what interests us in academic development. Philosophy has conventionally been divided into several major areas of enquiry – epistemology, metaphysics, logic, ethics or moral philosophy, aesthetics, philosophy of mind, political philosophy. This is what has been called the philosophical 'canon' but over time it has varied considerably, particularly as areas that were once not thought to be amenable to empirical enquiry become newly formed sciences – for example, sociology, psychology and linguistics.

A central area of philosophy relevant to academic development is epistemology. This includes enquiries into what is it to know something, what, if anything, can be known with certainty, what counts as evidence, what distinguishes different forms of enquiry or the 'disciplines'? In the defence of a subject-based approach to the curriculum or to academic development, the distinctions between disciplines becomes a critical issue, although one which is often ignored by those who advocate discipline-centred academic development.

The study of ethics considers questions about what are regarded as rights and wrongs and how these are justified; what are the ways in which humans should behave towards each other; what are our duties, our rights and responsibilities. In academic development relevant issues include: what are good/right/appropriate relationships between teacher and students; what are the ethical dimensions to the disciplines we teach; what moral duties do universities owe to their staff and students; is higher education concerned with the moral education of its students? An important contemporary ethical issue arising in academic development is the place of tolerance towards others and to alternative systems of thought or belief: how important is tolerance; why do we value it; are there limits to tolerance; can tolerance be taught (Rawls 1972)?

The study of values is closely related to ethics, but ranges beyond human relationships. As I have indicated above a key question here is what is worth knowing? What makes a subject important? How do we prioritize what students learn? Who has the right to decide – teacher, student, or society?

The philosophy of mind includes enquiries into the nature of a person, the relationship of mind and body, mental states and outward behaviour, the nature of intentionality, consciousness, emotion. Of particular interest in academic development are questions such as: what is it to learn something; how is learning different from a reflex, an instinct, or something that simply develops; are some ways of learning preferable to others; what assumptions are made about learners as individual subjects; is education about mental states or behaviour?

Social/political philosophy is concerned with questions such as what kind of society, political institutions, culture do we wish to aim for? It assesses the claims for different principles for organizing a just society, for example equality, social contract, rights and also examines the justifications for political systems such as democracy, anarchism, socialism, feminism and so on. Some key concepts include liberty, freedom, representation, the state, community, liberalism. Of particular interest in higher education are issues of access and equity, equality of opportunity, financing, significance of the sector to the state, social and economic goals of teaching and research, and the autonomy of universities (academic freedom).

This very brief summary of the relevance of philosophical issues and questions to academic development is intended merely to map out the scope of some forms of enquiry which a philosophical approach might include.

Schools of thought

Finally, a third approach could be based on the insights, arguments, style, and methods of particular philosophers or schools of thought. A good illustration of this approach is Webb's *Understanding Staff Development* (Webb 1996a) which compares positivist, hermeneutic, critical theory and postmodernist understandings of staff development. The approach in this case proceeds by consideration of a body of thought proposed by schools of philosophers often in a context not originally conceived as responding to issues in higher education, although in a minority of cases philosophers such as Plato, Locke, Rousseau, Dewey (pragmatism), Habermas (critical theory) and Russell have commented directly on education and its role in society. The aim is to take the ideas and ways of thinking of that philosopher and then apply them to the questions (or others like them) considered above.

Three examples will suffice to illustrate this approach – Rorty, Foucault and Habermas. We have already mentioned Rorty above. As a pragmatist he offers a particular conception of knowledge and enquiry which is characterized by a form of relativism in which truth, insofar as it is possible to use the term, is understood to be created through agreement between speakers within a community of practice. Inquiry must always be tentative, provisional and open to revision. Any understanding will always be only a possible reading, and never a definitive or exclusive account of an objective reality. It is always important for Rorty that the door is kept open for further conversation and further illumination. Badley (2001) argues that the academic developer is never in a position to deal in absolutes, to provide the final truth, or to describe an entirely objective reality. On the contrary in any debate on teaching methods, curriculum design or modes of assessment, the best we can achieve is to stimulate a conversation which attempts to create a vocabulary with which we can tell a more-or-less convincing story about what is happening or what could happen.

A second example of a philosopher who is influencing philosophical approaches to academic development is Foucault whose archaeology of knowledge explores how concepts and social cultures emerge through historical analysis of discourses. Foucault emphasizes that it is through discourse that social power is established, maintained and modified. Social control is not possessed by individuals or by social institutions, but rather is created by what he calls technologies of production, technologies of sign systems which permit the use of signs, meanings, symbols and signification, technologies of power, which determine conduct through types of domination, and technologies of the self, which allow individuals to behave or not behave in certain ways. Foucault traced the development of important social institutions such as crime, punishment and prisons, madness and psychiatry. He traces from the late eighteenth century what he regards as a key shift from arbitrary external control to internalized self-control.

Foucault's influence has been twofold. First, he has bequeathed a method, a way of approaching discourses to reveal the shifts in thinking, relations and behaviour over time. Second, he has suggested some theories about how power is established, about ways in which individuals become complicit in their own subjugation, and how knowledge is constructed through rule-bound 'truth-games'. Foucauldian analyses of academic development might explore the emergence of the learning and teaching discourses in higher education over the last 15 years and the place of academic development in that process. It would explore how and why it has become permitted to talk about teaching and learning as an important policy driver. Interesting topics for analysis, might include the rise of outcomes-based curriculum design, the growing popularity of 'reflective practice' and 'scholarship of teaching and learning', and how and why the learner and learning achieved the dominance which these concepts currently enjoy. Any attempt to utilize a Foucauldian approach will examine not only what can be said at any given time, but also what is being excluded, what is not being said or cannot be said. Webb (1996b) has argued that the current discourses in academic development are exclusionary in some important ways:

> The major categories and metaphors that are praised at present are those of 'reflective practice', the 'deep' and 'surface' metaphor and the idea of emancipation through collaborative action research. Those excluded comprise much of hermeneutics, humanism, post-structuralism including post-structuralist feminism, ethnically informed, localised and historicised research.
>
> (Webb 1996b: 64)

The challenge to academic developers is to face the accusation that significant issues in the curriculum and in debates about teaching and learning have excluded much of the theorizing about, for example, race and ethnicity, feminism, and power relations between staff and between students and staff.

Finally, I want to comment on another contemporary philosopher who has influenced thinking about academic development, namely the German philosopher, Jurgen Habermas. The importance of Habermas is his attempt to preserve the key objectives of the 'Enlightenment project' from the ravages of the postmodernist onslaught. He attempts to distinguish between rationality and various forms of interested discourse in which the search for truth is distorted by power relations. In his study of 'communicative action' he has described what he calls the 'ideal speech situation' in which participants in a conversation have an 'orientation to reaching understanding'. This requires that there are no hidden blocks to achieving a rational consensus, such as undeclared or unchallenged assumptions, failures in understanding of the language used, inequalities of power or a hidden strategic purpose held by one or other of the participants. 'A communicatively achieved agreement has a rational basis; it cannot be imposed by either party, whether instrumentally through intervention in the situation directly or strategically through influencing the decisions of opponents' (Habermas 1984: 287).

The possibility of communicative agreement is one that is of considerable interest to academic developers. In the interactions which academic developers have with staff, there are always important issues of power, communication, and negotiation involved. Habermas provides, not only an account of how rationality can be pursued, but also goals for social communities to which we can aspire and which can be achieved through 'communicative action'. The literature in adult education inspired by Habermas has been extensive (for example, Mezirow (1991 and 1995); Welton (1995)) and there have been some attempts to use Habermasian ideas as a theoretical frame within which issues of academic development can be discussed (Gosling 2000a).

Conclusion

In this chapter I have explored what we might mean by taking philosophical approaches to issues and concerns which are part of academic development as it is currently understood. I have made a plea for greater consideration to be given to questions of the goals and values implicit in discussions of, for example, 'active learning', 'key skills', 'professionalization', 'reflective practice' and so on. If the 'development' literature is to succeed in communicating more effectively with the wider academic community, greater attention needs to be paid to making explicit in discussion the underlying value assumptions. The long history of philosophy provides an enormous wealth of methodological devices, theoretical frameworks and discussion of ideas which are central to Western thought. To ignore the potential contributions of philosophy to academic development is to impoverish the level of debate and ultimately reduce its effectiveness in achieving its goals.

8

Alternative Perspectives on Professional Practice in Academic Development

Sarah J. Mann

Recent scholarship in the field of academic development has sought to investigate the philosophical and theoretical underpinnings of educational development practice. Most notably, Webb (1996a) has offered a critique of the philosophical assumptions underlying staff development practice; Malcolm and Zukas are undertaking a bibliographic and conceptual map of pedagogic models in use in higher education; and, SEDA (Staff and Educational Development Association) is currently undertaking a project to identify the theoretical ideas used by academic development practitioners to underpin their practice. More significantly, it has come to be taken as self-evident over the past few years that professional practice should be evidence-based. The ILT (Institute for Learning and Teaching), for example, includes this as a key criteria for good practice in teaching in higher education. And it is certainly the assumed model for best practice in secondary and primary school teaching, as well as in other fields such as health.

Whilst I fully support the need to identify and critically examine the theoretical assumptions underlying our practice, some part of me is made nervous by the idea that I as a teacher/academic developer, in order to be deemed professional, need to show that my particular practice is informed by published theory and research (i.e. is evidence-based). This goes against my own experience of practice as both a teacher and a teacher educator. My practice emerges in the here and now and is inextricably bound up with who I am, what I believe, what I value and what I know. Published theory and research, i.e. potential evidence to inform my practice, is interpreted by me from within the framework of my own particular personal stance; and only what is 'significant' to me is integrated, as it were, into my own developing frameworks for practice.

The dissonance I feel between my own experience of practice and the 'requirement' to account for practice in terms of published theory and research challenges me to consider the question of authority in relation to practice. On what authority do I base my practice? In order to pursue this question, I have been on a search for alternative ways of thinking about professional practice and the place, or authority, of theory and research evidence in such practice. The results of this reading and reflection are presented through three different perspectives – positivism, praxis and postmodernism, and an attempt is made to show where these perspectives locate the authority for practice.

The chapter is organized in three main sections according to this theme of authority – Authority of science, Authority of the practitioner, and Challenges to authority. It concludes by examining the practitioner's position in relation to these different perspectives and by elucidating what such a position implies for academic development practice and approaches.

Two points need to be made before proceeding with the chapter. First, the main focus is not on the relationship between theory and research (though at times this does come into it), but is on the relationship between 'authorized' or published ideas, theory and research evidence and the practitioner and their practice. (The term 'practitioner' refers here to both the academic developer and the academic as teacher.) Second, given that the scope of the chapter covers vast areas of theoretical and philosophical ground, it is the case that the accounts of these necessarily typify and reduce the complexity of these different perspectives.

Authority of science

The desire to establish the theoretical foundations of an area of practice such as educational development, and the call to professionalize university teaching by founding it on evidence, imply a need to authorize or legitimate such practice. Such a desire for legitimacy in itself implies an assumption that theory and evidence can in some sense provide an absolute ground from which principles, approaches and methods can be founded. Evidence-based practice in particular seems to imply the possibility of absolute knowledge. Hirst (1996) argues that systematic evidence from experimentation needs to inform practice so as to reduce prejudice and ill-considered ideology and that such evidence needs to be generated through public, not private, processes by significant social groups, such as educational researchers. The ESRC has recently established a research programme for the purpose of training educational researchers, particularly in quantitative methods, in order to produce trustworthy evidence which can be used for improving classroom practice. The DfEE has commissioned the Evidence for Policy and Practice Information Co-ordination Centre at the London Institute of Education to include education in its remit.

The desire for its foundation suggests a positivist view of research and the theory and evidence it generates. From a positivist perspective, the achievement of universal, objective and generalizable statements of truth are possible. Such truth, or knowledge, can be expressed as laws of cause and effect or explanatory theories which have predictive power and can thus generate hypotheses which can be tested through experiment and observation. The purpose of such an approach is to explain, to predict and thus to accumulate progressively a secure, objective knowledge foundation. Application of rigorous scientific method (involving value free observation and logical reasoning) secures the validity and reliability of evidence thus generated, privileging it over other forms of knowing.

Such a view, for example as stated by Hirst (1996), judges practitioners' knowledge to be local, particular, subjective, routinized and implicit, and therefore neither valid nor reliable for informing practice. The solution to making practice effective is therefore for practitioners to be informed of 'proper' evidence and to apply this to their practice. For such a view to 'work' it must necessarily assume practice to be devoid of context, value and difference, to be asocial, ahistorical, and atemporal. Thus both context and practitioner must of necessity be assumed to be neutral, and susceptible to control. From such a perspective, the practitioner is required to set aside his or her implicit knowledge in order to receive and apply evidence-based theory rationally to achieve goals or solve his/her practical problems most effectively. The practitioner thus gains authority for his/her practice by becoming a professional technologist through surrendering authority to external legitimacy.

Such a view strives towards 'the unity of science' by assuming that there is no significant difference between the natural world and the social world, such that the scientific method applied to researching the natural world is equally valid and applicable to the social world. Hence arises the need to reduce the social world to context-neutrality in order to assert the assumption that the social world can be explained through causal laws and explanations which can predict behaviour.

From this perspective, we split evidence-based theory and practice into a dualism where the characteristics assigned to theory are implicitly valued over those assigned to practice. Within this positivist perspective, we uphold the academic/researcher as the source of truth in relation to practice, and we marginalize any authority and validity practitioners' claims to truth might have.

The first challenge to the positivist perspective comes from within this 'naturalist' position. Popper argues against the possibility of absolute knowledge. He challenges the logic of positivism which states that if 'a hypothesis (*H*) implies an observation statement (*O*) and if (*O*) is true, then (*H*) is thereby confirmed' (Hollis 1994: 74). In Popper's view, the only logic which holds is one of falsification in which if (*H*) implies (*O*), and if (*O*) is observed to be not true, then it is possible to infer that (*H*) is not true also. Thus the task of science should not be to confirm or seek absolute knowledge but to falsify knowledge. From this view, all knowledge (or evidence) can only ever be provisional. The freedom of society can only be assured where research processes and outcomes are transparent and made public in order to be subjected to critical scrutiny from within the community of scholars. The practitioner, from this perspective, is required to take the stance of a rational sceptic towards research and to view its findings as provisional.

Stenhouse's (1979) argument for research-based teaching seems to be strongly influenced by this Popperian position. Stenhouse compellingly argues for the teacher's role to be one which encourages learners to see knowledge as always provisional and to enable them to develop as critical inquirers of the world around them. Stenhouse also argues for a view of educational research based on such a premise, and which fundamentally engages teachers in research of their own practice, where error and failure are valued as sources of improvement, rather than a seeking of certainty and the confirmation of approaches to practice.

Stenhouse offers a bridge to the next section as it both embraces the Popperian critique of positivism, whilst challenging both positivism and Popper's naturalist position by asserting the particularly social, situated and complex nature of the human world and educational process, in which an uncritical and reductionist technical rationality has no place.

Authority of the practitioner – praxis

The Aristotelian concept of praxis offers an alternative way of thinking about the relationship between research and practice. First, it dissolves the dualism implied by positivism between theory and research-based evidence, and second, in doing so, it reduces the distance between practitioner and researcher by locating the inquiry process with the practitioner. Carr and Kemmis (1986: 33) define praxis as 'informed action which, by reflection on its character and consequences, reflexively changes the "knowledge base" which informs it'. Neither theory nor practice is pre-eminent. Theory and practice inform each other through an iterative, cyclical and reflexive process in such a way that leads to both the enhancement of theory and practice. Praxis necessarily assumes practitioners to be goal-oriented and ethical, capable of engaging in rational and critical analysis of their actions in order to understand and improve them.

Practitioners are required to build actively their own theory of action through critical reflection on practical knowledge reviewed within communities of peers in 'free and open dialogue' (Carr and Kemmis 1986: 31). It is through this process that the potential for practitioner knowledge to be habitual, routine, irrational and ill-informed, can be overcome.

Such a view is based on a very different model of the human being to the naturalist one. Such a view is best described as interpretivism. Interpretivism argues that human beings do not act according to universal and predictable laws of nature but live in a world of significance and meaning in which social action and individual experience can only be understood according to the interpretations individuals make of their contexts and the particular social norms, rules and assumptions governing these. Reality achieves its characteristic of objectivity or truth by being brought into being, made real or constructed through the interplay of subjective meaning and the social rules and assumptions that govern what is taken to be true and appropriate. How people make sense of the world, assign significance to it and act in it, will all be influenced by each individual's particular experience and history, their values, beliefs and assumptions, their previous knowledge and their particular intentions, goals and desires.

Research thus needs to focus on understanding why people act in the way that they do, by finding out how people experience and make sense of their world and their particular context of action. Given that the researcher is by necessity implicated in this social world, no research evidence or theory can achieve the objectivity espoused by positivism. Research findings can only achieve validity through the criteria of coherence in relation to the meanings they reveal and the confirmation of their 'truth' by research subjects themselves (Outhwaite 1987; Hollis 1994).

From this perspective, practice is a complex and unpredictable social process made real and meaningful through the multiplicity of perspectives of the different actors engaged in any instance of practice and the particular norms and assumptions governing it. What is required of the practitioner is not to control and apply technologies to the realm of practice, but to seek to improve it, by understanding its meanings and processes, how it is experienced by others and how else it can be interpreted. Although it is ultimately the practitioner who is the source of authority for what is taken to be valid and meaningful, there is also a requirement on the practitioner to critique their understanding in the light of alternative perspectives.

The iterative nature of praxis, the meaningfulness of social action and the primacy of subjective meaning are implicit in approaches to professional development such as action learning (Revans 1983); reflective practice (Schön 1983b); and experiential learning (Kolb 1984).

These three positions are challenged by Carr and Kemmis (1986) from the perspective of critical theory and action research, and by Webb (1996a) from within the interpretivist tradition.

Whilst supporting the interpretivist assertion of the special nature of human action and the significance of meaning in this, Carr and Kemmis (1986) argue that processes of reflective practice and the attempt to understand social action through interpretation of subjective meaning are not good enough as a basis for professional practice. Such processes are likely to be blind to the role of power, its influence and expression through structural social differences and issues such as gender, race and class. Unless practice is critiqued under conditions of intersubjectivity informed by critical theory, it is likely to be conventional and normative. This view is based on the Habermasian assertion that norms, values and beliefs remain unexamined in 'ordinary conversation' (Furlong 2000). Only through a form of discourse which legitimizes the questioning of the validity of beliefs, assumptions, and evidence is it possible to achieve a form of practitioner knowledge which 'can be freed from its tendency to deteriorate either into subjectivity or into technicism' (Furlong 2000: 27). Carr and Kemmis (1986) argue that as well as these discoursal conditions, such critical discussion needs to be informed by critical theory which challenges purely subjectivist views of human action and includes attention to the role of historical and social conditions in also shaping human experience and action.

In contrast to critical theory and to the somewhat introspective and asocial emphasis in the idea of reflective practice, Webb (1996a) argues from a strongly humanist hermeneutic perspective for communication and understanding to lie at the heart of academic development. He suggests that the key task of the academic developer is to form empathic relationships with practitioners in order to enter into their worlds, and help them to make sense of them and establish similar relationships with their learners. The proposed process for developing this understanding is a hermeneutic one, described by Outhwaite (1987: 64) in reference to Gadamer as 'a fusion of one's own "horizon" of meanings and expectations ("prejudices") with that of the text, the other person, the alien culture'. Outhwaite argues that Gadamer's vision of hermeneutics, drawn on by Webb (1996a), is one which gives primacy to encounter and engagement. Thus according to Webb, rather than seeking continual improvement and development, the purpose of academic development is to foster relationship, communication and understanding between the different participants in the learning process, thus giving value and voice to each individual's own subjective experience. However, the strength of Webb's position is that, whilst placing relationship and understanding at the heart of the academic development process, he still requires of the developer to draw on both the critical perspectives of praxis and on the more challenging perspectives of postmodernism (see next section). In this section I have tried to show how praxis assumes practice to take place in complex social contexts in which individual actors act according to the meaning and significance they give to the particular context and action grounded in their own values, beliefs, assumptions and prior knowledge and the particular social rules and norms of the situation. Such a view privileges subjective experience, significance, and meaningful action. Although praxis seems to dissolve the positivist dualism between theory and practice, by establishing an iterative and reflexive relationship between these two, I have argued that it actually privileges practice and the practitioner over externally derived theory and research evidence. From this view, published theory and research is secondary to the primacy of practitioner experience and practical knowledge derived through critical reflection on practice. If authority lies with the practitioner, then the 'danger' is for practitioner knowledge to remain unexamined, conventional and solipsistic. Assuring the robustness of the validity of practitioner knowledge requires reflection (reflective practice); open and free dialogue with peers and the testing of reflection in action (action learning; action research); and critique of practice based on critical theory (action research, Carr and Kemmis, *op. cit.*). For Webb, this critical reflexive interpretive process is a delicate and sacred matter, arising as it does out of human communion and relationship.

The authority of the practitioner which assumes practice to involve rational goal-directed action guided by ethical judgement and humanist values is challenged in the following section; as is the authority of science and the scientific method.

Challenge to authority (both of science and of the practitioner)

Challenge to the authority of science

Kuhn (1970a) argues that science operates in two different ways – normal and revolutionary. The conduct of normal science depends on unexamined assumptions which take for granted certain axioms, beliefs, values, norms, rules and procedures as if they were true. These 'intellectual paradigms' are only challenged when unexpected results have to be made sense of by radically changing these usually unexamined assumptions or paradigms. Kuhn also argues that paradigms have an institutional dimension such that 'normal science is also kept on track by social mechanisms. It is highly organized activity, usually with a hierarchic power structure' (Hollis 1994: 86). Such a view was and is radical for it presents science not as a neutral, logical, rational and objective process but as one which is normative and implicated in relations of power. The neutrality of evidence is put into question by the intellectual paradigm which it presupposes and the vested interests which might support it.

As if this wasn't bad enough, Feyerabend (1970) argues against the view that scientific discovery arises from rationality. His analysis of the history of science suggests the significant role of rhetoric, persuasion, irrationality, and anarchy in producing what is taken to be true. Such a view suggests that 'truth' or evidence is more likely to be arrived at through anarchy and the possibility for play and creativity than through rationality. From this perspective, the practitioner would be required or rather invited to open up to play, looseness, creativity, and uncertainty, and to relax the need for mastery (see Phipps (2001) for how this might occur in practice).

Foucault (1970) argues for the representational view of language (which sees language as simply expressing a pre-existing reality) to be revised, in such a way that language becomes the means by which that which language refers to comes into being or is made 'object'. Thus discourse, which he views as historically formed and non-neutral, is seen as constituting what is taken to be real and true. From this perspective, theory and practice are ways of talking – discourse both brings into being the ways of thinking which set up a duality between theory and practice, and, by positing discourse as the process through which this 'reality' is created, thus dissolves the dualism. Furthermore, echoing Kuhn's (1970a) concept of the institutional nature of paradigms, Foucault argues that what is taken to be true or what we call knowledge is inextricably bound up with power. Power shapes knowledge and knowledge forms power.

Lyotard (1984) further challenges the authority of science by arguing that science has been governed by meta-narratives which legitimate what it is possible to assert as valid. He argues that the previously powerful meta-narratives of truth and of justice are currently being replaced by the meta-narrative of performativity. Rather than seeking to legitimize evidence according to criteria of truth or justice, we now seek to do so according to its performative validity or effectiveness: in short, in terms of whether it will work.

These four perspectives provide a resounding challenge to the view of research as an objective and neutral process whose evidence can be trusted because of its adherence to proper scientific method. Such views challenge the neutrality of the practitioner themselves and practitioner desires for certainty, predictability and authority. They require of the practitioner not only to question the ground on which published theory and research is based, but also to question their own ground. That is, they require the practitioner to seek out the assumptions on which published evidence and their own practice is based, to locate these within different paradigms or historical ways of knowing, and to be alert to the operation of power and vested interest in their construction and realization.

Challenge to the authority of the practitioner

The concept of authority suggests a number of things – authorship, expertise, origin or source, autonomy, rationality, mastery, self-knowledge. All of these underlie the idea of praxis and meaningful goal-directed social action and are challenged by the following perspectives.

Foucault and Lacan would both argue, in their different ways, that discourse is prior to the individual such that we are subject to it. There is no place outside discourse. It is through our place in discourse, for example how we are named, (Lacan) and through discoursal and disciplinary practices (Foucault) that we are made individual subjects. In this view, language cannot be used by individuals in order to express something essential about themselves, rather it is language which forms the kind of experience that human beings can have of their subjectivity.

Even if language could be viewed as a tool we use in order to express ourselves and represent our reality, the Freudian notion of the unconscious would posit that we can never achieve full knowledge and mastery of ourselves. Attempts at self-transparency, representation and mastery are nothing but illusion. To assert to know oneself is a deception as there is always something that will be unconscious and thus unknowable. Such a view challenges the critical self-reflection required in praxis and the authority of subjective experience.

The idea of authority is further challenged by the work of Barthes and Derrida. Barthes famously asserts the death of the author and replaces the idea of authorial authority with that of the validity of multiple realities and interpretations. Whereas Derrida, rather like Foucault, asserts that there is nothing outside the text. Each act of interpretation of a written text (such as this one) cannot aspire to be a statement expressing the truth of that text validated through reference to external reality, it can itself only be another text. Practitioner knowledge becomes just one among many possible multiple realities and interpretations. The task of the practitioner becomes one of not seeking to reduce meaning to absolutes, validated by original sources of authority, but to deconstruct their own and others' 'texts' of theory and practice.

To summarize this section, from the postmodern perspective, truth/authority becomes a relative notion arising out of social and discoursal practices, either agreed upon according to different paradigmatic assumptions, norms and rules or validated through meta-narratives; or even arising out of anarchy and irrationality. The dualism between theory and practice is dissolved through language, in such a way that language comes to constitute theory and practice, rather than reflect these as external realities. Closure and certainty are not possible, and the self cannot be transparent to itself.

Conclusion

So what can one conclude from the analysis of these three different perspectives for the possibility of authority and the legitimacy for practice?

If evidence-based practice is to be held out as the basis on which to ground legitimacy for practice, then the above analysis suggests six possible positions for the practitioner and their relationship to research-based evidence:

1. Practitioners uncritically apply to their own contexts of practice the research-based evidence generated by professional researchers. This view positions the practitioner as rational technologist (positivism).
2. Practitioners take a sceptical stance towards research-based evidence generated by professional researchers, applying it to their practice in the knowledge that it is only the best bet at the moment. This view positions the practitioner as sceptical pragmatist (Popperian position).
3. Practitioners inquire into their own practice, and the issues of power implicit in it, generating their own evidence, validated through critical reflection engaged in with communities of peers and informed by critical theory. This view positions practitioners as self-disciplining legitimators of their own practice (praxis).
4. Practitioners deconstruct the discoursal and disciplinary practices of education through critical discourse analysis to reveal how educational subjectivities are formed and what norms and assumptions validate different educational theories and research-based evidence. This view positions

practitioners as archaeologists of knowledge and critical discourse analysts (postmodernism – dominance of discourse and text).

5. Practitioners undertake psychoanalysis in order to become more aware of their own unconscious processes and dynamics and those operating in their classrooms. This view positions the practitioner as inquirer into unconscious processes through analysis (postmodernism – dominance of the unconscious).
6. Practitioners co-inquire with their learners/clients into their subjective experience of the educational process through the establishment of empathic relationships based on agape (compassion or unselfish love). This view positions practitioners as fosterers or cultivators of understanding (one of Webb's threads of argument – humanistic hermeneutics). It is important to note however, that although this position seems to be at the heart of Webb's view of academic development practice, he argues that this striving for understanding needs to be kept 'honest' by adherence to the positions of criticality and postmodernist deconstruction. His approach thus fuses these three positions.

All six positions imply different methods of inquiry, yielding different forms of evidence and different requirements on practitioners. If practice is to be evidence-based, then which kinds of inquiry and evidence can it most legitimately be based on?

According to the naive version of evidence-based practice, it should be possible to seek out evidence that would inform the decision one would make. And yet this paper has just shown how evidence can take many forms arising from the different modes of inquiry legitimated through different perspectives. It therefore seems to me that the key task for the practitioner is not to seek evidence upon which to make a judgement, but to make explicit the different values, beliefs and assumptions implicit in all accounts of educational policy, research and theory and in their own practice (Mann 1987). In this way, the practitioner may be more able to make a judgement as to which position they would most want to adhere to, and thus which forms of inquiry and evidence are most appropriate to their position. This last judgement can only be made on the basis of value, that is, it can only be made on the basis of what the individual practitioner takes to be the most appropriate models of human beings and human action for education, teaching, learning, and research into these. Such a position is an expression of value and belief about life and its purpose and not an expression of factual knowledge legitimated by evidence. This is a political issue and it is philosophical inquiry, that is inquiry into purpose and value, which needs to form the primary basis of the legitimacy for practice, not evidence. Education for the purpose of engendering democracy requires a quite different set of processes to those for an education whose purpose is conformity.

'At the heart of the decision-making process there must be a value judgement about how the mind should be cultivated and to what end' (Bruner 1986: 8).

This chapter has argued that a distinction needs to be made between practice that is evidence-based and practice that is grounded in a clear articulation of educational philosophy and value. It is the latter grounding which is required of the practitioner if the practitioner is to maintain a capacity for accountable professional autonomy and a capacity for critically engaging with policy, theory, evidence, practice and academic development processes.

Acknowledgements

My thanks to Glynis Cousins and Vicky Gunn for their helpful comments on this chapter.

I referred to a number of texts in this chapter. However, I would like to stress my particular debt to Webb (1996a), Carr and Kemmis (1986), and Usher and Edwards (1994). Webb argues against positivist and modernist views of staff development, arguing for it to be seen as a hermeneutic practice, informed by critical theory and postmodernism. Carr and Kemmis argue for a critical approach to theory and practice, and, in doing this, critique the possible contributions of positivism and hermeneutics to this. Usher and Edwards provide a thorough review of post-modernism and its implications for education.

Part 2

Research and Academic Development

9

Qualitative Research Methods in Higher Education Development

Peter D. Ashworth

Introduction

How is academic development work to focus on change which will be broadly beneficial, and will lead to the intended reorientation? One of the preconditions for avoiding unintended harm is that academic developers understand deeply what it is their activity is intended to change. Understanding in order to facilitate change, then, is an absolute priority. Too often our development work is based on superficial analyses; well-judged interventions by educational developers must be based on deep understanding. In this chapter, qualitative approaches to educational research are discussed in the light of the purpose of enriching understanding. I take the reason for their use to be to inform educational developers about the exceedingly complex human situations with which we are confronted. The kinds of qualitative methods to be discussed may be useful in other situations relevant to educational development, such as assessing the outcome of changes for evaluation purposes. But our focus here is on the elucidation of complex situations so as to understand them better and therefore to be enabled to facilitate beneficial change.

The meaning of 'qualitative'

A brief description of 'qualitative analysis' in chemistry will give us a standpoint from which we can become aware of the special way in which the term is used in education and the other social sciences. In the qualitative analysis of a material, the chemist focuses on *what is there.* Once it is known what elements and compounds are present, quantitative analysis answers to *how much of each of these there are.* So qualitative analysis in chemistry is concerned with the discovery of the makeup of the sample of material. Quality does not here have a connotation of value – 'high' or 'low' quality – and neither does it have such a connotation in education or the other social sciences.

As in analytical chemistry and commonsense, then, qualitative educational research is about the elucidation of the character of an entity or situation. However, the chemist's assumption is that, once having characterized a material, one can go on to measure the quantities of its various constituents. In educational research – and the same is true of the other social sciences – this assumption is controversial. Quantitative research presupposes that the makeup of the entity or situation can be expressed, possibly on the basis of prior qualitative research, in terms of a limited set of discrete variables, at least to the extent that appropriate measurements can be made and definite hypotheses tested. Certainly, some educational researchers are happy to accept this presupposition, and, like the chemists, see no conflict between qualitative and quantitative research. Educational entities and situations, for them, can be described in terms of systems of variables and quantification is possible. Many researchers in education argue, however, that studies of individuals, or of a group's behaviour, or of human situations generally, do not permit quantitative research. Such educational researchers would argue either (a) that quantitative research is not feasible because of the number of relevant variables and the complexity of their interactions, or (b) that analyses of situations or entities into sets of discrete variables would actually misrepresent the nature of these phenomena – human action is, instead, to be understood in terms of the meanings of situations for the individual(s) involved; since meanings interpenetrate with other meanings they cannot be bounded so as to be rendered measurable as such-and-such a numerical value of a variable. So in educational research, unlike chemistry, there can be a fundamental difference between qualitative researchers and quantitative researchers.

How this chapter reviews approaches to qualitative research

Though some qualitative researchers view their work as complementary to quantitative research, others regard qualitative research as a separate undertaking. And among the latter are some significant differences in methodology which I will outline. In particular, qualitative researchers sometimes view experience as a form of perception. That is, they elicit by interviews, focus groups, or observation, the way in which such people as students or teaching staff perceive their situation. Other qualitative researchers may use these same techniques but conceive of the information they obtain, not as perceptions, but as *conceptions or constructions* of the situation. This can be simply a difference in emphasis, but may sometimes lead to more fundamental divergences.

Another distinction among qualitative researchers differentiates those who regard constructions as *personal*, and those who stress the idea that constructions have their origin in the society of which students and staff are members – that they are *social* constructions.

Finally, in this chapter, though this by no means exhausts the kinds of qualitative research there are, I will indicate the viewpoint of those who see the individual as embedded in the culture to such an extent that research should take account of the whole group and its means of activity. An example of this standpoint, 'situated learning', does not see learning primarily as a matter of the individual cognitive acquision of knowledge, skills and understandings, but rather as membership in a group in which these things may be unevenly distributed between people and some of the necessary 'knowledge' is vested in equipment, written documents, etc.

In the rest of the chapter, these varying approaches to qualitative research will be discussed with illustrations from the transcripts of some interviews on student cheating and plagiarism (Ashworth, Bannister and Thorne 1997). This illustrative material is obviously ready to hand; but it also draws attention to precisely the kind of area, seen as a problem by university authorities, in which educational developers could well be called upon to intervene. Intervention may possibly not lead to a diminution in the level of cheating unless the educational developer has a deep understanding. So this is precisely the kind of complex situation in higher education in which qualitative research should be undertaken in order to inform the developer.

Take the following as an example of the material. It consists of two sections from different points of the same interview with a second-year undergraduate in English.

> I mean, the actual exam at the end isn't a test of . . . I mean, it allows me to go further – it allows me to do whatever I want to do, so I've got to do, you know, work in that direction. But I don't think I would . . . not unless I really thought I was going to fail and it wasn't a subject that I was planning to specialise in. It was, you know, just something I needed to get to that level. Because, if I thought I was failing on the subjects that I wanted to continue on, then I don't know whether I'd even be able – I'd want to carry on, because I'd want to be able to do well, without an incredible amount of problem, or I'd decide that it wasn't the course for me if I couldn't do it . . .

> Yeah – like I'm prepared to help [interviewee's younger brother] in his GCSEs because I see it as just in order to get to something that he could do easily, you know, and sort of shine in – the GCSEs are just a way of testing that doesn't suit him, but is necessary and, you know, is below him – but is necessary for him to get somewhere where he, you know, and he can't do this, he has a problem with this method of, so yes, yeah, I'd be prepared to help him cheat. Like, helping him with assessments.

Qualitative research as the discovery of relevant variables

I have indicated that qualitative research is often seen as an initial stage in a research programme, for it has been suggested that science is a two-stage process. Reichenbach (1938: 382) named these the 'contexts' of *discovery* and of *justification*. Qualitative research is sometimes understood as appropriate mainly for the first stage, that of discovery. What is to be discovered – on this view – is the set of variables about which one may formulate hypotheses. In the later stage, the variables are conceptualized in such a form as to allow measurement ('operationalized'), and the testing of hypotheses is undertaken; this is the realm of justification, the quantitative stage. Quantitative research is viewed as a more precise and rigorous stage, allowing the researcher to produce scientific laws.

On this understanding of the role of qualitative research, our research interviews concerning cheating would be expected to allow the tentative discovery of relevant variables, on the basis of which we could formulate some appealing hypotheses about the nature of student behaviour. The resulting hypotheses might be tested by structured questionnaires including rating scales designed to quantify the variables which have been indicated as possible factors in the decision to cheat, or by other quantitative approaches (cf. Roberts and Toombs 1993; Franklyn-Stokes and Newstead 1995).

The underlying assumptions about educational research which are embedded in this view of qualitative research are positivist. Positivism takes it as axiomatic that there is one, unequivocal real world which has determinate characteristics, and the purpose of science is to model this world in its theories. These theories will show how certain variables interrelate, especially how they relate to each other in a cause-and-effect fashion. Mathematical formulations of the relationships between variables are to be sought if at all possible. The purpose of research is to generate and later test hypotheses regarding relationships between variables, and to reach, by closer and closer approximation, theories which can begin to be regarded as having the status of scientific laws (Polkinghorne 1983).

The qualitative interview data from the cheating study could very well be treated in a positivistic way. For example, it would be possible to analyze the interviews so as to identify the variables which could later be built into hypotheses concerning the likelihood of cheating. In the interview data I have already introduced, the first paragraph has the interviewee saying that she would differentiate between units which matter as a basis for further studies and those whose content is not relevant in this sense to her longer-term interests. She believes it would be foolish to cheat to avoid failure in units which are important (from this point of view) because her future academic progress would become increasingly difficult. In the next paragraph, she says that she would be prepared to help someone cheat (and, we may infer, cheat herself) if a taught unit were merely a hurdle to be surmounted in the process of getting onto units which 'matter'. She talks about this in the context of her brother's problems with the modes of assessment in certain school exams.

So, in positivist mode, the qualitative interview data provides evidence of variables which we can tentatively hypothesize as related to the likelihood of cheating.

- If the person is having difficulty with a unit, this increases the likelihood of cheating in the unit.
- If the person sees the unit as unimportant to their longer-term interests but merely a hurdle to be surmounted, this increases the likelihood of cheating in the unit.
- If there are apparently arbitrary features of the unit which artificially increase the difficulty of passing, this increases the likelihood of cheating in the unit.

Qualitative research as the elucidation of meanings

What is the nature of the scientific product at which qualitative research is aiming? It plainly varies. Positivists aim at specifying some set of features which are part of the underlying lawful reality of the human social world. But other educational researchers view efforts to turn qualitative research into the discovery of variables whose lawful relationships are supposed to make up the human social world as mistaken. The researchers to whom we turn now, emphasize the idea that the world of education is not to be taken as a system of variables, but as a field of interpenetrating meanings.

The elucidation of meanings; that is, individual perceptions

What if we take qualitative research as being concerned to elucidate the meaning of a situation or entity in terms of *how it is perceived by the individual person*? This is indeed the focus of much qualitative research in higher education – for example, that which investigates 'student experience'.

The most rigorous approach to individual perceptions of situations and entities is derived from phenomenology. The founder of philosophical phenomenology, Edmund Husserl (1859–1938), had a fundamental aim to provide a firm foundation for the disciplines – sciences, arts and humanities – by establishing their basic concepts. The method he developed involved an extraordinarily thorough explication of those *human experiences* which were related to the subject matter of a given discipline. Now, Husserl's philosophical aim is not generally followed in educational research, but his attention to the details of experience does provide a valuable model, and – taken together with its later existentialist elaboration in such authors as Heidegger (1962) and Merleau-Ponty (1962) – is of importance in qualitative research (see, for education, van Manen 1990).[1] It is of some concern that, though much research in higher education purports to be of participants' experience, little of it is rigorously phenomenological.

The aim of phenomenologically-based qualitative research, then, is to elucidate individual experience. There are several things which need to be said about such elucidation of individual perceptions.

Intentionality

Husserl (e.g. 1931) developed the view that all mental life involves a link between 'inner' consciousness, and the entity or situation that one is 'conscious of'. The technical term for this relational form of all experience is 'intentionality'. As far as qualitative research in higher education is concerned, the law of intentionality means, for example, that student experience should be considered in these two ways: (a) what is the experience of? and (b) what is the manner in which it is experienced – is it perceived? or also judged? are feelings involved?

In our example, let's take this snippet:

> I mean, the actual exam at the end isn't a test of . . . I mean, it allows me to go further – it allows me to do whatever I want to do, so I've got to do, you know, work in that direction. But I don't think I would . . . not unless I really thought I was going to fail and it wasn't a subject that I was planning to specialise in.

The interviewee is contemplating cheating as a personal possibility. The experience is one of, let us say, theoretical imagination. What is the imagination of? Plainly it is of a certain kind of cheating situation in which she personally might act to pass a test illegitimately. The imaginary situation allows her to discourse on the circumstances in which she would or would not cheat. We see that her imaginative awareness of such situations is one in which a sense of 'academic biography' (the way in which she relates to the total degree programme, with subjects which are more or less 'relevant' to her interests and ambitions) is very much to the fore.

Appearance

The founder of phenomenology was concerned that analytical attention should be directed to *things as they appear*, as given, or as the research participant – the student or university teacher – experiences them. So the premature search for causes of the experience, or the underlying motives for the experience, or how the experience is to be understood theoretically, must all be set aside. The focus is on elucidating the experience itself as it appears. What, for instance, is cheating in the experience of this student, solely as they perceive or conceive it?

Attending to experience 'in its appearing', without straightaway making interpretations, is actually a hard discipline. One aspect of the task is often referred to as 'bracketing presuppositions' (Ashworth 1999). In the work on cheating, it was often difficult consistently to bracket various presuppositions. That cheating is wrong, for instance, was a presupposition that, for various reasons, I held and still hold. It was certainly necessary to set this aside in order to see that, for some research participants, this was not necessarily part of their experience. For the student quoted before, cheating was a possibility which was by no means ruled out as 'wrong'.

Lifeworld
A particular experience lies within the whole lived world (Husserl 1970). So, in the quote above, the interviewee's experience of cheating engages, at one point, with her affection for her brother and her willingness to be helpful (as she understands it) and to do work for him that would be presented as his. In general, the meaning of an experience can only be understood within an understanding of its relevancies to other parts of the person's subjective world. Cheating is often experienced in the context of what we called 'fellow feeling'. In other words, 'assistance' to another student in their work was often related experientially to the wish to be helpful and kind to them.

The elucidation of meanings: the repertoire of conceptualizations of definite aspects of the world; phenomenography[2]

Phenomenography (e.g. Marton and Booth 1997) is a little hard to place within the range of qualitative methods. The name links it with phenomenology, and Ursula Lucas and I (Ashworth and Lucas 2000) are among those who have tried to indicate how phenomenographic research might be improved by taking this link seriously. The objective of phenomenographic research was indeed to see the world from the student's perspective, though it was recognized that the emphasis was on experience that has been reflected on to the extent that it could be discussed and described by the experiencer (Marton 1981; Uljens 1992).

> The empirical study of the limited number of qualitatively different ways in which various phenomena in, and aspects of, the world around us are experienced, conceptualised, understood, perceived and apprehended.
> (Marton 1994: 4425)

The results of phenomenographic research – its 'outcome space' – are categories of description, in which different ways of understanding an entity or situation are logically and hierarchically interrelated to establish a typology. Phenomenological concerns with intentionality and lifeworld are not prominent. Since a person could have more than one understanding of the entity or situation and could change over time, what is arrived at in phenomenography is a 'repertoire', within the research population, of ways of conceptualizing the entity or situation.

Phenomenography has had a considerable, but perhaps under appreciated, impact on higher education research. It was the basis for the considerable research effort concerned with deep and surface approaches to learning (a brief review is in Marton and Booth (1997: 168–171)). But perhaps the most characteristic studies are ones in which students' conceptions of some basic concept within their discipline are drawn out. Typically, it is found that the variation in understandings can be treated as a hierarchy of partial understandings and misunderstandings.

To revert to our own study of cheating and plagiarism, I think that it is students' understandings of plagiarism that could most easily be analyzed phenomenographically. The variation within the outcome space includes the following:

> Plagiarism is simply neglecting to use the conventions of citation and referencing which we have been taught. ['Plagiarism of text.']
>
> Plagiarism is a worry: it would be possible to plagiarise accidentally, if you absorbed somebody's view and made it your own. Then you could put it in an essay not remembering that the idea wasn't yours. ['Inadvertant plagiarism of an idea.']
>
> None of us are going to really do something original on this [natural science] degree. Our work's always based on some scientist before. [Plagiarism as irrelevant because originality is impossible. All is reproduction.]

The understandings might all be seen as showing a different partial grasp of the complete concept – of which, indeed, some students may have a fully realized construct.

The elucidation of meanings; that is, social *constructions*

The phenomenological viewpoint – and perhaps the phenomenographic one – has, embedded within it, an image with the individual ego on one side and the world on the other. This image is built in, as it were, to the law of intentionality. Many qualitative researchers have been critical about two aspects of this image. Firstly, it is *individualistic*; secondly, it is *representationalist*.

In attacking representationalism Gergen[3] pointed to what he regarded as the mistaken assumption that experience is to be understood as a kind of direct perception of situations or entities. In asserting that this is not so, he sides with the constructivists. Indeed, in Gergen's view, qualitative research does not reveal a lifeworld (either subjectively perceived or constructed). Instead all that can be discovered by qualitative research is a kind of network of elements, each of which gains its meaning purely from its position within the total system. Individuals' conceptions do not touch reality. All is construction.

Beyond this, Gergen is a social constructionist. The accounts that people give of entities or situations are derived (probably entirely) from the materials that society has currently available for accounting for such entities or situations. These materials may be termed *discourses.* (This is, as Gergen himself points out, a central notion of postmodernism.)

In the qualitative method of *discourse analysis* (Potter and Wetherell 1987), the accounts that people give are interpreted as expressing one or more local cultural and linguistic forms available to participants – culturally-available discourses. The research participants are the channels through which the discourses flow, rather than the originators of personal constructions of the world (though the issue of *agency* is controversial). It is the research intention to discover in the participants' accounts the implicit or explicit structures of meaning, or latent themes, which are understood to be both constitutive of and constituted by the wider social reality.

Here, again, the meaning of data is transformed by the approach which is adopted to qualitative research. In the interview material on which we have been relying for illustration, there are certainly discursive themes worthy of note. The most obvious one is a moral discourse. Sometimes students immediately dismiss cheating as a form of wickedness – but we have seen that this is not always so. In general, it seems that student experience is informed by a morality of fellow-feeling, so that cheating is described as ethically justifiable if it seems to reduce the misery of a fellow student in dire circumstances. On the other hand, some discourses which might be found in the repertoires of lecturers (the maintenance of the validity of assessment and the meaning of the award) were rarely if ever seen in the interviews with students.

Discourse analysis moves qualitative research firmly away from concern with the individual as such to the view that data (though emanating from a particular person) is to be seen in the context of the culture as a whole.

The elucidation of meanings; that is, interpretation of the total social setting

We have been moving in an increasingly collectivist direction, and we now come to a viewpoint in which the meanings of situations and entities are specifically *not* vested in the individual. Indeed aspects of the situation – including especially the language in which the situation is framed – pre-date the individuals who have to do with it. The individual finds themselves a participant in a situation whose meaning and structure are not up to them to construct, but are simply inherited or adopted – and their activity is both facilitated and constrained by this fact. Moreover, the realization of the situation or entity may be the *joint* product of a number of people – different people making separate contributions and no individual participant having a total awareness of the constitution of the activity. It can be that some 'knowledge' and 'skill' essential to the activity may be vested in tools, instruments, or written records.

With slightly different emphases, action theory, situated learning and critical realism have this awareness of the total – present and historical

– circumstances of the situation (see, for example, Lave and Wenger 1991; Chaiklin and Lave 1993). As Hutchins (1993) writes, in introducing a classic study of the process of learning maritime navigation:

> Looking at navigation as it is actually conducted aboard ships . . . brought home to me the extent to which cognitive accomplishments can be joint accomplishments, not attributable to any individual. Another absolutely apparent feature of this setting is the extent to which the computational accomplishments of navigation are mediated by a variety of tools and representational technologies.
>
> (Hutchins 1993: 35)

Key terms for those whose qualitative research takes this type of approach are *setting* and *practice*. For this analysis of higher education requires that the researcher views the total physical and social situation (probably with something of its history) as a complex whole, and treats the thing to be investigated as a social practice.

Can cheating and plagiarism be treated in this way? I certainly think that plagiarism as a social practice would enormously repay investigation.

- Historically, the emergence of plagiarism as a problem is of relatively recent origin (prior to the printed book, I imagine, there was little need for the specific citation of authorities since all readers and hearers would know very well to whom one was referring). Plagiarism relates to available technology of communication, and the internet has merely moved an existing type of problem onto another level.
- The social meaning of the ownership of ideas, the concept of originality, and the ideology that lies behind the insistence that assessment be individual – all these have a bearing on the existence of plagiarism as a possible problem.
- Within different disciplines, varying emphases on such things as (a) personal creativity, and (b) art or science as a collective activity in which new participants build on the work of their forebears, lead to different conditions for plagiarism.

Conclusion

It has been the aim of this chapter to emphasize the way in which qualitative research divides into a number of distinct forms of investigation, each with characteristic ways of viewing the meaning of the data. In surveying the area in terms of overarching philosophical orientation, I have made no mention of techniques of data collection such as interviewing, or of general techniques of analysis such as 'grounded theory' (e.g. Strauss and Corbin 1990). These techniques are of some use to all the methods discussed in the chapter. But it is especially the meaning of the overarching method which must be considered carefully if the research is to provide that deep understanding of the situation or entity which will enable the educational developer to intervene relevantly. The distinctions between kinds of qualitative research may appear subtle, but it is fundamentally important to realize that the *method of research is part of the theory* of the thing being investigated. Any assumption of the research method becomes a theoretical assumption regarding the thing being investigated. Errors are very often made because this is not sufficiently understood.

Notes

1. For a valuable website, maintained by Max van Manen, see http://www.phenomenologyonline.com/
2. A very useful website, maintained at the Goteborg home of phenomenography, is http://www.ped.gu.se/biorn/phgraph/home.html
3. A good representative account of Gergen's social constructionism is on the web at http://www.swarthmore.edu/SocSci/kgergen1/text12.html

10

Pedagogical Research in UK Higher Education: An Emerging Policy Framework

Mantz Yorke

A policy *terra incognita* no more

Not so long ago, this chapter would probably have been more white space than text. Pedagogical research has always taken place in higher education, of course, but without much by way of an overarching policy framework. Indeed, it was largely undertaken by individuals or by small groups of enthusiasts, and was relatively unremarked. It does not figure in McNay's (1997) study of the impact of the 1992 Research Assessment Exercise (RAE), save for references to Jenkins' (1995) small-scale survey of academics in geography departments that indicated *inter alia* that research into the teaching of geography was not being valued. Until recently, pedagogical research has lacked many advocates to press its case for recognition. A key reason may be that, as Elton argued,

> . . . such research is at present very little understood by most people outside those who are practising it, for the simple reason that such people rarely if ever have had any pedagogic training, let alone carried out pedagogic research.
>
> (Elton 1995: 47)

This may account for the minuscule amount of recognition that was given to pedagogical research in the consultants' report[1] that fed into the *Review of Research* organized through HEFCE (HEFCE 2000b).

The situation is changing to the advantage of pedagogical research as – *inter alia* – the RAE is giving greater emphasis to it in the various Units of Assessment, the Learning and Teaching Support Network (LTSN) is shaping its contribution to pedagogy in higher education, and institutions are being required to produce learning and teaching strategies (in which pedagogical research clearly has a role to play).

A policy framework is beginning to emerge from a scattering of components. It is as if parts from a construction kit are being bolted together, though the model has yet to assume more than a skeletal form. In this chapter, a number of components are identified, some existing connections are pointed out, and some thoughts are offered regarding a shape that might emerge for the framework.

What is pedagogical research?

First of all, there is a need to identify what is being subsumed under the heading of pedagogical research. There is a gradation of educational interpretations. At one end lies the relatively narrow, predominantly instrumental, focus on the practices of teaching, learning and assessment, and how they might be made more effective (and possibly more efficient). Pedagogical research here would tend to be empirical – even technicist – in character, trying to determine 'what works' or possibly 'what might work better'. Here, there is a risk of disconnection with theory. There is – it must be said – considerable danger in an uncritical acceptance of 'what works', since circumstances vary in education (and *a fortiori* in higher education).[2]

At the other end of the scale is a more-encompassing perspective within whose purview anything that might influence teaching, learning and assessment might be found. Within this broader perspective philosophical, sociological and psychological conceptions about values, conditions and purposes will be made apparent in a way often not appreciated by the narrowly-focused empiricist.[3]

Pedagogical research is a special case of discipline-based research. For educationalists, it is a significant part of their discipline (more accurately, subject area). For others, it is the research analogue of a second language: whilst the researcher's disciplinary base may be, say, history, he or she is researching pedagogical issues by drawing on concepts and methodologies drawn from education or the social sciences. Pedagogical research in higher education is, unlike other research, directed inward towards the system in which it exists. Perhaps it is for that reason, coupled with its dispersal across higher education, that it receives less recognition within the higher education sector than does research into matters such as the practices of the medical profession.

There are also a couple of political dimensions to pedagogical research. The first derives from a governmental concern that teaching and learning in higher education should be maximally effective and optimally efficient – a value for money issue, at root. The drive for 'better' pedagogy implies not only new pedagogical research but also syntheses of the findings from what is known in the relevant literature. With a few exceptions, such as Bligh's (1998) appraisal of the research on lecturing, the latter is not exploited as fully as it might have been. Higher education knows more than it is generally able to tell, though there is potential for the LTSN in particular to mitigate this weakness.

The second political dimension relates to the fact that there is no obvious grouping which can press the case for valuing pedagogical research – those to whom it is important are to be found dispersed across the higher education landscape. Communication between pedagogical researchers in, say, medicine and engineering is difficult. In contrast, those who engage in broader studies of the nature of higher education (for example, Becher 1989 and Barnett 1999) can locate their work under existing categories of research. They have a clear intellectual 'home'. This is an important issue, since recognition of the value of pedagogical research will depend to a fair extent on having an interest group that is prepared to argue for it.

Pedagogical research in higher education is embryonic in theory terms. It is generally not well understood; there is uncertainty regarding principles and regularities; and there is a lack of certainty regarding concepts and models. The corollaries are that pedagogical research is a contested construct, and that it is difficult to specify rigour in simple terms when there is no single research paradigm. Even with its much longer tradition, schools-related research (much of which has been pedagogical in character) has not lacked controversy, with the findings of critical reports such as Tooley with Darby (1998) and Hillage *et al.* (1998) being contested by the British Educational Research Association (see Rudduck and McIntyre 1998). Schools-related research is blessed with a theoretical pluralism, and there seems little reason why pedagogical research in higher education should be different in this regard. Grand theory regarding pedagogical research is therefore probably far too optimistic a goal (as has turned out to be the case in the social sciences more generally), not least because of the particularly heavily context-inflected nature of pedagogical research in the sector. There is a need for a generous notion of what pedagogical research might be, if the trap of a narrow and perhaps atheoretical empiricism is to be avoided.

It is a concern about academic *locus* that presses this chapter towards the narrower end of the gradation noted earlier, at the risk of it being construed as pragmatic and technicist. Some, no doubt, would have preferred the broader perspective. The point must be made, however, that broader considerations are not absent: there are many opportunities for them to irrupt into pedagogical research – at times, uncomfortably for the narrowly empirical researcher.

Contemporary encouragements towards pedagogical research

The Research Assessment Exercise (RAE)

The RAE has exerted a considerable effect on higher education in the UK. Ratings are important to institutions because of the funding they attract, and because of the reputational value that accrues. Hence a lot of institutional effort is devoted to preparing a 'good RAE submission' in the various Units of Assessment.

The position of pedagogical research in the RAE is evolving. In the 1996 RAE it was considered under the Education Unit of Assessment, by a sub-panel whose membership was dominated by academics with particular interests in continuing education. Little opportunity was taken to 'bundle' pedagogical research from across the disciplines into a coherent institutional submission to the Education Unit of Assessment, as was done with some success by Sheffield Hallam University. Where pedagogical research was submitted, it seems to have been sent in under the particular subject discipline to which it was being applied. This placed it in the hands of subject-specialist panels whose expertise in pedagogical research would have been adventitious, and whose valuing of pedagogical research may not have been high. Some academics were dissuaded from undertaking pedagogical research in the run-up to the RAE on the grounds that it would not 'count' as much as research in the discipline itself, and that the choice of research topic would have implications for future careers.

Since then, interest across the sector in pedagogical research has risen, concomitantly with a concern for teaching and learning that has gathered momentum following the publication of the Dearing Report into higher education (NCIHE 1997). However, few institutions have followed the lead of Sheffield Hallam University in coalescing pedagogical research within a specialist unit – the Learning and Teaching Research Institute (LTRI). This has led to the formation of seven research groups, some of which have bid successfully for external funding, and some are influential in innovation in their own schools. Within the LTRI framework, approximately 80 people across the university are undertaking pedagogical research.

In 1999 a task group set up by the funding councils advised that pedagogical research focusing on higher education should not be singled out for special treatment in the 2001 RAE, and that such research would normally be expected to be submitted to the education panel (Task Group on Education Research 1999, paras 4–5). This constituted a rather narrow perspective on pedagogical research that failed to set it in a broader context of institutional policy relating to the student experience. Yorke (2000), in criticizing the task group's recommendations, suggested a number of policy options through which pedagogical research might be encouraged via the RAE.

In the event, RAE panels were instructed as follows regarding their treatment of pedagogical research:

> Research into the teaching and learning process within higher education (pedagogic research) is regarded by the funding bodies as a valid and valued form of research activity. It will be assessed by all subject panels on an equitable basis with other forms of research.
>
> RAE Circular 5/99, para 1.10 (available at website http://www.rae.ac.uk/Pubs/5_99/)

If they did not contain expertise in pedagogical research, panels were expected to co-opt appropriate persons to act in an advisory capacity. It remains to be seen whether this has permitted pedagogical research relating to Subject X to compete on an equal footing with research into Subject X itself: however, anecdotal reportage suggests that the disciplinary bias against pedagogical research has not been entirely dissipated, and the likelihood is that relatively little pedagogical research will turn out to have been submitted within the disciplinary Units of Assessment other than that for Education.

There are two problems for those who would want to see pedagogical research achieve a higher profile in the RAE. First, it will be particularly difficult to assess the extent to which pedagogical research may have been discouraged within subject disciplines in the lead-in to the RAE. Second, without some detailed research it would be difficult to identify how pedagogical research was actually treated by the RAE panels.

Regarding the second problem – and to some extent the first – John Rogers, the manager of the 2001 RAE, indicated that the treatment of pedagogical research would be evaluated during the RAE process, using a three-strand approach.

- He would be observing panels at work on their assessments and would be paying particular attention to issues such as their treatment of pedagogical research.
- The profile of pedagogical research submitted for the 2001 RAE would be checked and compared against that for the previous RAE in 1996: this would enable a view to be taken regarding the effectiveness of the funding councils' new measures for the encouragement of submissions of pedagogical research.
- A post-assessment survey of panel chairs and members would include a specific question about the treatment of pedagogical research submissions (Rogers 2001).

The outcomes of Rogers' evaluation may have a significant influence on the development of pedagogical research, particularly if there is another RAE in 2005–2006.

The ESRC Teaching and Learning Research Programme

In 1999 the Higher Education Funding Council for England (HEFCE), the Scottish Executive, the Welsh Assembly and the Department for Education and Employment together provided £12.5 mn to support research into teaching and learning across the whole of the education spectrum. Phase 1 of this funding was primarily provided for research networks in which synergy was clearly expected. The larger Phase 2 sought to support large-scale research projects. Although there were a number of bids for research into higher education, only one of these was funded.[4] This created some dissatisfaction across the higher education sector since the bulk of funding was coming from its own funding bodies.

Perhaps in part acknowledgement of this, Phase 3 of the initiative (for which a further £10.5 mn was committed in March 2001) gave particular emphasis to projects focusing on post-compulsory education, work-based learning and lifelong/adult learning. The remit of Phase 3 also covers people moving between learning in different sectors, including transitions from school, and teacher/trainer education. Pedagogical research in higher education, as a consequence, has in theory a greater chance being funded: however, the relative underdevelopment of the field and the dispersion of both protagonists and fields of interest together weaken the prospects of success.

The Fund for the Development of Teaching and Learning (FDTL)

The FDTL was established in England by HEFCE in December 1995 with the intention of spreading good practice relating to the student learning experience in higher education (see HEFCE 1995). Projects supported by this fund are ultimately overseen by the HEFCE Teaching Quality Enhancement Fund Management Committee.[5] In order to be eligible to lead an FDTL project[6] an institution had to have had its provision in the relevant subject area identified as 'excellent' when its quality was assessed through the peer review system of 'quality assessment' then operating. When a revised methodology for teaching quality assessment was implemented, institutions were awarded scores out of 4 in each of six areas: the award of a '4' in an area was the criterion of eligibility to lead a project under FDTL.

The bidder for an FDTL project was required to identify an aspect of its practice that was highly regarded and to propose ways in which this expertise might be spread around the higher education system. The original purpose of FDTL, therefore, was dissemination rather than pedagogical research. However, the dissemination of good practice was not entirely straightforward, since practice tended to develop over time as a consequence of research-like activity. In HEFCE's invitation for bids for the fourth round of FDTL funding, the ground has shifted towards pedagogical research:

> **Research and innovation.** We will build on the substantial innovation in learning and teaching already taking place in UK higher education, and identify other areas where investment in research and development can best contribute to the learning experience of students.
>
> (HEFCE 2001c: para 12c)

The shift constitutes a recognition that even highly praiseworthy pedagogy cannot stand still, and that the possibility of incorporating a research dimension to an FDTL project is likely to be attractive to academics with an eye on a possible future RAE.

The Learning and Teaching Support Network (LTSN)

The LTSN consists of a Generic Centre (whose brief, in summary, subsumes aspects of learning and teaching that cross subject disciplinary boundaries) and 24 Subject Centres tasked with supporting developments in learning and teaching within particular subject communities (or groups of communities). The original documentation leading towards the establishment of the LTSN concentrated on the Network's capacity for sharing practice identified as being good. The projected programmes of the Subject Centres (which were created through a bidding system) varied considerably in the extent to which they embodied support for pedagogical research. Through the developing partnership relationship of the LTSN with its Subject Centres greater attention is being given to pedagogical research across the LTSN. The next move for the LTSN is to find a way in which it can ensure that pedagogical research has the widest impact for the investment being made in it.

The Institute for Learning and Teaching in Higher Education (ILT)

Anyone with a responsibility related to learning and teaching in higher education is potentially eligible for full or associate membership of the ILT. The applicant has to make a case for recognition, which is considered by assessors appointed by the ILT. Pedagogical research is not a requirement at this stage, since the focus is on the professionalism of an applicant's teaching, with emphasis being given to the quality of reflection and how this is used to inform practice. It is expected that, in due course, an ILT member's accreditation will be 'refreshed' through a demonstration of the further development of professionalism in respect of learning and teaching. At this point pedagogical research is likely to come more into the picture.

Institutional developments

(a) Inhouse educational development projects

For many years, some institutions have implemented schemes through which relatively small amounts of money are made available to support projects that seem likely to be of benefit to teaching and learning. These have tended to be developmental in character (for example, the creation of teaching materials), but have often had something of a research flavour through the evaluation of the effectiveness of the development in the field.

There have been three main problems with this approach. First, projects have tended to be pragmatic, in the sense that they respond to identified local pedagogical needs. At an invitation workshop on pedagogical research held in Coventry in March 2001 the charge was made that, at times, pedagogical research was small in scale and badly done.[7] Second, projects tend to be localized within the disciplinary area concerned, and transfer to other learning milieux has been limited. In other words, the 'bang for the buck' has not been as big as it might have been. Third, the research potential has probably not been exploited to the full, with connections to theory and other empirical findings being made to only a limited extent.

(b) Institutional learning and teaching strategies

In 1999 HEFCE began, under its Teaching Quality Enhancement Fund, the process that led to institutions in England producing formal learning and teaching strategies (for details, see HEFCE 1999). An analysis of the position at that time showed that a few institutions had already developed something akin to a formal strategy, but that these were in a small minority (Gibbs 1999; Gibbs *et al.* 2000). In support of this HEFCE initiative, Graham Gibbs led a number of regional workshops designed to support senior managers in the writing of such policies. The majority of institutions produced full strategies from the outset, but some institutions opted to present an interim 'emergent' policy which would be followed a year later by a fully-fledged version. Policies reflected institutional needs and priorities, and were not tied to a fixed set of expectations.

A number of institutional policies took existing policy features and developed them further. In some, the recognition and reward of teaching, already contained within institutional policy frameworks, was strengthened. In others, the use of inhouse R&D projects was extended. The development of institutional policies gave greater attention to the pedagogical side of higher education, with consequent potential for the promotion of pedagogical research. At the time of writing, it is too early to judge the extent to which institutional commitment to pedagogical research has been affected.

At Coventry University there is a scheme of secondments for curriculum and pedagogical development in subject areas, which is linked with various post-experience awards: the intentions of the scheme are partly developmental, partly research-oriented. Large-scale commitments such as this take time to demonstrate a return, but institutionally the initiative has already led to an annual conference on learning and teaching, and could be expected to have an influence on pedagogy in the longer term.

Quality assurance

Quality assurance merits a brief mention in this chapter, since one of the key quality assurance questions asks (or ought to ask) how practices might be enhanced. There are obvious supplementary questions relating to evidence-based and/or theory-based practice, and – by further extension – to how pedagogical research might be contributing. Any institution committed to the enhancement of pedagogical quality is implicitly committed to engaging with pedagogical research – at minimum, by becoming informed about what is emerging from other places, and at maximum by engaging in pedagogical research itself.

Where external quality scrutiny under the aegis of the Quality Assurance Agency is concerned, it seems probable that pedagogical research has not figured to any significant extent at the level of institutional review. The situation is different at the level of subject review, where reviewers pick up any threads relating to pedagogical research that are woven into the institutional documentation. Reviewers test not only whether the curriculum, and teaching, learning and assessment, are up to date in terms of subject content but also whether they reflect contemporary developments in pedagogy. The latter may involve pedagogical research conducted within the institution, engagement in projects such as those sponsored by the FDTL, and involvement in the work of the LTSN.

A spectrum of engagements

There is, implicit in the preceding subsections, a spectrum of engagements (actual and potential) in pedagogical research. At one end lie the small-scale and homespun studies conducted by individuals who are concerned to understand and improve their personal pedagogical practice. At the other (but noticeable by their sparseness) are programmatic studies designed to provide robust and potentially transferable evidence regarding aspects of pedagogy. Each kind of approach has its rationale, but it is inappropriate to 'read off' one in terms of the other.

Most academic appointees to higher education lack a formal background in pedagogy – hence the various institutional schemes for new lecturers. These schemes necessarily engage lecturers in an appraisal of pedagogical practice and typically require them to undertake some kind of small-scale investigation as part of reflective practice. Herein are the first, probably tentative, steps towards work that could be graced with the title 'pedagogical research' – but the primary aim is pedagogical understanding and the enhancement of practice. The uniqueness of the study's setting constitutes a simplifying factor, but at the expense of potential generalizability. Theory may be present, but perhaps in rather general terms: details of the theory and associated research methodology may at this point be relatively sketchily appreciated. For example, many lecturers are routinely faced with Marton and Säljö's (1976) distinction between surface and deep learning, but it is less likely that they will be exposed to its full theoretical richness or to the phenomenographical approach that underpinned its elucidation.[8]

The main problem at the other end of the spectrum is contextual diversity. Take, for example, the desire to establish which aspects of formative assessment might be the most powerful contributions to student learning. Formative assessment cannot 'cleanly' be detached from confounding variables such as the whole approach to teaching and learning, the institutional (perhaps departmental) ethos, the teachers' pedagogical expertise, and the backgrounds that the students bring to the assessment situation. Educational research is relatively weak as regards the cumulation of qualitative findings. There seems to be a need for the development of a robust methodology for cumulation that will allow the strength and direction of the wind to be estimated from the movement of a number of discrete straws of (to some extent) diverse characteristics.

Is a programmatic approach to pedagogical research needed?

The stance of this chapter is an unambiguous 'yes'. This is a 'yes/and' rather than a 'yes/but', since it does not seek to deny the value of the local and parochial because the local and parochial can provide starting points for more ambitious projects. However, there is a need for research that spans contexts, that can indicate where generalizable outcomes might be found, and that can – because of contextual variations – suggest where the apparently generalizable may require adaptation.

There are at least four ways in which a programmatic approach might be approached: major projects (possibly, but not necessarily, funded by the ESRC); linked smaller projects funded through a sectoral coordinating body such as the LTSN; linked projects run within one or more institutions; and whole-department research on one or more topics.

Major projects

The ESRC Teaching and Learning Research Programme is the paradigmatic example here. This programme seeks large-scale projects that have a high probability of producing research outcomes that are of broad applicability. In satisfying academic and user referees, at least two challenging problems need to be surmounted – first, the methodological difficulty relating to contextual variability (noted earlier) and, second, the relative lack, amongst those who are likely to be the most interested in pedagogical research, of a strong track record in educational research.[9] The environment of major funding is one into which newcomers find entry difficult. For many pedagogical researchers, this will prove to be 'a step too far' at the moment: their work will need to be pursued by other means. That said, the 'building capacity' aspect of the TLRP offers the possibility of a sustained programme of learning opportunities for those who are interested in pursuing pedagogical research to a high level of sophistication but who need to develop their research skills if they are fully to achieve this.

Linked projects, sectorally funded

This is where the LTSN has an opportunity, through the activities of its generic centre and subject centres. There is a growing interest in pedagogical research within the LTSN, which reflects not only the need to share research findings across sometimes insular subjects but also the need to be involved in the conduct of pedagogical research into aspects of broad sectoral relevance. Although there is a lot (of varying quality) in the educational literature, there is relatively little *consolidated* knowledge of – for example – the most efficacious uses of information and communications technology within 'standard' curricula; of how to optimize the development in students of 'employability'; and of the most productive ways of giving feedback on student work. A programmatic approach to issues like these could engage a broad swathe of academics across higher education in projects that were linked via the 'hub' of the LTSN.

Intra-institutional pedagogical research

In many institutions there exists a body of research expertise in a Department of Education. The emphasis of such departments tends to be on school education and the training of teachers. Relatively rarely is their expertise drawn upon for the benefit of the wider institution. In a few institutions there is a group of staff expressly charged with supporting educational (and, by interpolation, pedagogical) research – Sheffield Hallam University stands out as an example.

There are a number of influences bearing on institutions that have implications for pedagogical research, amongst them being learning and teaching strategies and the (in many cases related) expectations that staff will become members of the ILT, with all that that implies for continuing professional development. Some institutions provide funding for projects related to learning and teaching, but – as was noted earlier – the emphasis of these projects is often developmental rather than on the research aspect. The harnessing of relevant 'inhouse' expertise has the potential to develop pedagogical research capabilities in those who wish to develop them, to enhance the quality of the findings from projects, and to contribute to the sharing of findings across the institution. In this context, 'programmatic' may embrace a variety of pedagogical research studies under an institutional commitment to the development of pedagogical practice and its transfer intra-institutionally (and possibly inter-institutionally).

Intra-departmental pedagogical research

A department might decide to concentrate its pedagogical research efforts on one or two topics instead of taking a *laisser-faire* approach. This would have the potential benefit of gathering sufficient weight of findings regarding the topic(s) to produce a substantive report. The sort of investigation might, for example, relate to the particular subject area. For example, there is scope in Engineering to study the causality of poor progression and completion,[10] and in Art and Design to study why some students seem to be unhappy with their learning experiences even though they appear to have no reservations about the choice of their subject of study.[11] Briggs *et al.* (2000) briefly describe an intra-departmental approach – but it should be noted that this is within a Division of Education in which relevant research expertise can be assumed. For some departments, it might be wise to engage methodological support from appropriate sources within the institution.

A variant of this approach might be for two or more cognate departments to get together to research a particular pedagogical issue.

Risking accusations of being an advocate of a *dirigiste* approach to pedagogical research, there is the beginning of a framework here, in that there are stages through which new pedagogical researchers might progress until they reach the peaks of pedagogical research capability as represented by gaining major external funding. However, few will get beyond the foothills if pedagogical research is not valued generally within the sector. Yorke (2000) put forward some policy options that in varying degrees might facilitate the generation of support for pedagogical research. These suggestions were largely predicated on the assumption of the continuation of the RAE in its present form, but could be adapted for an RAE-free environment.

The time is perhaps approaching when a new method of valuing institutions' contributions to the sector can be contemplated. The 1999 RAE-type exercise in Hong Kong (see UGC 1999) was more inclusive than those of the UK in that it was based on Boyer's four scholarships (of discovery, integration, application and teaching).[12] Boyer's argument has, over the past decade, encouraged the emergence – albeit a slow one – of a broader perspective on research and scholarly activity.[13]

The separation, in funding mechanisms, of teaching from research has encouraged institutions to converge in their strategic thinking, and has contributed to the undervaluing of pedagogical research. If diversity in the sector is to be valued in reality (as well as in the rhetoric), is the time perhaps nearing when – as Ryan (2001) suggested in a letter to *The Times Higher Education Supplement* – teaching and research assessment are brought together under a single review process, with the consequential funding being a substantial part of the overall institutional allocation? Pedagogical research, which forms a bridge between teaching and research, would probably be a beneficiary as – more importantly – would pedagogy itself.

Notes

1. See JM Consulting Ltd *et al.* (2000).
2. This was one of the many criticisms levelled at the National Educational Research Forum's consultation document on educational research (NERF 2000).
3. The diversity of view is captured in the reports of two *ad hoc* meetings on pedagogical research that were held at Coventry in November 2000 and March 2001. These reports, together with associated documents, can be found via http://d153.arch.cf.ac.uk/~Pedagogical-Research/login (there is a formal logging in procedure).
4. Projects were also funded in the areas of further education and postgraduate employment (for details see the TLRP website: www.ex.ac.uk/ESRC-TLRP/).
5. The National Co-ordination Team, based at the Open University, has a direct overseeing role.
6. If institutional provision was not deemed to be excellent, the institution could nevertheless be a partner in a bid led by an eligible institution.
7. To which the riposte might be that pedagogical research often was in a position analogous to formative assessment – it would assist the development of thinking about the matter in hand without seeking the finality and closure that would be associated with summative assessment. To a researcher concerned with theoretical and methodological rigour, the riposte would be considered too loose.
8. As the ex-editor of *Studies in Higher Education*, I recall submitted papers that claimed a phenomenographical base which, on close scrutiny, seemed to amount to little more than an airy wave in the direction of Marton and Säljö's article.
9. Many interested parties will, of course, have considerable expertise in applying the outcomes of research to teaching and learning situations, and in transferring their knowledge to others.
10. This is evidenced in the performance indicators published by HEFCE (2000a), and some possible causes can be found in Yorke (1999: 50–1 and 135–6). Further pointers to the adverse impact of an academic environment on student learning can be found in a large-scale qualitative study of science, mathematics and engineering that was undertaken in the US by Seymour and Hewitt (1997).
11. See Yorke (1999, loc. cit.).
12. Boyer's four scholarships appear in a number of publications: see Boyer (1994) for one such appearance.
13. Though not in the *Review of Research* (HEFCE 2000b). Set against that report, however, are events such as the conference on the Scholarship of Teaching and Learning held at the University of East London in June 2001.

Acknowledgements

The writing of this chapter has been influenced by the discussions that took place at two exploratory workshops held in Coventry in November 2000 and March 2001. Colleagues who were present at the workshops may recognize fragments of these discussions, and some would undoubtedly have taken a different tack regarding the topic.

I also thank the following for helpful comments during the drafting of this chapter: Carole Baume, Mick Healey, John Rogers and Peter Williams. They cannot, of course, be held responsible for what I have written.

11

Practitioner-centred Research on Academic Development in Higher Education

Trix Webber, Tom Bourner and Suzanne O'Hara

This chapter focuses on *practitioner-centred* research because we believe it to be an approach which has much to recommend it to the readership of this book. Three characteristics can be identified which make it attractive to those concerned with research on academic development in higher education. First, its aim is the conduct of research which *influences* practice, rather than research which seeks to find out more about practice. It can thus have a direct influence on academic development. Second, it is a research methodology which gives due weight to the impact which the individual practitioner has on action. Finally practitioner-centred research involves practitioners as researchers more fully than is usually the case with other methodologies.

The chapter first identifies who the researchers on academic development are. It then goes on to consider the merits and limitations of three approaches to the conduct of research in this area, each of which is associated with the generation of particular types of knowledge. The dissemination of practitioner-centred research is then discussed in more depth.

Researchers on academic development

A distinction can usefully be made between two types of researcher on academic development in higher education. The first is the *educational developer,* that is the person who runs courses in teaching and learning for university teachers. Academic development is likely to be the main research interest of members of the academic community who occupy these roles. They tend to be experienced researchers, capable of using a range of methodologies and usually have resources available for conducting cross-institutional research as well as smaller scale 'local' studies. For these reasons they can be thought of as *professional researchers* on academic development.

As well as conducting their own research, educational developers are usually responsible for encouraging academic colleagues to conduct research on academic development and offering advice on how they might go about it.

The second type of researcher is the university teacher for whom educational developers design courses. The main research interests of members of this group usually relate to their teaching subject areas. Their involvement in research on academic development tends to be limited and to focus on improving their own practice. The studies which they carry out are usually small scale and aim to achieve local improvements in learning, teaching, assessment and knowledge creation. They can, therefore, be regarded as *researching professionals* (Bourner, Katz and Watson 2000) on academic development, rather than professional researchers.

These two groups of researchers, the professional researchers and the researching professionals, will have quite different needs and aims when conducting research on academic development. The educational developers, the professional researchers in this context, are likely to employ a range of research methodologies, of which practitioner-centred research will be just one, in order to generate new theories and develop new practices. The researching professionals, in contrast, have more limited aims and for them practitioner-centred research is likely to be an obvious choice.

The conduct of research on academic development in higher education

We suggest that three approaches to research in the area can be identified. Before outlining these, however, an explanation of what we mean by research on academic development is perhaps useful. In this context we define research as the intentional creation of new knowledge of how academic development occurs and how it can be enhanced. By academic development we mean achievement of the desired outcomes of higher education. These we identify as the effective education and development of individuals; the creation of new knowledge; and the enrichment of society. While there is now considerable diversity in the outcomes which universities and the learning communities within them strive for (Otter 1982), they can all be encompassed within these three broad headings. The main focus of the chapter will be the first two.

Academic development is achieved by the activities in which academic staff and learners engage in order to achieve these outcomes. Research on academic development is wide ranging – how learners learn, which teaching and learning strategies are effective in which contexts, and the impact of assessment regimes on learning are just a few possible themes. Much research in this area concerns the practice of higher education teachers – the academic 'practitioners'.

While many research methodologies are employed to realize this range of aims, they can be grouped into three approaches: research into academic development; action research on academic development; and practitioner-centred research on academic development. The following sections of the chapter offer an outline and comparative critique of these three before discussing the reporting of practitioner centred research in greater depth.

Research into academic development

The first of the three approaches, research *into* academic development, requires the researcher to stand metaphorically outside the arena of investigation and adopt the role of a detached observer. This approach is rooted in the tradition of scientific enquiry and is based on empiricism, induction and objectivity. Bourner, O'Hara and France (2000) define empiricism as enquiry which seeks evidence from the physical world, through observation or experience, rather than 'inner' sources such as intuition. Inductive research aims to 'develop theory from the observation of empirical reality' (Hussey and Hussey 1997: 13). General inferences are deduced from particular instances and patterns found in the evidence. Objectivity is based on the assumption that the world is external to the researcher and research is independent of the influence of the researcher's values and beliefs.

Research aims are likely to focus on reaching conclusions which can be applied to a wider population, and from which general recommendations can be formulated. Useful methodologies are likely to be surveys, structured interviews or highly structured activity logs, which standardize data collection and so yield comparable data. Quasi-scientific research designs may be useful, such as comparisons of subgroups of a population or 'before and after' studies.

Research *into* academic development aims to produce propositional knowledge, that is theories and models which enable us to understand the nature of what is being investigated. Ryle (1967) terms this type of knowledge 'knowing that' in contrast to 'knowing how to'. An important vein of research into academic development, for example, concerns how students approach learning tasks. Marton's (1975) finding that students engaged in two levels of cognitive processing, deep and surface, became the basis for much subsequent research. A deep approach occurred when: 'students tried to understand the message by looking for relations within the text or by looking for relations between the text and phenomena of the real world . . .' (Marton and Säljö 1997: 43). A surface approach, in contrast, was characterized by 'a blind spasmodic effort to memorise the text' (Marton and Säljö 1997: 43).

Eraut (1995) terms this type of knowledge 'conceptual knowledge' and suggests that it can have different degrees of 'formality'. The theory of deep and surface learning has attained the status of 'formal' conceptual or propositional knowledge – it forms part of a widely shared body of knowledge on student learning and will almost inevitably be referred to in any scholarly work on the subject. Its reliability stems from the fact that it is the product of research which has been conducted and recorded systematically, then subjected to the scrutiny of other researchers. This can be contrasted with informal theories, for example theories shared by one group of people about other groups, which are based on the attitudes and experiences of group members rather than systematic research. They are not usually recorded and are often not subject to external scrutiny.

When people speak of 'evidence-based practice', they are usually referring to evidence collected through research into practice. Research into academic development aims to develop, through the use of appropriate methodologies, formal theories which can be widely shared, scrutinized and critiqued. Its strengths and limitations can be summarized as follows.

The strengths and limitations of research into academic development

Research into academic development is valuable because it provides a widely shared foundation of knowledge which forms much of the bedrock upon which professional practice of any sort is based. The general applicability of results means that theories and facts can be interrogated by later research, as well as by critical dialogue within the academic practitioner/researcher community. Moreover, research into academic development is the only approach which can capture the broad sweep of data and use sampling to find out that which is generally true.

The limitations of research into academic practice arise in part from the quantitative methods often employed, which, in aiming for breadth of data, standardization and objectivity, exclude the meaning and purpose which people attach to their activities. Moreover the search for objectivity can be challenged as being an impossible and inappropriate goal in social science research. Guba and Lincoln (1994: 107), for example, suggest that 'facts are facts only within some theoretical framework'. What we call 'facts' are really interpretations of one theory or another.

Other concerns focus on the limited and indirect effect on practice of this type of research and four main reasons for this can be identified. The propositional or conceptual knowledge which it yields raises awareness, but does not necessarily lead to action. Practitioners may not be able to, or feel motivated to translate this knowledge into improvements in their own practices. Currency of the knowledge may be a further problem, since the considerable time lapse between starting a large scale piece of research and disseminating the outcomes may mean that the issues have changed and the results can only help practitioners to become 'proficient in the practices of yesterday' (Revans 1984: 16). There is, also, an inevitable trade off between wide applicability and relevance to the individual. Higher education institutions vary widely and even within an institution there is enormous variance in teaching and learning practices. Bourner *et al.* (2000)

make the point that professionals need to be assured that a practice will work in their specific context and for them personally. Finally, there is the question of ownership of and involvement in research. Research into academic practice tends to remain the province of the professional researcher in the field, since it often involves extensive data collection and analysis. Its findings may therefore remain distant from academic practitioners, the researching professionals.

Action research on academic development

The second approach to conducting research on academic development encompasses a range of research methodologies for which 'action research' has come to be an umbrella term. Bourner *et al.* (2000: 233) define action research as 'a form of social research that, typically, involves making changes to resolve a problem that exists in a social situation'. The development of action research as a deliberate and systematic approach is generally credited to Kurt Lewin (see, for example, Kemmis 1988). It usually involves a collaboration between researchers and those immediately involved in the situation, which starts with a joint definition of the problem, definition of the desired improvement and selection of an investigative framework. Data are then collected and analyzed, providing the basis for further collaboration to agree action for implementing change. A parallel aim in this cycle is to develop new conceptual frameworks as well as achieving change. The cycle may then need to be repeated in the light of the learning gained. Dickens and Watkins (1999: 128) describe the process as:

> . . . ever deepening surveillance of the problem situation . . . and a series of research informed action experiments.

The researchers are usually professional researchers from outside the immediate problem situation and the involvement of participants in the situation varies. They may be involved in the early stages of research design or brought in at a later stage when the parameters are already defined. Once started, researchers and participants are 'inside' the research process, however, rather than the researchers being objective observers. The process challenges the assumptions of all parties and involves all in:

> . . . mutually opening themselves up to an enquiry process that seeks to unfreeze the assumptions underlying their actions.
>
> (Raelin 1999: 117)

Action research on academic development produces propositional knowledge, but this will be local and contextual since it is based on in-depth interpretative enquiry of one situation. It also, however, results in what Ryle termed 'knowing how to' since the research itself involves trying, evaluating and improving elements of practice. Eraut (1995) calls this 'process knowledge', of how to do things or get things done. While not unproblematic, action research has much to offer those who seek to enhance academic development.

Strengths and limitations of action research on academic development

Action research on academic development has the advantage of being responsive to the changes in people and the environment which occur while research is in progress, since its iterative approach allows issues to be revisited and develops a 'slow, continuous cumulative understanding' (Cronbach *et al.* 1980: 47). Moreover as the action research cycle involves developing and trying out new possibilities for action, it has a direct influence on practice. The research is grounded in 'real' situations and if the cycle is repeated, changes in practice are evaluated systematically. Involvement of the broad community that surrounds a situation is an additional strength, since 'most action is determined by a pluralistic community, not by a lone decision maker' (Cronbach *et al.* 1980: 84). The bias of action research towards inclusion therefore further enhances its chance of influencing practice.

While the action/reflection cycle is a strength, however, it can also prove problematic. Finding the optimal balance between action and analysis may prove difficult in practice. Dickens and Watkins (1999) suggest that frequently, projects either become stuck at the diagnosis stage, or the participants become so immersed in action that they neglect to analyze and evaluate the ensuing data. It is, also, an unwieldy methodology. Although able to respond to change, action research requires time for in-depth, iterative enquiry, while academic practitioners may be under pressure to produce rapid results. Its thorough and prescriptive nature may, therefore, make academic practitioners disinclined to embark on an action research project.

A partial mismatch between the aims of action research and those of research on academic development is a further issue. Action research is designed to improve problematic situations, whereas research on academic development has a wider range of aims. Action research will not, therefore, always be appropriate. Alternative methodologies such as 'appreciative enquiry' were, in part, developed as a reaction against the problem-focused orientation of action research. A significant dimension of this problem focus is the emphasis in action research on whole situations, whereas in research on academic practice, the individual practitioner may be a legitimate and useful focus of attention. Bourner *et al.* (2000) make the point that research has the most impact on practice when a practitioner is able to decide from reading about it, that the ideas for improvement can work for her/him as an individual. A final point is that, like research into academic practice, involvement of the researching professional may be limited. While action research involves academic practitioners as the participants in the situation being researched, they tend not to have equal status with the outside 'professional researchers' who orchestrate the enquiry.

Practitioner-centred research on academic development

The third approach, practitioner-centred research, was developed in part as a response to increasing expressions of concern about the limited impact which research on professional practice had on the practice of professionals (Bourner *et al.* 2000). This limited impact has been an ongoing preoccupation for the research councils and for government departments which fund research of this type. Charles Clarke, the then minister of state at the DfEE, stated in 1998 that: 'Findings must be presented in an accessible form so that a wide variety of practitioners can translate the implications into their contexts'. In contrast to the other approaches discussed, the question which practitioner-centred research seeks to answer – 'how can professional practice be enhanced by research?' – focuses specifically on practice.

The argument made here is that practitioner-centred research fulfils a function which is outside the scope of research into academic development and action research on academic development. Taken together, the three provide an extensive repertoire of approaches to fulfil a broad range of research aims. Practitioner-centred research aims to create improvements in professional practice by adding to the stock of usable knowledge of professional practice. It is the intentional creation of new knowledge of professional practice of a kind that can be applied by other professionals to their own practice. Practitioner-centred research starts from the following premises:

- research on professional practice has had too little effect on professional practice;
- professional practitioners have much discretion over whether or not to adopt new professional practices;
- in deciding whether to adopt a new practice the question 'Does it work?' is less important than the practitioner-centred question: 'Can it work for me?'

If we start by considering an idea for an improvement in practice, there are three core questions that academic practitioners need to be able to answer in order to accept and adopt the putative improvement. They need to know whether the idea is generally workable; whether it can work in the context of their own professional practice; and whether it can work for them personally?

The concept of 'professional judgement' gives practitioners a great deal of discretion about the practices they use, and academic practitioners are no exception. This can be illustrated by the practices employed by two economics lecturers from our own faculty to help students to understand macroeconomics. Working to identical learning outcomes, one uses a PowerPoint presentation and the other allots roles to students and has them rushing around the room replicating the interactions between elements in the macroeconomic environment. The professional decisions that academic practitioners take, and the practices that they choose to adopt, are thus based on their educational values and beliefs as well as their skills and professional knowledge. There are likely to be tacit aspects of the practice that are influenced by their beliefs and values. Practitioners will be reluctant to adopt new practices if the beliefs and values that are embodied in the new practice are much different from their own.

Beliefs and values will also influence the criteria they use to judge success or failure. A current debate in our own faculty concerns the criteria which should be used to assess masters degree dissertations in management. While all agree that sound business reporting and academic rigour are both vital, views differ on how they should be combined and the relative importance of each. Professional practice is thus mediated by values and beliefs in many ways.

Practitioner-centred research is a systematic approach to generating and disseminating process knowledge, Ryle's 'knowing how to', which is specifically related to professional practice. Bourner *et al.* (2000) term this 'knowledge of practice'. In higher education, a lecturer's knowledge of practice would typically include a range of specific practices plus more general principles, for example how to change teaching processes in response to the rising size of seminar groups.

The conduct and dissemination of practitioner-centred research

In this section of the chapter we consider how knowledge derived through practitioner-centred research should be disseminated. Criteria for a practitioner-centred research report are identified and illustrated with reference to three examples.

An academic practitioner's personal knowledge of a new practice in higher education teaching, learning or knowledge creation which he or she has developed will include a clear rationale for developing the new practice, which might relate to the limitations of current practices or the desire to expand learning opportunities. It will also include the aims and intended learning outcomes of the new practice. He or she will know from experience, as well as from a theoretical basis, what the merits of this particular practice are in relation to the practitioner and the learners. The practitioner's procedural knowledge will encompass many aspects of using the new practice such as timing of activities, the materials required and procedures to follow. Knowledge of the value of the practice will have been gained from reviewing the experience of carrying it out.

In order to translate this personal knowledge into practitioner-centred research, it needs to be disseminated in a way which will enable other practitioners to decide whether the practice is appropriate for the context in which they work and whether they personally would use it. The disseminated account therefore needs an explanation of the beliefs and values which underlie the practice as well as contextual information. We suggest that a practitioner-centred research report will include each of the following three elements:

1. Sufficient information about the emergent professional practice *per se* to replicate it in the type of context where it has proved successful.
2. Sufficient information about the contextual factors on which the new practice depends to enable other practitioners to decide whether they can apply it in the context(s) of their own practice.
3. Sufficient detail of the beliefs and values that underpin the practice to enable other practitioners to decide whether they will adopt it in their own practice.

The second element is likely to comprise information about the context of its origin – the type of contextual information that would be expected in sound case study research. The third element is likely to take the form of information about the beliefs and values of the originator(s) of the new practice. A practitioner considering whether to adopt a new practice needs to be able to answer the question 'Am I enough like the originator(s) to be able to share their successful experience with a new practice?'.

In much the same way as scientific researchers have to be explicit about the physical context of their research results and social researchers have to be explicit about the social context of their research, so practitioner researchers have to be explicit about the personal context of their research. Professional people use themselves as the instrument of their work and they themselves provide a personal context to the practices they employ.

Table 11.1 sets out the characteristics of a sound practitioner-centred research report, using three examples of practitioner-centred research as an illustration. The first is 'The use of magic in teaching organizational behaviour' (Krell and Dobson 1999). The other two are from our own experience.

'Hi-fidelity case studies' in management education (Flowers, O'Hara and Reeve 1997) were developed as a way of overcoming the 'low-fidelity' of the traditional case study approach. In 'hi-fidelity' case studies, students, who are also practising managers, offer their own real, current managerial problems to small teams of other students who act as consultancy groups. These groups produce individual, customized solutions to the live problems and generate genuine management learning. The hi-fidelity case study was developed and refined over a number of residentials on the Brighton MBA programme. It has been written up in sufficient detail, including contextual factors such as the history of its development and the characteristics of students, to enable other educational practitioners to judge whether they would wish to use it. Published accounts of hi-fidelity case studies include an examination of the values and beliefs which underlie the practice.

The third example is 'Forming action learning sets in management education programs' (Webber and O'Hara 1997). The practice advocated here,

Table 11.1 Characteristics of a practitioner-centred research report

The contextual or historical reason for developing the new practice	A	Other techniques rely on possibly inaccurate assumptions about students
	B	Traditional case studies are removed from students' experience
	C	Choosing action learning sets had proved problematic in the past
Relationship to other relevant work	A	Link to previous work on how magical effects act as memory hooks and the use of magic in therapy
	B	Link to other case study method
	C	Link to other accounts of set formation and group dynamics
Educational goals of the new practice	A	To heighten awareness of the complexity of organizational life
	B	To develop consultancy, team working and problem solving skills
	C	To develop understanding and ownership of group process
Values and beliefs which underpin the practice	A	The importance of emotional response in learning
	B	Valuing of students' experience as a vehicle for learning
	C	Belief that students should participate fully in group process
Why this practice	A	Magic creates powerful parallels with organizational learning events
	B	It engenders an intense and exciting experience
	C	It creates a powerful learning experience without the problematic elements of other methods
Detailed description of the practice including how it is managed, necessary materials, timing, past experiences of using it		This is self-explanatory in each case
Analysis of the practice to the wider context of learning	A	The general principle that links magical effects to organizational behaviour
	B	The transfer of learning from management courses to students' work situations
	C	Other instances of group inclusion and exclusion in organizational life

A 'The use of magic in teaching organizational behaviour' (Krell and Dobson 1999)
B Hi-fidelity case studies
C 'Forming action learning sets in management education programs' (Webber and O'Hara 1997)

of involving learners fully in group process, resulted from a number of occasions when dividing a cohort of students into action learning sets, small groups of six or seven which would work together for the year, had proved problematic and even distressing for some students.

Strengths and limitations of practitioner-centred research

The strengths of practitioner-centred research lie in the ownership of the research by practitioners and the individual focus. In contrast to the two other approaches discussed, the research process in practitioner-centred research is managed by the academic practitioner, the *researching professional,* focusing on his or her own practice, rather than an outside professional researcher. Practising professionals are in a privileged position in engaging in the process as they are able to test out and refine their ideas through application to their own professional practice. Once clear that the idea can work, they are in a position to disseminate the research in a way that will enable other practitioners in their field to try, evaluate and possibly adopt the new development. The individual and contextualized nature of practitioner-centred research means that personal learning can be converted into useful professional knowledge. The personal learning from new developments in professional practice can be translated into knowledge that other professional practitioners can use, adding to the stock of knowledge available to all practitioners. An assumption that underpins these strengths is that the individual practitioner/researcher and the research are not separate, independent entities.

Potential drawbacks stem from the subjective nature of the research and the fact that unlike action research, there is no built in scrutiny. Whereas action research prescribes scrutiny of research results by the community of researchers, practitioner-centred researchers must build appropriate scrutiny and critiquing into the process themselves. It must also be recognized that an inherent danger in subjectively based research is a self-indulgent over emphasis on reflexivity at the expense of creating knowledge which will be of use to others. Both potential pitfalls can, however, be avoided by appropriate research design and procedures.

Conclusion

Traditionally, research has been undertaken by professional researchers. We believe that there is considerable scope for research to have more impact on practice through the work of researching professionals. While we recognize the role of *evidence-based practice* in academic development, we also see a role for *practice-based evidence.* It is through practitioner-centred research that researching professionals can generate practice-based evidence.

Academic developers are likely to find practitioner-centred research a useful approach to recommend to colleagues wishing to improve their own professional practice and share their knowledge.

Practitioner-centred research is not, of course, a new invention and journal articles appear regularly which meet the practitioner-centred research criteria which have been identified in this chapter. Our aim has been to propose practitioner-centred research as a distinct and intentional approach, with its own discipline and criteria by which it should be judged. We are not suggesting that it should replace other ways of researching academic practice, nor are we making any comparative evaluations between the three approaches which have been examined. We see all as valuable and having a place in contributing to academic development. Practitioner-centred research as presented here is relatively new. It will be developed and refined through further researching as well as dialogue with the community of those committed to using research in the cause of academic development in higher education.

12

Researching the Training of University Teachers: Conceptual Frameworks and Research Tools

Graham Gibbs

Introduction

In the UK there are currently in excess of 70 training programmes for teachers that are substantial enough to be Postgraduate Certificates, or accredited by the Staff and Educational Development Association or the Institute for Learning and Teaching. These programmes differ widely in their length, their design, the topics they cover and in the teaching and training methods involved. They also differ in their underlying rationales and in their intended outcomes. Interviews with trainers about their goals has revealed a wide range of underlying beliefs, values and intentions (Coffey and Gibbs 2001). There is currently little evidence about which of these course designs or processes works best or indeed if any of them achieve anything at all. In some instances programmes have adopted specific training methods without:

- a theoretical rationale for using their particular methods;
- insights from the literature about why these methods might not always work;
- using research tools, in their evaluation, which are suited to identifying the impact of these methods;
- convincing evidence of the effectiveness of these methods on their programme.

Training now, however, is much more extensive and high profile than previously. It features in the 'learning and teaching strategy' of half of all 134 English institutions (HEFCE 2001b) and the Institute for Learning and Teaching is a prominent component of national policy. This national policy, and the attitude of institutions to investment in training, is open to influence by various vested interest groups. In the absence of evidence concerning whether current training provision works, or why, current policy and practice may turn out to be vulnerable. The Institute for Learning and Teaching, for example, has made the policy decision that to be accredited by the ILT an initial training programme has to be at least at the level of a postgraduate certificate course (carrying 60 M-level credit points). This is in excess of the scale and level of many previously existing programmes and imposes on all such programmes the need to undertake a very formal assessment of each teacher. This policy will cost many institutions substantial additional sums, every year, to implement and the employment implications for individual teachers of 'failing' such a formal course have yet to be fully realized. There is currently no evidence available about the relative impact of short or long training programmes which could justify this policy decision. It might have been sensible, but we have no research programme in place at institutional or national level to find out.

It is argued here that it would be to the advantage of educational developers to:

- use research evidence to select training methods;
- use models of the development of teachers and conceptual frameworks to select aims for programmes;
- exploit insights available in the literature so as to understand better some of the phenomena and problems encountered during the operation of programmes;
- use research tools and methodologies when we evaluate our programmes;
- obtain evidence of the overall impact of our programmes on the quality of teaching and learning so as to justify our practice and defend the investments our institutions make in our programmes.

What is training attempting to achieve?

Before attempting to answer a question such as 'does training work?' one has to be clear about what kind of outcomes might be achieved and what trainers say they are trying to achieve: what 'working' might consist of. Interviews with trainers about what they are trying to achieve have revealed a wide range of goals (Coffey and Gibbs 2001). A questionnaire study has attempted to quantify trainers' priorities amongst these goals. The questionnaire listed five of the most common goals identified in the interview study and asked trainers to allocate 12 'points' amongst these goals in a way which indicated their relative importance on their training programme. By way of illustration, Table 12.1 shows the way two different trainers, both from UK institutions, allocated these points.

What is clear here is that while Trainer A has a clear priority, and should presumably seek some kind of measure of reflection in order to evaluate the success of the programme, Trainer B has no such clear priority. It is much less clear what Trainer B should be trying to evaluate. Some existing measures for these five different goals exist, and new instruments are being specially developed for this purpose (see below).

Table 12.1 Variations between trainers

The course is concerned with . . .	*Trainer A*	*Trainer B*
Reflection	5	3
Student learning	2	3
Repertoire	2	0
Conceptions	2	3
Skills	1	3
Total	**12**	**12**

Does training work?

We often believe our training works and can probably think of individual teachers who we are convinced made great strides while on our programmes. We may have atheoretical evaluation evidence, from home-made questionnaires or informal interviews, that show a reasonable level of satisfaction, on the part of those we have trained, with our programmes. Some of this evaluation evidence has been written up and published. Rust (1999), for example, has reported a range of evidence based on self-reports from teachers who have been through a programme at Oxford Brookes University. But this kind of evidence may not be sufficient to convince those who form training policy or make resource decisions. The Rust study, for example, reports no independent evidence employing any measure of teaching effectiveness, and no evidence from students.

A recent issue of the journal *Teaching in Higher Education* contained several articles which argued that the whole enterprise of training and staff development for university teachers was inherently incapable of achieving anything useful. These articles contained not a single scrap of evidence but nevertheless posed a real challenge to trainers. There are few studies of the overall effectiveness of attempts to improve new teachers in higher education. Two examples are given here that highlight some of the methodological problems associated with them.

In Australia, Nasr *et al.* (1996) compared the student feedback ratings of teachers at their institution who had completed postgraduate programmes for teachers (programmes at their or any other institution) with those who had not. They found that trained teachers received significantly higher ratings. While this is encouraging, in Australia it is usual for such programmes to be voluntary, so this difference may simply be between teachers who are keen and conscientious enough to volunteer to take formal courses and those who are not. There was no 'before' measure to see if these teachers would have had better student feedback ratings without taking the training programme, simply as a result of either their characteristics or of their experience of teaching. There was also no evidence about what the goals of these postgraduate courses were, and whether these goals even included the improvement of student feedback ratings. The feedback ratings were from a locally designed questionnaire that had not been tested for its reliability or validity and which had no underlying theoretical model of what good teaching consists of. These are fairly substantial methodological problems.

Giertz (1996) has reported a follow-up study of the impact of a training programme at the University of Uppsala. The study used depth interviews and teachers were given the freedom to define for themselves what kinds of changes they believed had taken place. The report makes interesting reading and the quotes from teachers would encourage any trainer. However there is no corroborating evidence of these self reports of any kind – from student feedback, from student performance, from observation, or from colleagues. There was no 'before' measure. Several studies (e.g. Murray and Macdonald 1997) have highlighted the difference between teachers' accounts or intentions and what they actually practise in their teaching. In the Approaches to Teaching Inventory (ATI) there are separate questionnaire items for teachers' intentions and for their strategies (Trigwell and Prosser 1996a). This difference, between what Schön has called 'theories of action' (e.g. *post hoc* explanations a teacher might give for why they teach in the way they do) and 'theories in use' (e.g. the teacher's implicit model which must be driving their observable teaching behaviour) bedevils research into professional practice which relies on self-report without triangulation with evidence from other sources.

These studies are amongst the few which provide any evidence that initial training makes any difference. Understanding their methodological difficulties, however, helps to illuminate what kind of studies are required if we are to place more confidence in our evidence.

The selection of training methods

As well as there being a lack of evidence of the overall impact of training there is also a lack of evidence about the efficacy of the most common training methods we choose to adopt in our programmes. For example, American reviews of the literature on faculty development (such as Weimer and Lenze 1997) have been uniformly scathing about the reliance of faculty developers on the use of workshops as a change process, in the absence of evidence of their effectiveness. The usual criticism is that there is little 'transfer of training' from the workshop to the classroom. Studies of the impact of 'microteaching' have highlighted this problem: behavioural change induced under workshop conditions may not be reproduced in the classroom. Academic development in the UK relies on workshops almost as much as do those in the USA. Should we be using workshops at all?

In the UK, Chris Rust is responsible for a national programme of workshops which have been running for more than a decade under the auspices of the Oxford Centre for Staff and Learning Development (OCSLD). In the face of criticism of the potential usefulness of these workshops he undertook research into the impact of OCSLD's activities (Rust 1999). In addition to end-of-workshop feedback on a large number of workshops, using a feedback questionnaire of a kind which many trainers would recognize, he followed up participants some months later with questionnaires and telephone interviews. He found that:

- Participants often report having made changes to their teaching after having attended workshops.
- Ratings at the end of the workshop predicted outcomes at a later date, in that participants who attended workshops which received better ratings were more likely to subsequently report having made changes to their teaching. What are often termed 'happiness ratings' may indeed have some usefulness, though some of these ratings had less predictive ability than others.
- 'Intention to change' ratings, in the end-of-workshop feedback questionnaire, predicted outcomes reasonably well, in that if a participant said at the end of a workshop that they were likely to introduce some changes, then they were likely to report having actually introduced change at a later date. To some extent we can trust such end-of-workshop intentions.
- Some features of workshops predicted impact more than others, and this data can help us to pay attention to the influential features as we design and run our training. For example, the extent to which plenty of practical ideas were discussed in the workshops predicted impact better than the extent to which the workshop presenter was considered knowledgeable in the topic.

There are problems with this kind of evidence in that:

- Those who attended the workshops were largely self-selected, as were those who replied to questionnaires.
- All change was self-reported change, with no independent corroboration.
- There is no independent evidence that the changes produced beneficial effects, for example from student feedback data or from student performance data. It is perfectly possible that these workshops fostered innovation that had no useful impact or even that it was harmful.
- There is no way of knowing whether these teachers would have brought about these changes anyway. Certainly some feedback from participants reported the workshops to have confirmed them in their beliefs and practices rather than actually introduced them to new ideas.

We can be slightly more confident in using workshops and slightly better informed about what to pay attention to in designing, running and evaluating our workshops, as a consequence of Rust's research. However, this is not the same as having hard evidence that workshops are a suitable method for trainers to adopt.

There is also evidence available about the effects of use of some other components of our programmes such as evidence of the effects of video feedback on teaching behaviour (Dalgaard 1982) and the effects of use of student feedback questionnaires (Marsh 1987). But how many programmes' choice of methods is informed by this research evidence? For example, most programmes in the UK probably encourage teachers to collect student feedback. However, few training courses encourage the use of feedback questionnaires that have established reliability or validity, such as the Student Evaluation of Educational Quality (SEEQ) which has been validated for use in the UK (Coffey and Gibbs 2000b). The evidence is clear that mid-term use of such feedback questionnaires, and consultation with an educational expert about the results, greatly increases the likelihood that the use of such feedback questionnaires will improve teaching (Marsh 1987). But how many programmes use this evidence and arrange for teachers to use questionnaires half way through courses (rather than only at the end of courses) and how many undertake a consultation with teachers about their student feedback? The University of Lincoln in New Zealand took this research seriously and required teachers to visit the educational development centre and have a chat about their student feedback. This was the only way to obtain the feedback and it encouraged most teachers to seek this consultation.

Consultation is shown to have long-term positive effects on student ratings, especially if this consultation is accompanied by observation or meetings with students (Piccinin *et al.* 1999). How many training programmes use either observation or consultation backed up by meetings with the trainee teachers' students?

Finally, there are studies which report on the effectiveness of training programmes with very specific goals. For example, Schreurs (1998) reports how a training programme was developed for tutors in a problem-based medical course. Very specific tutor behaviours which were considered desirable in problem-based tutorials were identified and a highly structured series of intensive workshops were designed to train tutors to use exactly these behaviours. Every teacher new to the institution, no matter how experienced or senior, was obliged to undergo this training, so it was important to be able to check that such a policy was justified. They used video as part of the training and also to evaluate whether the tutors had adopted the desired behaviours. It is not common for training programmes to have such specific goals that they can evaluate their success in this way. However, it is unclear what can be generalized from such studies other than that such behavioural change is possible.

Using research to develop and implement rationales for programme design

As reported above, trainers have many different rationales for the design of their courses. One such rationale will be explored in detail here to illustrate the potential of research to conceptualize the issues, provide assistance in programme design, and provide research tools with which to evaluate the impact of training.

Some training programmes attempt to re-orient teachers from a teacher-centred approach to a student-centred approach. For example one trainer reported:

> I can think of an instance where I was observing somebody . . . and this . . . member of staff said to me 'when I first came on the programme, all I could think about was me and how I was performing. What this programme has made me think about is 'are students learning?' . . . we provide a programme, we do it to the best of our ability, but somehow they have got to make that transition themselves.

This difference in focus has been studied in Australian universities (e.g. Trigwell *et al.* 1994). Teachers have been interviewed about their approach to teaching, just as Marton interviewed students about their approach to learning (Marton *et al.* 1993). A questionnaire has been developed (the ATI: Approaches to Teaching Inventory) which identifies the extent to which teachers are teacher-focused or student-focused. Other studies have shown that teachers who are teacher-focused are more likely to have students who take a surface approach to their studies (Trigwell *et al.* 1999) and we know that students who take a surface approach understand less and forget more quickly. Teacher-focused teachers also have a narrower repertoire of teaching techniques while teachers with a student focus score better on a student feedback questionnaire (the SEEQ) (Coffey and Gibbs, under review). So we know that changing teachers' approach is an important goal for training. But can such approaches be changed by training?

Ho (1998a) has reviewed the literature on conceptual change as it applies to professional contexts, and to changes in conceptions of teaching in particular. She designed and implemented a programme for new higher education teachers consisting of ten activities, designed according to these principles. Using depth interviews, before and after the course, and analyzing transcripts using the Trigwell and Prosser categories of approaches to teaching, she has demonstrated changes in teachers' conceptions between the start and end of the programme (Ho 1998b). These changes also translate into teachers' action and impact on student learning.

Changes in teachers' approach from the start to the end of training programmes have also been reported, using the ATI to measure teachers' approach (Coffey and Gibbs, under review). ATI scores were found to correlate with student feedback ratings using the SEEQ, with the approach students took to their studies and to the repertoire of teaching methods the teacher used. The findings demonstrated that variable changes in approach to teaching are clearly possible. Training programmes, in 20 institutions in eight countries, have been found to move teachers to a more student-focused approach and a less teacher-focused approach, while a control group, who experienced no training, moved in the opposite direction (Gibbs and Coffey 2001).

In the example discussed here a particular rationale for a programme has a theoretical framework, an empirical basis and empirical evidence of impact based on the use of a purpose-designed research tool (the ATI), using properly designed studies (including a control group).

Using research to make sense of problems

Research can be used to understand what is going on when training does not work as well as it might. For example, Isaacs and Parker (1996) ran an initial training programme for new teachers at the University of Queensland which was oriented towards improving student learning outcomes and reflective practice. It operated in an intensive block right at the start of the academic year. Evaluation showed that the participants did not like it at all and would have preferred an emphasis on getting the basic skills right, such as lecturing.

To help us make sense of what was probably going on here there is a growing literature about the nature of the changes that take place as teachers in higher education develop over time, especially at the start of their careers. Two models of development, in particular, provide helpful clues for researchers about what to look for in tracking the development of teachers over the course of an initial training programme.

The best researched scheme (Nyquist and Wulff 1996) was derived from qualitative research at a number of US universities and colleges, and informed by models developed in the context of school teaching. It plots a developmental shift of teachers' focus of attention from *self* to *skills* and then to *students.* A second scheme (Kugel 1993) which has come out of work at Harvard University and Boston College, describes the first stage as involving a focus on the self: whether one is liked or seen as competent. Kugel defines an additional stage in which the focus is on the subject – characterized by over-preparation and overfilling lectures out of anxiety about being on top of the material. Kugel then describes a focus on the student which develops in three stages: from a focus on the student as passively receptive, to being active, and finally being independent. Kugel also emphasizes key transitions which take place and these transitions are identified in Table 12.2 which integrates the Nyquist and Kugel schemes.

The first transition described is from a focus on the content of what teachers teach to a focus on how to teach it. The implication is that it may be difficult to get new teachers to pay much attention to methods until they feel reasonably secure in their knowledge of their subject. The second transition described is from a focus on teaching to a focus on learning. This is a transition many teachers never make and it is difficult putting models of reflective practice into operation if teachers pay no attention to learning outcomes and to what students do as a consequence of their teaching. Recent longitudinal work, following new teachers over an extended period (Nyquist and Wulff 1998) has identified a lack of reflection, or indeed any ability to 'thematize' teaching, as accompanying failure to develop.

Table 12.2 Stages and transitions of the Nyquist and Kugel developmental models

Stages
Stage 1: Focus on self, including own knowledge of subject
Transition from focus on content to focus of process
Stage 2: Focus on methods: how should I teach?
Transition from focus on teaching to focus on learning
Stage 3: Focus on outcomes: what have students learnt? Am I effective?

The problem the University of Queensland programme experienced was probably associated with the teachers being at too early a stage in their development to be able to focus on students and learning outcomes and hence the focus of the training programme passed them by. Theoretical frameworks, and the empirical evidence which accompanies them can provide insights and explanations to help evaluate training programmes and to interpret evaluation evidence.

Research tools

At the SEDA Staff Development conference in Manchester in 1997 a medical school reported in a workshop how they had developed a new tool for evaluating interactive teaching sessions through observation. Their observation schedule was based on an informal survey of what items teachers and management in the school would like to see included in it. In the seminar participants were asked to use the observation schedule as they watched a video tape of some small group teaching. It proved impossible. There was no agreement about what the observation categories meant or whether particular things had been observed or not. The observation schedule had not been developed in a way that could possibly make it reliable or valid.

There is a substantial literature on what aspects of teaching can be reliably judged, emphasizing the importance of focusing on 'low-inference' teaching behaviours where the observer is having to make as few subjective judgements as possible so that observers watching the same thing find it easy to agree that a teaching behaviour has happened (see Murray 1983). Well-developed observation schedules already exist, accompanied by evidence of high levels of inter-observer reliability as well as evidence of validity in that what can be observed relates to important student learning outcomes. Why do we try to invent our own tools and devise our own evaluation questionnaires when there are well-developed research tools already available?

Table 12.3 Goals of training, their focus and associated measures of outcome

Goals	*Focus*	*Associated measure of outcome*
Behavioural change	Classroom teaching behaviour and the improvement of skills.	The Student Evaluation of Educational Quality (SEEQ) (Marsh 1982, Coffey and Gibbs 2000b) which measures low inference classroom behaviours.
Conception of teaching	Movement from a preoccupation with content to a focus on learning. Personal conceptions of learning and teaching.	The Approaches to Teaching Inventory (ATI) (Trigwell and Prosser 1996) which measures the extent to which a teacher is teacher-focused or student focused (in both intention and strategy).
Reflective practice	Ability to reflect on practice. Responsiveness to context and student differences. Freedom from habitual and traditional methods. Ability to innovate.	The Teaching Methods Inventory (TMI) (Coffey and Gibbs, under review) which measures teaching repertoire and reflection.
Improving student learning	How students approach learning. Focus on learning outcome rather than teacher input.	The Module Experience Questionnaire (MEQ, based on the CEQ) (Ramsden 1991) which measures students' approach to learning and response to features of course design.
Development of self-confidence	'Teacher efficacy' and confidence in their ability to teach effectively and to use new methods.	The 'Teacher Efficacy' questionnaire (Gibson and Dembo 1984).

Table 12.3 summarizes the main goals of training identified by UK trainers (Coffey and Gibbs, under review) and the research tools currently available to measure the impact of training on the achievement of these goals.

The Centre for Higher Education Practice has been undertaking an international study since 1997 in which the SEEQ, MEQ, ATI and TMI have been used in a total of 24 institutions in eight countries, at the start and end of training programmes, in an attempt to identify the relative impact of training programmes of various kinds. The institutions studied include four where no training is undertaken, in order to separate the effects of experience from the effects of training. The trainer responsible for each programme has also completed a 'Training Rationale Questionnaire' in order to be able to see if training with different goals has different impacts. Preliminary evidence from 10 programmes includes a positive impact of training on five of the six scales of the SEEQ after only three months of training (Coffey and Gibbs 2000a).

While the four instruments used provided valuable data, there were a number of problems:

- They were too long and time consuming to complete. Both teachers and their students were asked to complete two instruments on two occasions and this substantially reduced return rates. Making the student questionnaires shorter is particularly important as about 20 students are required to complete this questionnaire for each trainee teacher.
- They each involved a different layout, structure and rating scales, making it difficult to understand how they should be completed and this introduced errors in responses.
- Statistical analysis showed that a much smaller number of items was required to obtain reliable scores for each measure and that some subscales were unnecessary.
- The TMI did not work sufficiently well to measure teachers' repertoire and failed to distinguish teachers in terms of the level of their reflectiveness.

By 2002 work was completed to develop two new short instruments to replace the four used previously, and to do this in a way which made them easy to use and score by trainers without access to specialist research or statistical support. Table 12.4 lists the scales the instrument contains.

If these questionnaires are administered to teachers, and to their students, at the start of training and a year later, after it is complete, scale scores may be able to be used in the following ways:

- Scores on Scale 1 can indicate the extent to which training changes classroom teaching practice, as perceived by students.
- Scores on Scales 2 and 3 can indicate the extent to which training changes the way teachers' students approach their studying.
- Scales 4 and 5 can indicate the extent to which training changes teachers' approach from a teacher focus to a student focus.
- Scales 6, 7 and 8 can indicate the extent to which training changes teachers' reflection, repertoire and self-efficacy, respectively.

With these two questionnaires trainers should be able to identify any impact of their programme and the nature of that impact, in relation to their training goals and methods. The Centre for Higher Education Practice at the Open University have made the Training Effectiveness Toolkit available for free use, together with instructions for its administration and scoring. Where possible, data and norms from the use of these questionnaires will also be made available so that trainers can compare their teachers' scores, and the impact of their training programme, with those of others in their own or other countries.

Table 12.4 The Training Effectiveness Toolkit (the toolkit contains two questionnaires)

Questionnaire for teachers' students

1. Classroom teaching (*c.* 10 items) (two items from each of five key scales taken from the SEEQ)
2. Surface approach (*c.* 6 items) (from the MEQ)
3. Deep approach (*c.* 6 items) (from the MEQ)

Total: 22 items

Questionnaire for teachers

4. Teacher-focused approach (*c.* 8 items) (from the ATI)
5. Student-focused approach (*c.* 8 items) (from the ATI)
6. Reflection (*c.* 8 items) (new items)
7. Teacher efficacy (*c.* 8 items) (derived from Gibson and Dembo 1984)
8. Repertoire (*c.* 8 items) (new items)

Total: 40 items

Conclusions

This chapter has argued for a more scholarly and rigorous approach to evaluating the impact of training of university teachers. It has reviewed some of the existing evidence, and the limitations of this evidence and the methodologies which produced it. It has attempted to show how use of theoretical frameworks and empirical evidence can inform training decisions and help to diagnose training problems. Finally it has reported on the development of two questionnaires developed specifically for the purpose of evaluating the impact of training, based on existing theoretical frameworks and existing research tools.

If trainers were to collaborate in using these questionnaires, and to pool the evidence from this research, we would have a substantial basis from which to influence policy on training, both within our institutions and at a national level.

13

An Action-research Approach to Strategic Development: A Case Study

Liz Beaty and Glynis Cousin

Background context

Higher education has been subject to a great deal of change in recent years. In the UK these changes have included a move from an elite, slim line system for the high flying few, towards a mass system, catering for almost half of school leavers and an increasing number of mature students. The imperative to educate many more people to the highest level has altered the nature of university provision. The ending of the binary divide between polytechnics and the older universities in the UK brought a new competition within the system with all institutions competing for research funding and student numbers. On top of these structural changes, there has been an unprecedented focus on accountability and a number of important systems for quality assurance and quality assessment have been put in place on top of the old peer review systems. Institutions of higher education have found it increasingly important to articulate their mission and to have a strategy to manage change. A third aspect is technological change around information and communications technology (ICT). The 'electronic revolution' has altered the way in which academics communicate, it has offered new possibilities for gathering management information and, most importantly, it has offered creative opportunities for the development of teaching and learning methods. These three sets of changes together create a dynamic and challenging environment for educational development.

The challenge is, however, heightened by the fact that few new resources have been found to support this growth and development in the system. The context for radical change exists within a framework constricted by a lower unit of resource for teaching, and increasing competition both within the UK and internationally. In July 1997 the report from the National Commission of Inquiry into Higher Education, chaired by Sir Ron Dearing, was completed (Dearing 1997). The Dearing report focused attention on the need for universities to think strategically about teaching and learning and one tangible result has been the HEFCE funded Teaching Quality Enhancement Funding which includes funds given to sector institutions specifically earmarked for teaching and learning strategies.

In the light of these contextual changes the management of change requires a strategic view of the needs of a more diverse set of learners, an approach to teaching characterized by attention to appropriate course design and effective use of the whole range of learning technologies, including appropriate infrastructure and working practices to support this. It also requires sensitivity to the scale and structure of necessary change. Elton (1993) has dubbed higher education 'the last cottage industry'. Specialization, team working and institutional strategies need to replace the current tendency of individual amateurism and ad hoc management.

Educational development and the management of change

Whether educational developers have seen themselves as change agents or as educational consultants their role is always associated in some way with enabling change. Because educational development supports change at both the levels of professional practice and of organizational development it needs to carry with it a scholarship in educational and organizational theory. It is no surprise, therefore, that when higher education self-consciously embarks on radical change, for example, from elite to mass higher education and the adoption of learning technologies, educational developers are given strategic positions within universities.

Recent writers have described variation in orientation to educational development work and demonstrated how this maps on to different images of change (Jenkins *et al.* 2000; Land 2001). How developers see their role has consequences for their functional position within the organization and for how they approach institutional change. Whatever position is adopted it is clear that in the early twenty-first century, educational developers in the UK and globally have increased influence. In a comparison of educational development units between 1995 and 2000, Gosling (2001) clearly demonstrates the improvements in the position and resourcing of units in the UK and suggests that the 'fledgling tribe of educational developers have come of age'. He points to the increase in the number of units, the influence on national higher education policy and the growing literature and research on development issues and theory.

Educational developers can, however, find themselves caught in a dilemma: wanting to use the opportunities within the contextual changes to support innovation and creativity but being asked to do so within a general call for efficiency gains and accountability procedures. If we stay at the periphery supporting innovation on the ground, being a critical friend and mentor to individual academics, we may become the first casualty in restructuring or downsizing. If we become the arm of the management, tied to accountability procedures, then we may find a great deal of work to do in these times but will not be well placed to foster the educational developments which make a real difference to the experience of learning. Furthermore, we could alienate our natural constituency of academic colleagues. To be effective, academic developers must work both top-down and bottom-up within the organization. Metaphorically speaking they are the filling in the sandwich between policy and management on the one hand, and innovation and practical action on the other (Beaty 1995).

This chapter aims to show how educational developers can meet the challenge of managing change by the adoption of an action-research approach at both micro- and macro-levels.

Interweaving two levels of action research

A conventional scientific paradigm sees practice as flowing from theory whereas action research posits a dialectical relationship between theory and practice in which the one is constantly influencing the shape of the other. According to this relationship, theorizing proceeds through practice and the Aristotelian concept of praxis (which is counter-posed to pure theory) is mobilized to capture this dynamic. Action research starts with a problem for which a provisional remedy is formulated that is then tested for its effectiveness. All variants of action research involve a cyclic or spiral process in which research, action and evaluation are interlinked (see for instance, Carr and Kemmis 1986; McNiff 1988, 1993). Importantly, action research is also founded on a research relationship in which those affected by the change are invited to participate in the research process, particularly with respect to the reflective elements of it.

Action research then, is *problem-focused, context specific and future-oriented* (Hart and Bond 1995). It is a framework that allows you to research as you field test a problem with an eye on the future shifts in practice such testing suggests. Most action research begins with the innovator researching his/her own practice (McNiff 1993). Beaty *et al.* (1995) describe a triadic model of action research where local innovation is supported by a professional educational developer and a dedicated researcher. Our approach has been to extend this model to encompass institutional as well as course level change. Figure 13.1 shows this dual process. The smaller spirals represent course level action research (task force projects) where the intention was to undertake development projects underpinned by scholarship and reflective inquiry. The larger spiral represents the broader action research into using educational development for strategic change. Our intention in undertaking action research on the institutional level was not merely to inquire into its effectiveness but also to support the development of the strategy itself. This strategy is formally speaking the university's teaching and learning

Figure 13.1 Action research at micro- and macro-levels

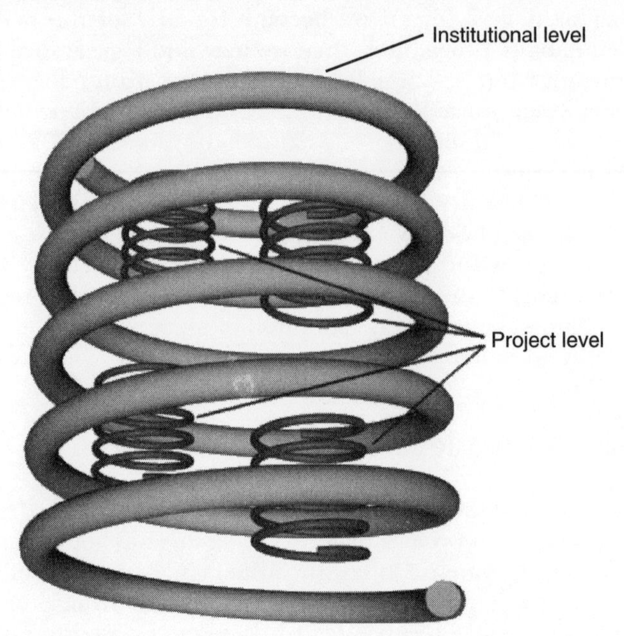

strategy. It is the task force together with educational developers who have played a key role in animating it.

The case study – Coventry University

Implementation of Coventry University's teaching and learning strategy can be described in three phases which correspond to different foci in the management of change.

- *Phase 1*: Initial design of the strategy based on the establishment of a supported critical mass of innovators.
- *Phase 2*: Development of task force projects supported by action learning and action research.
- *Phase 3*: Development of cross-university work – embedding in a community of higher education researchers and developers supported by a new Centre for Higher Education Development.

Phase 1: Initial implementation of the strategy

In 1997 the Pro Vice Chancellor Professor Gareth Thomas surveyed North American practice in the use of Information Technology which fed into his design of a teaching and learning strategy. The aim was to encourage innovation in teaching, learning and assessment practice. The strategy was based around the creation of a task force of seconded academic staff to undertake development projects within their subject areas under the direction of the first author. The task force members' role was to:

> Keep abreast of global developments in resource-based learning by networking with other agencies and individuals. Evaluate relevant materials and methodologies and share good practice and disseminate this widely in the university.
>
> (Coventry University 1997)

Each member of the task force had a development project which was supported within their subject group. Projects included the development of a work-based learning masters course within the business school, interactive multimedia package for chemistry teaching, computer-based assessment developments in engineering and web-based interface design for students' access to course information and materials. Many of the projects were not new ideas in teaching and learning, rather they were bringing these innovations into courses and to staff and students who would otherwise not have the time or resources to use them.

Critical success factors in Phase 1

At this stage the visible support of the PVC was essential to gain the trust of task force members and to force broader policy or infrastructural changes. The educational developer's role was to create a team approach to the work, forming subgroups with specialist interests and support groups around the projects. After seven months the task force was working effectively with some cross-departmental activities. One example of this was an exhibition of teaching and learning developments put on for a day in early April. The exhibition and related symposium discussions had over 200 visitors, mainly university staff.

The task force unearthed and made visible the problems that could have stopped innovation progress. During this phase various infrastructural issues emerged, for instance lack of communication between academic and support areas in particular computing services. The educational developers fed these kinds of issues into the university decision-making process and increased the interaction between the different groups. One useful way of doing this was through the creation of a task force support group comprising colleagues in the library, computing services and student services. As a critical mass the task force and its supporters were able to perform a path-clearing function allowing innovations to develop alongside structural changes at institutional level.

Phase 2: An action-research approach to task force projects

Evaluation of the work of the task force was seen as crucial to its efficacy. In Phase 2 the members of the task force were encouraged to see the importance of disseminating their work. The second author was appointed to undertake two key roles (in line with the triadic model mentioned above). The first was to research the student experience of the innovation projects and the second to support the reflexivity of the task force.

A further important element of reflexivity was the action-learning sets which supported cross-disciplinary conversation and collaboration (McGill and Beaty 2001). The task force members were grouped into four action-learning sets which met regularly to progress their individual projects and to explore issues and links.

This dual structure of a dedicated researcher and of action-learning sets ensured that the effect of the projects was greater than the sum of their parts.

Critical success factors in Phase 2

The success of the task force depended as much on the outcomes associated with the various projects as on the wider changes which came about as a result of the synergy between them. Thus networking and communication became increasingly important. The development of task force members as educational researchers and developers had to be thorough. They needed to disseminate their work within their subject group and increasingly beyond. This required new skills and knowledge.

It was important that regular away-day workshops provided for feedback to individual project members, discussion of wider implications of educational change and external consultants for workshop activities. A crucial function of these days was building a community of change agents and supporters through the exploration of educational ideas and development processes. The days were often fun and the enjoyment of social interaction increased the willingness of members to work as a cross-disciplinary team.

By having action research and action learning as primary processes in managing innovation and change, reflexivity and collaboration were integral to the strategic development.

Phase 3: Embedding the community

The larger question facing the university at the end of the third year was how to resource a continuation strategy when the task force completed its work. If individual projects were successful in embedding useful course developments within subject groups, how could this be sustained without the remission time required by the task force? The solution was found first in a formal restructuring of the resources to fund eight school-based half-time positions as teaching fellowships. These were promotions from within the staffing to principal lecturer to support local educational developments. A smaller number of project-based task force projects continued. This provided a firmer basis for educational development throughout the university.

Second, it became clear to the authors in analysis of the institutional level action research data that the critical mass had moved considerably beyond the locus of the task force. For instance, in reviewing attendance at what had become an annual conference on teaching and learning it was clear that the active constituency included participants of the postgraduate programme, pedagogic researchers from across the university working on their own and colleagues involved in the online learning developments. A Higher Education Research Group was established to provide a network for these colleagues.

Critical success factors in Phase 3

It was clear to us that the groupings identified above had the potential to form a community of practice but that we needed to support them actively. The actions in Phase 3 therefore became focused on a wider group of people whom we could support in a variety of ways. The umbrella for this became the Higher Education Research Group which is a loose affiliation supported by regular seminars and networking activities. The establishment of the Centre for Higher Education Development in a new building was conducive to this, providing a hospitable and identifiable environment for the group.

The restructuring of the original task force has forced a reconceptualization of the teaching and learning strategy including a refocus on new ways to support its implementation. It has been important to continue support for a task force and also to support the new teaching fellows, to provide a place for ex-task force members and new inclusive arrangements for the growing community of interested and active colleagues.

Understanding the process of change through action research

Metaphors for development

The action research at institutional level was undertaken primarily by the authors through regular review meetings using information from project progress, analysis of issues raised in away-day meetings and interviews both formal and informal with task force members and other staff and students of the university. At each stage the questions we were asking were evaluative ones. How well is the task force working? What are the effects and where are the blocks to change? What processes or actions could improve the effectiveness of the task force on institutional change. Who needs to be involved in this?

We worked with metaphors to help us think through strategies and tactics for moving on. In the first phase the metaphor of hubs and spokes helped to communicate with the task force about their role and the function of away-day and action-set meetings. At the end of this phase the PVC introduced the idea of forming the rim of the wheel which helped to articulate the need for task force members to work across and between the school-based structure of the university in dissemination of their innovations. By the end of this phase we were less enamoured of the wheel analogy and our review indicated that we needed a richer metaphor and we started working with the idea of building a community of practice. This metaphor both allowed us to analyze what was happening through this prism but also indicated actions we could take to strengthen the task force as part of an educational community and also to focus on negative side effects such as exclusivity and cliquishness.

Constructing dialogue through action research

Many of the problems that come with adopting new educational ideas can not be solved at the course level; they require structural changes and regulatory support systems within the organization. Resources must be allocated differently and staff work accounted for in more appropriate ways. Thus innovation cannot be embedded without changes at the organizational level. Similarly, strategic changes which are seen as necessary to respond to broad educational trends and national policies are useless if left in policy documents. A model of educational development that is top-down inhibits ownership of change by most people in the organization. It can also very easily become blocked by what Perkins and Wilson (forthcoming: 5) refer to as 'blow up factors':

> Anyone who has participated in processes of organizational change knows that defensive routines or the organizational immune system inevitably come into play. The behaviours thereby generated might be called blow-up factors. They tend to cause the process to blow up altogether, or induce small glitches that greatly slow it down.

Engaging sensitively with these factors requires dialogue and learning from all of those involved in the change effort including the developers themselves. Everyone needs to be positioned as a learner particularly in this context. As Handy (1989) has remarked – to be better at change one has to take learning seriously. As we elaborate below, action-research fits the need for a learning culture because it values communication and learning throughout a deliberate process of change which involves all the actors within the change, supporting their communication and valuing their contribution. In short, action research is a method by which developments can be both underpinned by scholarship and dialogue and takes an evaluative and problem solving approach to change management.

The issues that change brings are often difficult to predict. They have to work themselves out in practice. It is the quality of the dialogue within an organization which affects the extent to which people can grapple with these issues. If this dialogue does not occur change will create vulnerability for the organization and the various groups within it. An important strength of action-research methods lies in its promotion of a network of relations built from the conversations and reflections it generates.

Reflection and action research

Management of change theories tend to offer prescriptive, technicist models for effecting change in which conditions conducive to change and procedures for effecting it are schematically set out (Robbins and Finley 1997). Arguably, these are outcomes-based theories whereas an action-research approach is more about the journey and the human factors that determine its course. While an action-research project needs to have a sense of purpose and of hopeful outcome, the reflective cycles embedded in it ensures that there is less risk of closure on what needs to be done or of slavish adherence to the stipulated processes of a model. As we have noted, although we began working with a 'hubs and spokes' model of change, the action-research framework within which we implemented this model and the reflective processes this framework allowed, led us critically to appraise our generative metaphor of 'hubs and spokes' as new information and observations came to hand.

A further strength deriving from the reflective processes within action research concerns its inclusive character. Reflection is *with* those involved in the issue to hand rather than *on* them.

Action research and collaboration

Action researchers reject a view of research in which its 'subjects' become its 'objects' through the distancing of the researcher from the researched. As McNiff (1988) puts it, 'there is no subject–object dichotomy in action-research' because all the stakeholders to a researched area become enlisted as co-researchers. This is an important issue for educational developers because it means that they can avoid the difficulties Webb (1996a) points to with respect to the implied hierarchy in a 'the developer' and 'the developed' binary. This principle has operated at two layers in our project first, it encourages colleagues to innovate *with* their colleagues and second, we have been exploring the effects of change with a growing constituency of involved and interested colleagues. In brief, the imperative to share the research and its analysis helps to generate a community of practice of action researchers.

Action research must involve a change intervention

The concept of praxis, namely the treatment of theory and practice as unified rather than sequential, drives action-research methods. Getting a cross-disciplinary team to appreciate that doing something can be research has not always been easy, particularly if colleagues' own disciplinary background resists this concept. The management of change 'change intervention' has been precisely the use of action research to motor innovations capable of creating ripples within schools. Enabling this framework for innovation has involved the generation of supportive web-based guidelines and literature on action research (http://www.ched.coventry.ac.uk) and the one-to-one support of a dedicated action researcher for the project. In the event, some colleagues have veered more towards development than research and a few have preferred to stay within a more conventional 'hypothesis testing' model of research. A good number, however, have come to appreciate the great benefits of marrying research with development.

Action research puts 'R' and 'D' together

For the majority of colleagues who did operate within action-research frameworks (some weaker than others), the benefits were considerable. First, perceiving their projects as research ones, meant that they felt able to present their findings to an academic community and to publish their results and analysis (generated by explorations of the student experiences of all the innovations were an important part of this). Indeed the task force has produced an impressive range of conference papers and journal publications. Thus while there were difficulties in 'selling' action research as serious research (Cousin 2000), once colleagues adopted it, they quickly saw its advantages both in terms of animating change and of raising their profile as practitioner-researchers.

Action research contributes to the learning organization

By using action research as a method of evaluative research at the institutional level, we involved large numbers of colleagues in our reflections on what we were doing, its efficacy, difficulties, successes and failures. Action research at the micro-level combines research with continuing professional improvement; at the macro-level, it ensures spirals of reflection rather than closed phases of them and collaborative rather than managerialist thinking.

Conclusion

In this chapter we have attempted to outline some of the important principles of action research and their application to a case study which addresses the implementation of a university's teaching and learning strategy. We would like to conclude by stressing the messy nature of the work and processes we have described. Committing an experience to print often gives it a neat and tidy appearance and the foregoing perhaps errs in that direction. Inevitably, the truth is more complicated than our narration of it. No project, including our own, can be run according to 'rational' processes and strategies, not least because human frailties and idiosyncracies inhibit this. Moreover, we are in an age of risk, uncertainty and of runaway change and no research method is going to be able to capture all of its features, difficulties and surprises. What we hope we have provided, however, is some kind of practical guide to our agency in supporting change through action research within the current context of higher education in Britain.

14

Realizing Academic Development: A Model for Embedding Research Practice in the Practice of Teaching

Gregory Light

Introduction

This chapter is concerned with describing a model of academic (faculty) development that is both focused on the practice of teaching and is characterized by research practice. The central assumption of the model is that significant change and development in how we understand and practice teaching in higher education will only occur through deep and transformative learning experiences in which the faculty member is substantially engaged in a problem that they care about. For academics such experiences and encounters normally happen through the challenges and opportunities presented by research and scholarship. Indeed, research and scholarship characterize much of how academics approach and understand the world. They are synonymous with the idea of academic learning. One notable exception, however, is how faculty come to understand and learn the practice of teaching.

Commonly – even traditionally – academic development of faculty teaching has primarily occurred through two paradigms of academic development: the 'ad hoc' paradigm and the 'skills' paradigm (Light and Cox 2001: 9–10). In the former, individual faculty development of teaching occurs in an ad hoc way, through a combination of teaching traditions and styles experienced as a student, observations of other colleague's practices, 'natural affinities', trial and error, and the passage of time. The collection of tactics and techniques gained this way are used more or less skillfully as personal and situational factors permit. The skills focused paradigm, on the other hand, tends to understand the development of teaching in terms of the often-formal acquisition of a repertoire of performance, communication and associated technical tips, skills and competencies. Neither of these two paradigms reflects in any significant way the essential nature of academic learning. They capture neither the richness of the experience nor the depth of the engagement of the finest research and scholarship that describes and defines academic excellence.

In this chapter I shall present a strategic model for realizing a third paradigm of academic development that draws upon the best practices of academic learning. By and large, this third paradigm may be described as *professional* in terms of its character and wider collective goals. Like most professions, the location of the *professional* paradigm extends beyond the practitioner's self and institution to embrace broader social questions and concerns. Professional status, here, 'rests primarily on three propositions . . . that society attaches value to higher education; that specialized knowledge is involved; and that there are higher order intellectual judgments and skills required in the largely independent acquisition, extension, and application of that knowledge' (Bennett 1998: 44). This professional paradigm is not detached from the core academic and professional activities of the academy but rather reflects them and embraces the same critical requirements and standards with respect to knowledge, theory, values and practice.

The aim of academic/faculty development in this professional model goes beyond the acquisition of various skills towards encouraging a change in the very way in which faculty conceive of or understand teaching. Such conceptions are not the result of innate personal traits or cognitive characteristics but are, rather, 'theories' – often undisclosed or intuitive 'folk' theories (Bruner 1996) – in accordance with which the particular 'world', here the student–teacher encounter, is interpreted and practiced. Kember (1997) describes five and Prosser and Trigwell (1999) describe six general conceptions of teaching in higher education. In both cases, these conceptions fall under two broad categories: teacher-focused/content-oriented versus student-focused/learning-oriented conceptions. In the former the teacher is focused on his/her ability as a teacher to transmit content while in the latter the focus is on developing the student's understanding of the material. The 'research' model presented in this chapter describes a strategy that supports academic/faculty change from the former to the latter category of teaching conception. It is referred to as a 'research' model because it embeds the development of teaching in the academic traditions of active research and scholarship. Such an approach, Zuber-Skerritt (1992a: 115) reminds us, 'is likely to have a more powerful effect on the improvement of learning, teaching and staff development than research (solely) produced by educational theorists'.

Research practice and the practice of teaching

The following discussion employs the term 'research' in a broad sense – including both quantitative and qualitative approaches and incorporating a wide range of empirical, scholarly and creative perspectives drawn from across the range of disciplinary cultures. It also regards 'research' as intrinsically fused with theory insofar as it informs theory, modifies theory, subverts theory, embodies theory and/or generates new theory. It includes both the wide range of subject based (disciplinary, interdisciplinary or transdisciplinary) research and scholarship which constitutes the academic focus of individual faculty, and the research and scholarship related to the practice of teaching and learning in higher education. This latter research may broadly be grouped into four categories.

The first category concerns relatively new research looking at the practice of teaching. It includes, for example, the kind of research briefly described above which looks at faculty conceptions of teaching in higher education, and includes their approaches, strategies, intentions (Prosser and Trigwell 1999) and so on. The second category draws together the increasing fund of research and scholarship on adult and student learning in higher education and includes approaches to learning, conceptions of learning, experiential learning, learning in disciplines etc. It is research that 'describes more clearly how learning takes place in higher education . . . (from which) teachers should be able to draw their own conclusions about how to facilitate their students' learning' (Entwistle 1997: 3). The third kind focuses on research of more specific relevance to what have been called individual 'genres' of practice (Light and Cox 2001). Here the research focus has been on particular aspects of teaching, including course design, lecturing, facilitating small group work, assessing students, innovating with technology, evaluating teaching and so on. The fourth category draws upon scholarship and research concerned with the professional issues facing learning and teaching in higher education. It addresses the social and epistemological issues and values and principles of the professional role of teaching within academic practice in higher education institutions and society in general (Light and Cox 2001). It challenges academics to reflect upon and think about their teaching in the changing wider social, political and economic contexts in which it is situated. 'What', for example, 'is it to educate at the highest level' (Barnett 2000: 153) in a 'postmodern' society?

These categories offer a wide range of research that can be drawn upon in the development of the practice of learning and teaching. They do not describe a practical framework for understanding the different relationships between research and practice in the realization of professional practice. In the following, I offer a schema for considering and managing these relationships. Again, it is not intended as an authoritative or prescriptive programme, but rather as a conceptual tool for reflecting upon, developing and improving practice. Figure 14.1 illustrates four ways in which research and teaching practice may be conceptualized in the realization of teaching within a professional, scholarship centred, paradigm of academic/faculty development: *practice defined by research; practice versus research; practice informed by research, practice as research.*

Figure 14.1 Realizing professional practice

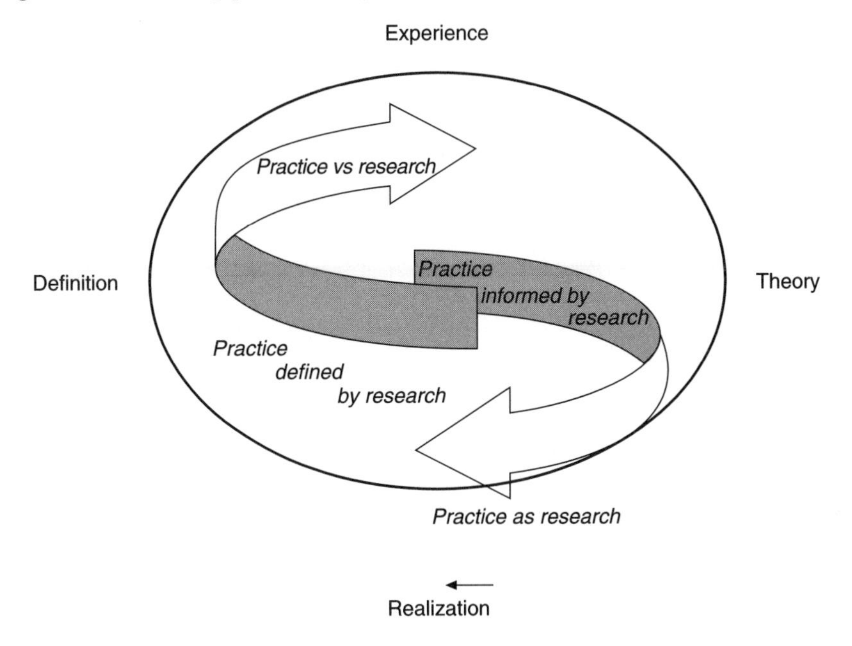

In this schema, these four ways of conceiving research and practice are four phases or movements in the realization of the reflective professional. They do not describe a necessary sequential order. As the cyclical design of Figure 14.1 suggests, the realization of practice will always be a recursive process in which teachers will individually and collectively reflect upon and rethink their practice in the light of their various academic and personal experiences.

Practice defined by research

The initial movement which may be referred to as the 'definitional phase' challenges teachers to reflect critically upon their own implicit, often unspoken, definition or conception of teaching practice in respect of research and theory. In the first instance, this reflection will likely consist of the relation of teaching to issues of learning and knowledge. Watkins and Mortimore (1999: 3), for example, define pedagogy or teaching as 'any conscious activity by one person to enhance learning in another'. But making the link between teaching and learning is not, of itself, sufficient. It does not take a huge critical leap to recognize such a relationship. What does demand a more critical approach is our personal examination of the nature of that relationship. Traditional perceptions of teaching tend to understand its relationship to learning as essentially linear, one in which teaching 'causes' or 'produces' learning. The definitional phase looks for a reversal of this perception in favour of one which views teaching as an outcome of learning, or as defined by learning. Teaching 'is authenticated only by the authenticity of the student's thinking (learning)' (Freire 1972). If there is learning – if there is a 'genuine' and deep engagement with 'knowledge', with ideas, concepts, facts, theoretical perspectives and so on – the teacher can be said to be teaching. If, on the other hand, learning is not 'genuinely' occurring, then irrespective of the teacher's efforts, one may legitimately question the right to the use of the term 'teaching'.

Re-centering the practice of teaching does not necessarily mean that teachers need to be formally aware of, or schooled in the literature and research on student learning. There are numerous examples of excellent teaching by teachers who have not studied the literature. These teachers have, however, focused their activities on student learning. Indeed, in a study looking at what the best teachers do, Bain (1999: 1) found that all these teachers 'had at least an intuitive understanding of human learning that bore an uncanny resemblance to the ideas about learning which have been emerging from the research in the learning sciences'. This first phase, then, challenges both the faculty/academic developer and the not so excellent teacher to redefine teaching for themselves – to centre student learning in their practice – by engaging with the research and scholarship and re-constructing it in their discipline for both themselves and their students.

There is, of course, no necessary connection between knowledge of the central role of learning in teaching and improved, let alone, excellent teaching. Such a redefinition of teaching in terms of learning immediately raises questions, particularly with respect to our understanding of the nature and character of learning and knowing. In addition, a thorough knowledge of a practice, even a critical knowledge of how the research can be used to improve practice, is nothing if the practitioner lacks interest, concern, motivation, the will power or ethical stamina to carry out this practice. These latter factors are complex and situational. Teaching and the development of teaching in many institutions – particularly those research institutions defined by or pursuing 'prestige' through research output (Goldman, Gates and Brewer 2001) – is regarded suspiciously. Faculty focusing on their teaching may even be doing themselves a career disservice.

These two issues are not so divorced as they might appear at first glance. They lead us to the next two phases or movements of the model we are considering, addressing the teaching practitioners' experiential and conceptual/theoretical understandings of learning.

Practice versus research

The juxtaposition of the second and third phases is not, as suggested above, a straightforward sequential matter. They do not occur separately or consecutively but are significantly interlocked in both development and ongoing improvement. The point of their separation here is to emphasize the commonality of learning at the heart of all our academic practices (Light and Cox 2001). We start with the experiential phase – and follow with the theoretical phase – to highlight the deep and rich experiences of learning that faculty bring to the learning and teaching situation. Through their own academic research and scholarship, they are able to bring to the encounter with their students, a shared experience of the struggle and exhilaration of learning. This includes considered and expert exemplars or models of its achievement in an academic environment. Unfortunately, all too often we leave the potential wealth of this common learning experience of scholarship/research and teaching untapped and unexplored. More ominously within academic practice generally, teaching and research are frequently, even habitually, regarded as rivals: time and status pitting the 'learning' of one against the 'learning' of the other.

As indicated above, the relationship between subject-based research and the practice of teaching a subject in higher education is characterized by a problematic, often deeply uncomfortable relationship. Both research and teaching have traditionally focused on the distinctive nature of the particular subject or discipline, rather than their mutual aspirations in learning and their shared aims in the construction and extension of knowledge. One way to conceptualize the idea of teacher-researcher is to recognize that both the practices of teaching and of research/scholarship are not ends in themselves. They are both aimed at encouraging, facilitating and improving learning. In the first instance this is primarily the learning of students and in the second the learning of the faculty member and his or her colleagues. This focus on the common goal of learning and the advancement of knowledge reveals that research and teaching are essentially the same practice, providing exemplars and models of learning for one another and, notably, for the student.

In this respect, this second phase in our model of academic faculty development takes us beyond our initial recognition that learning is the central feature of teaching to the further recognition that our research and scholarship practices can provide us with an experiential understanding and representation of this learning. In addition, it helps to bring about a rapprochement between the methods of enquiry which faculty engage in while doing research/scholarship and those methods of enquiry that they are engaging in and developing with their students. This phase challenges the teacher/scholar to examine critically this 'rivalry of learning' and the associated fragmentation of 'learning' within the academic community that ensues. The issue for the teacher-scholar is to go beyond the academic tension of researcher versus teacher to establish a comprehensive culture of learning that encourages active engagement in learning by all in the community. The teacher-scholar develops ways to integrate his or her own learning with that of their students in a 'culture of inquiry' (Clark 1997).

The model focuses, then, on the development of teaching practice within a broader conception of disciplinary research/scholarship, which includes a more thorough understanding of the learning characterization of research and its relationship to the context of both research and teaching practice. The language of professional practice does not simply draw upon generic understandings of teaching/learning but also draws upon and augments disciplinary languages of disciplinary research/learning. Reflection on practice includes reflection on disciplinary research as a learning practice. 'How do I and my colleagues learn in this discipline?' How do we collaborate? What does learning consist of in this subject? How can we improve this learning? What impedes it? How does this learning embrace, engage and extend the learning of our students? How can we collaborate with our students to improve learning? It is characterized by the idea of an inclusive, critical language of practice and the overcoming of the rivalry of learning – indeed the former is aimed at the latter. This in itself has repercussions for how a faculty member conceptualizes learning and teaching but also how he or she conceptualizes his or her own role as an academic, in particular the tension between research and teaching.

If the experiential phase of the model challenges faculty to reconceptualize teaching in terms of learning, and to do so in terms of their own conceptions of learning through disciplinary research and scholarship, the next phase challenges them to theorize and articulate their experience of learning through an understanding of the research and scholarship on the nature of learning and its facilitation. It is a challenge to become professionally 'literate' with respect to learning and teaching generally and in particular with reference to learning in their field.

Practice informed by research

This 'theory' phase of integrating research and practice has sometimes been referred to as the practice of 'scholarly' teaching. Hutchings and Shulman (2000) distinguish it from excellent teaching on the one hand and the 'scholarship' of teaching on the other. Excellent teaching is essentially best practice in which practitioners focus on student learning but do not formally draw upon the literature on learning and teaching although, as Bain suggests above, they may have a tacit understanding of what learning consists of. The 'scholarship' of teaching, first elucidated by Boyer (1990a), suggests an inquiry into 'some or all of the full act of teaching . . . in a manner susceptible to critical review by the teacher's professional peers and amenable to productive employment in future work by members of that same community' (Shulman 1998: 6).

Scholarly teaching 'is informed not only by the latest ideas in the field but by current ideas about teaching the field' (Hutchings and Shulman 2000: 48). Informing practice with research and scholarship goes beyond 'current ideas' to develop a practical understanding of the research and conceptual frameworks that characterize these ideas and implementation. I particularly draw upon the surge in recent research in student and adult learning and widespread employment of this research in both the design and content of training and development programmes for teaching staff in higher education. The development of individual and collective practice, however, is not limited to any one or two categories of research and theory. It will draw upon all four of the categories of research described above. It will also inquire about and explore others, particularly those from other disciplines, other practices and other professions that are of special significance and relevance to the individual practitioner.

Teaching informed by relevant research, by theory, by specialized knowledge, by expert and critical ways of understanding is a vital ingredient of reflective and professional practice. It provides the knowledge and the conceptual scaffolding for reflecting upon and 'critiquing' one's knowledge, practice and common experience as a learner. In this, it describes a phase of educational and professional 'literacy'. Such 'literacy' embodies the development and practice of a common and comprehensive 'language' of learning and teaching. Characterized and informed by research, theory and scholarship, such a language offers opportunities for:

- sharing a common understanding of learning with colleagues and students;
- moving beyond the mere acquisition of a series of communication and performance skills, and specialized teaching competencies;
- re-positioning academic practice within a deeper and more critical understanding of professional life, practical engagement, reflective skill development, 'genre' refinement and continuing professional development etc.;
- conducting personal micro-research – or even larger scale collective research – as part of professional and academic development;
- reconciling academic practice, through common experiences of learning and through a shared academic discourse of theory, evidence, argument and conceptions of rigour;
- managing uncertainty and change;
- improving personal scholarship on practice;
- improving personal learning in the practice of research and scholarship;
- raising new and powerful questions about learning, teaching and academic practice.

Practice as research

The concluding phase of the model – 'practice as research' – is not an end result so much as the bringing together of the phases into a process/method of practical realization. It articulates a strategy for professional realization that incorporates and integrates the other three phases. The strategic form presented here describes a process of becoming critically engaged through action research. In this respect, it aims at 'professional realization' by transforming 'academic practice' – habitual or customary action – into *'academic praxis'* (Zuber-Skerritt 1992a: 113) – informed, critical and committed action. This is achieved through 'critical and self-critical reflection that help practitioners to emancipate themselves from the often unseen constraints of habit, custom, precedent, coercion and ideology' (ibid).

Action research differs from more traditional forms of educational research in the degree to which it involves issues such as critical practice, improvement, participation, and the actual environment or situation of practice. The main aims and benefits of action research are 'the improvement of practice, the improvement of the understanding of practice by its practitioners and the improvement of the situation in which the practice takes place' (ibid: 110). Carr and Kemmis (1983) describe three kinds of action research that address these issues, albeit at different levels of practitioner engagement. In the higher education context with which we are concerned, they are differentiated by the relationship between the researcher and the teacher: by the degree to which the teacher is or becomes the principal researcher. In the first, *technical action research*, the researcher who facilitates the process establishes and judges the standards for improving the effectiveness of learning/teaching practice. The teacher is mainly engaged in the process at a technical level. The second, *practical action research* also aims to improve the effectiveness of practice but encourages the teacher to engage more fully and self-reflectively in the research process to develop his or her practical understanding and professional development. The third type, *emancipatory action research*, encourages the full participation of teacher-as-researcher to explore critically the effectiveness of practice and its practical understanding within social and organizational constraints. Improvement, here, includes enlightenment with respect to the academic context in which teaching is situated and is characterized by a more inclusive practical and critical 'engagement'.

Action research in this more inclusive guise consciously and deliberately sets out to improve, enhance and realize practice through actions informed, but not constrained, by research and theory. It is flexible, open to change necessitated by experience and circumstance, and it is subject to the practitioner's critical and rational practical judgements. Kemmis and McTaggart (1988: 7) describe the implementation of this strategic action as a continuous cycle comprising:

- a plan of action to improve what is already happening;
- action to implement the plan;
- observation of the effects of action in the context in which it occurs;
- reflection on these effects as a basis for further planning, subsequent action and so on, through a succession of cycles.

In addition, the above strategy embraces three broad areas: situated practice, educational resource and research documentation. Neither teaching nor research exists in a vacuum. It is *situated practice*: the teacher/researcher is investigating practice within his or her institution, department and academic discipline(s). Academic development programmes and projects are not focused on helping faculty to compile evidence of generic skills and competencies. They are, rather, aimed at helping them identify, critically examine and develop expertise and skills embedded within their own discipline, department and institution. They shall, of course, draw upon a broad range of *educational resources* including the relevant research literature, workshops and training events, experts/consultants, mentors, colleagues, and students. While these are often associated with generic or cross-disciplinary aspects of teaching, they are not regarded here as 'answers' to teaching and learning problems, so much as tools for critically reflecting on and addressing the 'situated' problems which teaching raises.

Finally, the realization of practice will need to proceed towards the production of some form of *research documentation*, for provision of evidence of professional realization, for sharing with colleagues in the best tradition of peer review and for informing and developing ongoing development. The documentation commonly associated with programmes for the development of learning and teaching practice mainly consists of the development of a portfolio of evidence related to a number of carefully selected outcomes as promoted in the UK, for example, by the Institute for Learning and Teaching in higher education (ILT). This has often been interpreted as a professional record of achievement. Other approaches, such as the Scholarship of Teaching movement in the USA have occasionally interpreted such documentation in more traditional academic terms, as research papers and journal articles. The approach suggested here retains the developmental character of the portfolio – its outcomes, evidence, professional requirements, etc. – but interprets them in active research terms. In this way, the portfolio may be conceived as a research document providing critical evidence and theoretically informed analysis of those areas of teaching and learning relevant to the teacher's situated practice. It requires the identification of appropriate research 'questions and methods', the appropriate discovery, development and generation of a variety of evidence of learning/teaching practice and the critical analysis, assessment and presentation of this evidence within a substantive theoretical context. It needs to be open to public dissemination, critique and evaluation.

Conclusion

The model of academic/faculty development described in this chapter takes research/scholarship as its guiding theme and principle. It does not do so because of the status and recognition which higher education accords to research – often at the expense of teaching – but rather because it characterizes the nature and spirit of what we understand by learning in higher education. It seeks to draw upon the culture of enquiry and learning at the heart of the best conceptions and practices of research/scholarship and extend them to our conceptions and practices of teaching and student learning. Most importantly, it recognizes that the very best teachers and students have a wealth of *problems* at the core of what they do.

> In scholarship and research, having a problem is at the heart of the investigative process; it is the compound of the generative questions around which all creative and productive activity revolves. But in one's teaching, a 'problem' is something you don't want to have, and if you have one, you probably want to fix it. . . . Changing the status of the problem in teaching from terminal remediation to ongoing investigation is precisely what the movement for scholarship is all about. (Bass 1998)

The reconciliation of research and teaching in learning challenges the pervasive and insidious 'rivalry of learning' at the heart of so many academic departments. Indeed, it is central to the new paradigm of academic/faculty development.

Conclusion

15

The Future of Research and Scholarship in Academic Development

Angela Brew

One of the problems with teaching, Hutchings and Shulman (1999) suggest, is that it has no automatic way of improving itself. This is unlike the process of research, which automatically develops its methods and approaches and the thinking and actions of researchers through peer review and the supervision of the next generation of researchers. Hutchings and Shulman argue that the scholarship of teaching is an important way in which teaching can take on a systematic process of development.

The same may also be said of academic development. Like the scholarship of teaching, the scholarship of academic development is a relatively new phenomenon. This is not because academic developers have been too focused on their practice to engage in scholarship until recently. Neither is there an absence of methods and approaches to adopt, nor a paucity of theoretical orientations. Rather, like the scholarship of teaching, it arises through a growing recognition in higher and tertiary education of the importance of taking a professional approach to development and of basing such development on systematically obtained evidence and well argued logic.

The newness of the scholarship of academic development is reflected in this volume. Throughout the book we have witnessed the growth of a critical discourse about academic development. Research and scholarship have been seen as integral to the professional practice of educational and academic developers. A number of crucial questions about the nature and role of research and scholarship in academic development have been addressed in a variety of ways. For example,

1. What are academic developers trying to do and why are research and scholarship important to the academic developer?
2. What is the field of academic development? Is academic development a discipline or a collection of disciplines and how does academic

development relate to other disciplines? What are its theoretical and methodological underpinnings?
3. What is the role of research in academic development and in what ways is academic development practice informed by research?
4. What is the role and nature of evidence in academic development work?
5. How should academic development be organized to strengthen its research and scholarship?

Answers to these questions are as varied and as diverse as the set of individuals who call themselves academic developers. In this concluding chapter it falls to me to do two things. First, to explore the reasons why research and scholarship are becoming to be important components of the work of the educational developer and second to do some crystal ball gazing to speculate on where it might lead. The above questions provide a framework for outlining in broad terms where we are now and suggesting what academic developers need to be doing, and where they might be going.

What are academic developers trying to do and why are research and scholarship important to the academic developer?

Higher education is grappling with changes in its teaching and learning and also in its research structures to cope with the changing requirements within what Nowotny *et al.* (2001) call 'Mode 2 society'; a society where 'there is a high degree of uncertainty, there is no clear-cut direction but many competing ideas, theories and methods, and no one is in overall charge' (Nowotny *et al.* 2001: 115).

The increasing complexity and precariousness of society has highlighted the importance of developing in students what Barnett (1997) calls 'critical action'. In the future, students are going to need to be able to solve unforeseen problems on a daily basis, not only while at university but more especially when they leave it (Barnett 2000). Within Mode 2 society, having the skills of investigation is crucial. These include the skills of critical analysis, gathering evidence, finding and discriminating information, making judgements on a rational basis, and reflecting on how they have made those choices and why.

> What is required is not that students become masters of bodies of thought, but that they are enabled to begin to experience the space and challenge of open, critical inquiry (in all its personal and interpersonal aspects).
>
> (Barnett 1997: 110)

Within this context, universities and colleges of higher and further education are endeavouring to find ways to develop new alliances between teaching, research and scholarship. The old distinctions are changing. Indeed, Nowotny *et al.* (2001: 89) argue that 'under Mode 2 conditions' the distinction between teaching and research breaks down. Institution-wide and departmental initiatives as well as steps taken by individual academics which bring together teaching and research activities are accelerating (Jenkins *et al.* 2002). This is happening both in research intensive universities and in what have recently been termed 'access-oriented' universities (Nowotny 2001: 90). Moves to strengthen 'research-led teaching' as well as 'teaching-led research' are growing. Inquiry is coming to be centre stage and it is this context in which academic developers now find themselves.

Academic departments, disciplinary communities, sub-specialisms, or individual universities can be viewed in this Mode 2 context as communities of practice where students and staff as well as developers engage in what Lave and Wenger (1993) call legitimate peripheral participation. Students are not simply apprentices in this community; rather they participate as equal partners. Or as Light, quoting Burton Clark, puts it: 'The teacher-scholar develops ways to integrate his or her own learning with that of their students in a "culture of inquiry"' (quotation from Light Chapter 14).

The new relationships between teaching and research within a Mode 2 society (Nowotny *et al.* 2001) indicate why it is important for academic developers to be involved in various forms of research and scholarship. If, in the context of multi-complexity and uncertainty of Mode 2 society, academics and students are focused within communities of practice on inquiry as the centre of their practice, then clearly academic developers must be too. They need to inform themselves about inquiry-based learning and to have a repertoire of responses when academics ask for examples.

This book is the product of communities of practice of academic developers. It draws not only from their discussions and work in specific institutions of higher and tertiary education, but also from the broader academic development community through the bringing together of two of its professional organizations (the Staff and Educational Development Association and the Society for Research into Higher Education).

Yet academic developers not only participate in communities of practice with other academic developers and higher education specialists. They also engage in communities of practice with academics in a variety of disciplinary areas and institutional levels. The challenges which face developers, then, are on the one hand how they can most effectively contribute to the development of their own disciplinary community of practice (higher education and academic development) while at the same time also engaging in legitimate peripheral participation in those other disciplinary academic communities of practice in their development role.

There is nothing straightforward about this. Unlike any other disciplinary area, the relationship of the disciplinary focus within academic development *is* its context, i.e. it studies higher education while itself being inside higher education. This self-reflexivity is always problematic. The different power relationships which academic developers of necessity have *vis à vis* their institutional managers mean that they rarely have the authority to define their own agendas. Thus while academic developers have established a discourse on what academic development is and what it is trying to do, as this book has testified, this discourse has always to be tempered by the ways in which academic development is defined institutionally, often by those who have other ideas about what academic development can and should do, how it should be organized or ideas about the extent to which it can be held responsible, for example, for changing teaching within an institution. The scholarship of academic development always has to have one face turned to the ways in which others define its role and function while at the same time endeavouring to develop academically respectable arguments which extend those definitions in the interests of increased effectiveness and academic rigour.

What is the field of academic development? Is it a discipline or a collection of disciplines and how does academic development relate to other disciplines? What are its theoretical and methodological underpinnings?

Whenever someone asks me what disciplinary area I am in I say that I see myself as a practical epistemologist. I am interested, as epistemologists are, in questions about the nature of knowledge and how we come to know. But as an academic developer, I have an interest and a professional responsibility in putting what I know about this into practice to improve the role of academics and the learning of students.

Peter Ashworth argues in Chapter 9 that it is important to understand what it is that academic development is intending to change. Again, people in different areas of our institutions have different views on this. As institutional priorities shift, so universities' needs for development change. I have always held that it was my duty as a professional academic developer to be mindful of institutional development needs and to temper my own enthusiasms with a rationally or empirically derived sense of what was needed. Increasingly, however, developers and managers are coming to different views about the range of development activities which it is appropriate for the academic developer to pursue and the ways to pursue them.

If developers are not free to determine the scope and direction of their activities, are they then also not free to determine the boundaries of the field of academic development? When Rowland (Chapter 2) points out that there are a range of traditions on which academic developers draw and asks what the field of academic development is, he is asking a scholarly question about the nature of the field of higher education studies. This question illustrates a shift in thinking about academic development. Indeed, this volume has echoed this move away from a focus on academic development practice, towards a position where academic development is accepted as a scholarly endeavour.

This book has highlighted some of the domains of research which are particularly appropriate for developers to be interested in pursuing. For example, research into the policies, practices and strategies of higher education in general and in relation to specific disciplinary areas clearly informs many aspects of academic development. However, scholarly work in the field of higher education studies has been affected by the fact that many of its specialists are located in development units, many of which are viewed, particularly by institutional managers, as service units and not as academic departments and where many staff are not even on academic contracts and neither funded for, nor expected to do, research. Only very few specialists in the field of higher education studies have been located in academic departments of education and even fewer in specialist academic departments of higher education. Fortunately this is now changing.

In addition, and not unrelated to this, opportunities for funded research in this domain have been extremely limited. Indeed, funding for research into higher education has, by and large failed to recognize the need for the higher education system itself to be empirically examined, resulting in many university and governments' policies failing to take account of research evidence (Elton 2001).

To say that the field of academic development is higher education studies is not to say that all specialists in this field of investigation are academic developers, nor that all academic developers identify higher education as their field of research and scholarship; witness Mick Healey and Alan Jenkins (Chapter 5) who locate their disciplinary home in geography.

Indeed, new developments in UK universities, for example, have opened up the field of higher education and many who do not have training or background in academic development methods and approaches are now taking up leading positions in academic development bringing with them a rich variety of theoretical traditions, approaches to research and scholarship and to academic development practice.

Yet again, as we saw earlier, academic development is a reflexive pursuit. In the context of shifting perspectives on the nature of knowledge which characterize late modernity, the breakdown of disciplines within higher education, and the growth of inter-, multi- and trans-disciplinary studies, no single answer can be given to the question: 'what disciplinary area does academic development belong to?'. To ask this question, is to presuppose the kind of answer which academic development discourse specifically sets out to question critically.

When I say that academic development is concerned with the field of higher education studies, then, I have in mind that this is a multidisciplinary, eclectic, ever-changing field made up of a similarly shifting series of subfields. Higher education studies is a field defined within multiple contexts, by individuals trained in a multitude of disciplinary traditions, working in various kinds of institution, researching multifarious questions about the nature of higher and tertiary education processes and practices, and being interested in the people who work and live within them, the structures of their organization and their relationships with the wider community. Academic developers, unusually where professional practice is concerned, do not own their own disciplinary domain.

But again we come back to the requirements for practice versus the development of a theoretical discourse within academic development practice. Academic developers are pragmatists. They work with whatever theory or idea will advance their practice. This has sometimes been to their detriment because they have often been misunderstood as focusing only on a narrow view of practice and tips for practice as Rowland (Chapter 2) points out. Yet the pragmatism of academic developers is both a strength and a weakness when it comes to defining theory. In my own case I know that this leads to a tussle between a need to be aware of the implications of theoretical ideas and their use in practice on the one hand, and a desire to develop creative ideas which extend thinking on the other.

No one area of research dominates this domain. Academic development has always drawn on a wide range of literatures as befits a profession which recruits from, and which works with, individuals from many disciplinary areas. Basic research into student learning, teaching methods and their effectiveness, conceptions of teaching, conceptions of the subject matter held by students and their teachers, effects of particular aspects of the learning environment on students' learning experiences has been the mainstay of academic development work. While cognitive psychology has arguably had a special relationship to academic development owing to the fact that the main traditions of teaching and learning in higher education have been within that tradition, as David Gosling (Chapter 7) points out, this literature does not explain the social context in which such teaching and learning takes place. So the adult education literature has also been important, as has literature on personal and organizational transformation, the research on higher education policy, as well as more specific theoretical and practical literatures, for example situated cognition, cognitive change, critical theory, postmodernism and on specific aspects of teaching and learning: assessment, group work, information technology in teaching and learning, and so on.

Yet it is a curious fact that much if not most of this literature has tended to be invisible to the clients of academic developers, i.e. disciplinary academics, and also often to the managers whose decisions can profoundly affect academic practices. Many academics develop their teaching with no, or little, knowledge of the critical literature that would inform teaching and learning developments. Academic development has been viewed as a practical pursuit with little theoretical basis. This is now changing through the increasing involvement of disciplinary academics in research on their teaching, wider recognition of the role of scholarship among academic developers and new people coming into the field of academic development who are strengthening the critical questioning of its theoretical base.

Experiences of variation

In describing how a young boy learns the difference between a goose, a duck and a swan, Thomas Kuhn (1970b) argues that more often than not we learn what something is, by experiencing what it is not. Bowden and Marton (1998) make a similar point when they suggest that we learn from experiences of variation. Academic development practice has traditionally depended on this idea. A great strength of its practice has been its ability to bring together academics from a broad range of disciplinary areas and provide opportunities for them to experience and to learn from seeing variation in teaching and learning practices. More recently, heads of departments and deans are seeing the need for academic development subject specialists to work within specific departments or faculties. Institutional managers have, in some cases, dispersed their central units to faculties. We have also witnessed the setting up of specialist 'subject centres' within the UK with responsibility for academic development across clusters of disciplines.

These new varieties and forms of academic development will doubtless lead to new discourses and yet further forms of organization, new networks and new disciplinary allegiances. The field of higher education studies is already far too vast for any one individual to have more than a smattering of knowledge across its various domains. New specialists will doubtless emerge. Questions about the disciplinary domains of academic development are like attempts to catch the wind. The territory is dynamic: shifting, changing and multiplying. It will not be tied down with static descriptions.

What is the role of research and scholarship in academic development and in what ways is academic development practice informed by research?

Research and scholarship in academic development practice is, as we have seen, tied up with developments in higher and tertiary education. A number of factors have been influential in determining its current and changing roles. I want to mention three key ones: the developing interest in the scholarship of teaching, interests in bringing research and teaching together and the influence of accountability procedures.

The Carnegie theory of the scholarship of teaching in the USA, a central tenet of which is that it has to be defined within each disciplinary context, is of central relevance to the question of the role of research and scholarship in academic development. Mick Healey and Alan Jenkins (Chapter 5) draw upon Martin *et al.* (1999)'s definitions of scholarship of teaching as involving three elements: engaging with the scholarly contributions of others on teaching and learning, reflecting on one's own practice, and communicating and disseminating ideas on teaching. All of these define roles for research in academic development practice. Academic developers are, or at least should be, experts in what constitutes good teaching in higher education. Most have a role in both encouraging the development of such teaching and in exploring ideas of how it can be extended. Ranald Macdonald's introduction (Chapter 1) examines some aspects of the impact of the scholarship of teaching on academic development practice.

The second set of factors derives from attempts to bring teaching and research together, which I mentioned at the beginning of this chapter. I have argued elsewhere [IJAD 7:2] that this influences academic development practice but it also suggests a role in research and scholarship for academic development.

Discussions in faculties and departments about the relationship between teaching and research traditionally assume a teacher-focused view of teaching with an emphasis on the transmission of information to the students. Teaching and research take place independently, constantly jostling for resources including the time of academics. Student learning is conceptualized as taking place with no apparent connection with the research culture, research teams and activities or even with equipment purchased to carry out research. Since research is viewed in Mode 1 terms (Gibbons *et al.* 1994) as the creation or discovery of a body of knowledge describing a pre-existent reality (Mourad 1997), research-led teaching is interpreted as the desire for the best researchers to teach across all levels of students or to put the content of research into lectures. Students are viewed as an audience for the research (Zamorski 2000). According to this model, academic development feeds in findings from research into teaching development through, for example, workshops etc. Teachers are an audience for research in higher education studies.

However, these ideas are now changing and in Mode 2 society (Nowotny *et al.* 2001), knowledge is viewed as a process of construction in a variety of contexts both outside and inside universities (Gibbons *et al.* 1994). Conceptions of teaching are changing to be more student-focused and oriented towards conceptual change. Knowledge is being recognized as being more diffuse, constructed through communication and negotiation in a variety of contexts.

Here research-led teaching shifts away from students merely being an audience for the research, to becoming engaged in research activities themselves. The same is also true in academic development work; their clients, the teachers, are becoming actively engaged in research on teaching and learning, not merely an audience. The emphasis is on the construction rather than the imparting of knowledge. Students and teachers both become researchers and scholars in the field of higher education. Research here is conceptualized as a process of developing understanding and meaning. The person of the researcher is a key focus of attention, because research here includes the growth not just of socially useful knowledge but also of personal meaning. This context challenges academic developers to involve themselves more intimately with a more diffuse set of research activities and to increasingly encourage research on teaching as a form of professional development for academics.

Ideas about the role of research in academic development come, thirdly, from political and institutional imperatives. For example, senior managers are taking a strategic interest in data to inform policy and practice within their institutions. The demands of institutional managers dictate rather than merely suggest a role for research in academic development. Again, as with the other questions discussed in this chapter, academic developers are not wholly free to determine the role of research for themselves. Their view of the role is going to be different from their role in research as viewed by institutional managers. Developers have to decide how much time to spend carrying out strategic research to provide information for institutional managers and how much to spend on research which will bring the credibility and the rewards needed for promotion and career advancement. These competing tensions between different agendas have to be resolved on every level, with every research project, in every research context, by every individual developer and every research and development team.

So what does all this mean for academic development practice? It means, of course, that there are multifarious roles for research and scholarship in academic development. Like the field which characterizes it, approaches are pluralistic, expertise and interests are varied and its relationship to what Nowotny *et al.* (2001) call the contexts of application and the contexts of its implications are diverse. The role of research in academic development is different depending on whether one is focused on present needs or future developments, whether research is carried out for the developer's intrinsic interest in the subjects of study or principally to enhance their practice, the academic practice of academics with whom they come into contact, or to assist in the enhancement of student learning. The role is different depending on the needs, demands and roles of different stakeholders, and the purpose to which the research is to be put. Mantz Yorke (Chapter 10) argues that there is a whole spectrum of ways in which academic developers may engage with pedagogical research from small scale 'homespun studies' conducted by interested individuals on the one hand to large research programmes designed to provide evidence that can be applied in a variety of contexts. There are many ways in which academic developers engage with research and scholarship.

In considering the role of research and scholarship, I think it is useful to think in terms of the functions that research and scholarship perform in academic development practice. These functions clearly overlap and academic developers may at one and the same time perform a number of them. Some examples will illustrate what I mean.

Strategic functions

Demands for accountability in higher and tertiary education and increasing requirements for action to be strategic, point to a growing role for academic developers, and one which a number of practitioners are now experiencing in their institutions. That is, to provide advice to institutional managers about both requirements for development, and appropriate institutional structures and strategies for the most effective ways to carry it out. Such advice of necessity needs to be based on well-argued research evidence.

Further, senior managers need data on which to base strategic decisions. Academic development work is being harnessed to carry out institutional research to inform this process. Research and academic development go hand in hand here, the one informing the other. For example, at the University of Sydney a university-wide initiative was to improve students' experiences in their first year. Our 'First Year Experience' project set out to investigate the experiences of students, document good practice in support of students in their first year and areas for improvement and provide a staff development programme to address the improvement needs. So staff development was integrated with research on the experiences of first-year students.

We investigated strategies being used to enhance first-year teaching by means of a survey and also by conducting interviews and focus groups. Examples of good practice in other institutions and relevant sources in the literature were also collected. Data from the Students' Course Experience Questionnaire was used to add further findings. A website was set up to disseminate the findings.

These activities of a research and scholarly nature led to a number of staff development initiatives including a 'Vice-Chancellor's Forum' with approximately 80 participants, workshops and regular meetings for 'First-Year Coordinators' where successful strategies are shared. Now, a cross-faculty working group has been set up with members nominated by deans. Major factors in getting deans to acknowledge something had to be done about the first year was the report we prepared based on our research findings. I believe that this marriage of research and development indicates a direction academic developers will increasingly find themselves in for the future.

This is not entirely unproblematic. There are boundary issues when it comes to wanting to publish work coming from such university initiatives. For example, we had to agree with our managers that data had first and foremost to be presented within the university; we cannot just go out and publish it or present it at conferences. We also experienced criticism by one senior manager for ignoring the development of teaching, learning and curricula and 'doing too much research'. So it has been important for us to demonstrate tangible benefits from this research in terms of initiatives to improve teaching and learning.

Illumination

Greg Light's four kinds of research in academic development (Chapter 14) illustrate the role of research in academic development as illumination.

New research looking at the practice of teaching; research and scholarship of adult and student learning in higher education describing how learning takes place; research on different aspects of teaching practice (course design, small group work, assessment etc.) and research on aspects of the professional role of the academic may all illuminate the process of teaching and student learning and are all intrinsically interesting. Yet all have a role in changing teaching.

In discussing what the field of academic development research and scholarship is, I mentioned a number of areas which research in this area may illuminate and the ways in which it may do this. Individual academic developers have personal research interests and many have made substantial contributions to illuminating specific aspects of the field of higher education studies. However, like their colleagues in other disciplinary areas, they are increasingly being called upon to align these interests with the strategic priorities of their departments or units, to define research strengths and to conform to research assessment requirements. Yet while the research of academic developers may principally be to illuminate an area of inquiry that the individual researcher or group of researchers have an interest in, academic development research is never solely for the purpose of illumination. It always has to have an eye to its possible influence on practice. Thus all research of this nature has a political function. Its intention is to contribute to change and the direction of that change is not a matter simply of chance. Academic development practice is imbued with a set of values which it is impossible for research and scholarship to ignore. Value freedom is simply not an option for the academic developer.

Developmental functions

There are a number of ways in which research is now used as a tool for development. First, developers are increasingly being called upon to lead or participate in action research as an integral part of professional practice. The growing importance of this is demonstrated in a number of chapters in this book. Often referred to as practitioner research or participatory action research, action research describes the relationship of the researcher to those participating in the research. It is therefore most appropriate for working with teachers as they research the effects of their interventions on their own students. Much of the research into their own teaching and learning practices that academics are increasingly doing and which is often encouraged in certificate courses in higher education is of this type.

The second way research and scholarship are serving developmental functions is by using research carried out for illumination purposes to enhance the quality of development work. My colleagues and I, for example, have used research findings on conceptions of assessment. Our university set up a policy to change to criterion referenced assessment and, in response, we initiated a staff development initiative to inform and educate academic staff about the changes. During a number of workshops it became clear that there was considerable confusion about what a criterion was. So we set up a research project to investigate the variation in conceptions of assessment enshrined in the criteria people were using in their courses. The research enabled us to understand academics' misconceptions and help them to clarify their ideas in subsequent workshops. In addition, we have been able to present our findings in an international conference thus contributing in a small way to our own career development goals (Barrie *et al.* 1999). The research also had a strategic function in that we were able to use the knowledge we gained to influence the new policy which was subsequently accepted by our academic board.

Exemplars

Academic development practice has, by its very nature, to represent exemplars of good practice. Academics present one of the most challenging and exacting clientele that professionals are ever likely to meet. So, for example, courses designed to teach them about good teaching have to practice what they preach. If academic developers are to teach higher education teachers to develop in their students an inquiry-based approach and their courses are designed to encourage the acquisition amongst the teachers and lecturers of the skills of educational enquiry, then academic development practice has to embody, and provide exemplars of those skills.

So developers need to do research which is useful in academic development work. They need to be more systematically using research in development activities. This has to be done by exemplifying good research practice. For example, if development takes the form of participants engaging in inquiry into various aspects of academic practice, then academic developers need to ensure that they are exemplifying good practice in the domain of their expertise, higher education studies. Making sure that references to the literature are provided in workshops, that ideas are grounded in empirical evidence and making sure that handouts, papers and slides are appropriately referenced (i.e. conform to high standards of academic behaviour) becomes a necessity.

Recursive functions

Traditionally, academic developers have tended to focus primarily on development and only minimally on scholarship of their own practice. However, we are now witnessing a shift in these priorities. In the last seven years or so, there has been a growing awareness on the part of academic developers of the need to reflect systematically on practice in scholarly ways. This awareness has manifested itself in the growing number of books related to academic and staff development, the establishment of the internationally refereed journal, *International Journal for Academic Development*, and in schemes such as the SEDA Fellowship scheme which provides a professional qualification for staff and educational developers who have demonstrated the achievement of a set of specific objectives and values.

The implications of the bringing together of teaching and research and the development of the scholarship of teaching is that developers increasingly need to engage in researching their own practice. Indeed academic development practice is another focus for action research. While funding for such work is virtually non-existent, the penalty for not so engaging is that the power and authority to define their own professional discourse is dispersed among the academic community. As I have argued throughout this chapter, it is a space shared by institutional managers and others inside and outside our institutions of higher education. But it is a space which academic developers may have growing confidence to occupy in the future if they equip themselves with a more scholarly basis for their work.

Emancipatory functions

Teaching academics how to live in a climate of uncertainty and encourage their students to change conceptions radically cannot be done through a mere transfer of ideas from research. In a Mode 2 society, how research is done becomes as important as what is researched and as important as what is found. Engaging in inquiry takes the emphasis away from research products towards the processes of research. The driving force for this, as I said earlier, is so we can thrive in a complex and uncertain society. Academic developers need to be at the forefront of encouraging academics to be open to new problems and new questions and finding new ways of searching for new solutions.

So academic developers may be concerned to encourage research-led teaching amongst their academic colleagues. Research-led teaching means teaching is infused with and enhanced by research. However, as developers grow, their awareness of the ways in which research can be enhanced by what we know about teaching, means they may go beyond research-led teaching to teaching-led research. This means that research is enhanced by infusing it with ideas and practices of good teaching, for example, the importance of good communication, attention to the processes of learning and the importance of critical reflection on practice.

There is also evidence of a freeing up of notions of what research is and what it can do. That may mean working with faculty academics to understand what it might mean and where it might lead them to change their approaches to, and conceptions of, research. Teaching-led research points to the need to encourage a change of emphasis on the value of the processes of research not only to students but also to academic researchers. This is also true of developers. In this sense research on academic development has an emancipatory function.

In a world characterized by uncertainty, complexity and plurality, academic research has to develop new forms of research, to expand existing frameworks of knowledge and knowing. It is notable that the ideas which have perhaps most strongly influenced the theory and practice of academic development and certainly teaching and learning in higher education were based on the development of a new methodology: namely, phenomenography. There is a need for basic research into the validity, viability and scope of particular methods. If anyone has learnt how to operate in a context of uncertainty and super-complexity it is those new researchers who have pioneered the way to new research methods and new domains of discourse. Much pedagogical research presents challenges to conventional research methodology. Taking research seriously as developers, therefore, means we not only need to be doing research we also have to develop ideas about what research can be. There is a need to be open to new problems and new questions. We must be ready to define new rules for research within each research project we undertake.

What is the nature of evidence in academic development work?

It is a paradox that many academic developers take evaluation very seriously, always ensuring that they obtain feedback on their activities, and yet as Graham Gibbs (Chapter 12) has argued, the existence of evidence of the effectiveness of these activities has rarely been documented and the impact of training is only now becoming apparent.

Perhaps a reason for the paradox is that academic developers are frequently sceptical about the nature of easily obtainable quantitative evidence.

Developers are increasingly being called upon to engage in institutional evaluation. This is needed by the institution, and also furthers understanding of the factors, which need to be focused on in development work. This may include evaluation of policy and strategy, student course perceptions and evaluation of students' performance. One example of this kind of research being carried out in my own institution began in 2000 with a survey that we in the Institute for Teaching and Learning were asked by our Pro-Vice-Chancellor to carry out. We surveyed 29,000 undergraduates about their experiences of their courses and obtained a response rate of over 50 per cent. In 2001, the same survey instrument was used with approximately 10 per cent of the undergraduate students at the University of Sydney and, for benchmarking purposes, with students at the University of Oxford, UK. The information from this Sydney Course Experience Questionnaire (SCEQ) has been fed into the university's performance indicators on which funding based on teaching performance is being allocated across the faculties. This research was not simply an exercise in providing data for senior managers. Academic developers had a role in advising how it should be done, working through the educational implications of doing it, and contributing to how the resulting data is presented, both internally and externally. Yet we did not have the freedom to decide what data to collect nor the theoretical basis of the work.

In Chapter 8, Sarah Mann argues that what constitutes evidence will depend on the theoretical and methodological tradition adopted, and, as Peter Ashworth (Chapter 9) reminds us, theories are intimately related to methodologies. Several writers have examined what the theoretical underpinnings of research on academic development are and what traditions they draw on; all agreeing that such approaches are necessarily eclectic. So, for example, following Mann, we can say that evidence in academic development may range from positivistic 'objective' evidence, through evidence derived from the personal experience of practice (praxis), discourse or psychoanalysis, to subjective understanding based on cooperative inquiry.

One of the major problems developers have is that what many faculty researchers and managers think research evidence is, and how they believe it should be found, cannot address the kinds of things which academic developers are interested in. For example, we have seen in this volume that the use of laboratory experimentation, double blind crossover trials and computer modelling are not suited to the kinds of questions needed to inform staff and educational development. Several of the authors have drawn attention to the limitations of notions of objectivity when seen alongside ideas about how to influence practice. Research questions which have to catch and bring together complex, multi-faceted phenomena are not always easily accommodated within conventional methodologies. Action and practitioner research is frowned upon in some academic contexts as being uncritical and, as one senior academic in my institution described it, 'not really research'. So there are problems in providing evidence of the effects of our practice. Yet as Sarah Mann argued, we need a variety of approaches if research in academic development is not to ignore contextual and intellectual factors that bear upon it.

Following the medical model there are now demands for well-argued empirical evidence of the impacts and effectiveness of educational interventions and changes. This is likely to grow. There is growing interest in evidence-based practice in higher educational contexts and academic developers will increasingly need to respond to that. However, it will be naive to assume that medical models of evidence-based practice can be readily applied in the higher education context. Academic developers will need to develop new ideas and models of evidence-based practice applicable to their profession.

How should academic development be organized to strengthen its research and scholarship?

Finally, we come to the question of how academic development should be organized if research and scholarship are to be central to the role of developers. Fortunately there are now a growing number of academic development departments in higher and tertiary education as institutional managers come to realize the need for research and scholarship related to issues of teaching effectiveness. Academic developers need, like their academic colleagues, to be on academic contracts. They need time for research and reflection, including periods of study leave where they can visit other institutions and examine best practice.

Mantz Yorke (Chapter 10) has set out the forms of organization if pedagogical research is to be integrated into academic development practice. Pedagogical research can, as he suggests, be carried out at a number of different levels. There is a role for a central academic development department to coordinate and disseminate developments across the university, bringing people together from different areas to share ideas and practices.

Since academic development departments, by their very nature, focus on higher education as the subject of their study and since their 'students' are more often than not academic staff themselves, they have to have a cross-institution focus. The institution-wide focus is illustrated here by Liz Beaty and Glynis Cousin (Chapter 13) who show how academic developers have been involved in a project where action research has been used as an integral part of an institution's change strategy. This kind of leadership would be difficult if not impossible to achieve from inside the faculty structure. This sets academic development departments apart from other academic departments.

So again in the organization of academic development we see its 'Janus' face. On the one hand is the need to be an academic department, organized like any other. On the other hand, there is a need for independence and a cross-institution view. This is a further tension developers have to live with.

Conclusion

In gazing into my metaphorical crystal ball in this chapter I have argued that in order to be credible as agents for change in a higher and tertiary education context where the boundaries between research and teaching are breaking down, developers are having to take research and scholarship seriously and become credible as researchers and facilitators of research on teaching. I have suggested that as teaching becomes increasingly viewed as a process of developing academic professionalism and the skills of inquiry in students so that they can cope with a world of complexity, developers need to work towards integrating their own research and teaching. As managers' hunger for data grows, developers must acquire the skills needed to respond quickly and effectively. Individual's research projects need to be developed with an eye to these demands. In addition, they need to do research which is useful in academic development work and should be using research in development activities. Developers have also to be mindful of ways in which what we know about good teaching can inform the research process; encourage researchers and their students focus on the processes of research and help them to develop new forms and conceptions of research.

Many developers may feel that the kinds of research and scholarship which this book has discussed, is not the kind of research which is rewarded in our institutions. For example, the idea that what is needed for promotion is evidence of single-minded attention over many years to one particular, perhaps narrow, subject of study on which one has made a reputation, does not sit easily with the eclectic careers of many developers who, of necessity, have had to range over a broad range of issues in higher education teaching and learning. Developers' research has to have one eye on the needs of the institution and the other on their own need to develop a coherent research track record while at the same time pushing the boundaries of what research can be within an academic development context.

Developers will continue the tussle between getting on with practice and engaging in the development of theory and the carrying out of empirical research work. They will continue to struggle with the Janus face of academic development as it looks at the institutions in which it is situated. Their research may perform strategic or developmental functions, it may function to illuminate or provide exemplars of practice. It may perform a recursive function, feeding back into academic development practice, or it may endeavour to go beyond current practice performing an emancipatory function. Academic developers have to balance the concerns and considerations of different groups within the higher education spectrum. An increasingly important and troublesome aspect of academic development practice in the future is that not only should it be based on research, but that the nature and use of that research extends beyond its immediate professional context.

The extent to which it is successful will depend on the levels of trust in the profession exhibited by senior managers and those who make decisions about its future.

However, we have seen in this chapter that the changing demands in society are requiring students to acquire research skills needed in their future employment and their lives. This, together with the growing importance of inquiry in higher education and the move to bring teaching and research closer together all place inquiry centre stage in higher education. Developers are re-thinking their relationship to research and its role in teaching and learning. The research that developers do is likely to challenge critically their own assumptions about teaching and learning. Critical challenge means changing and being prepared to change conceptions and world views, sometimes so radically that the ways we have seen teaching and learning and staff development before, are completely overturned (Brew 1993). Further, through the research developers do, there is a need to be ready to push the boundaries of what we understand research to be.

There is an enormous amount of work to be done.

References

Andresen, L. (1996) The work of academic development – occupational identity, standards of practice and the virtues of association, *International Journal for Academic Development*, 1(1): 38–49.

Andresen, L. (2000a) A useable, trans-disciplinary conception of scholarship, *Higher Education Research and Development*, 19(2): 137–54.

Andresen, L. (2000b) Teaching development in higher education as scholarly practice: a reply to Rowland *et al.* 'Turning Academics into Teachers', *Teaching in Higher Education*, (1): 23–31.

Ashworth, P.D. and Lucas, U. (2000) Achieving empathy and engagement: a practical approach to the design, conduct and reporting of phenomenographic research, *Studies in Higher Education*, 25: 295–308.

Ashworth, P.D. (1999) 'Bracketing' in phenomenology: renouncing assumptions in hearing about student cheating, *International Journal of Qualitative Studies in Education*, 12: 707–22.

Ashworth, P.D., Bannister, P. and Thorne, P. (with members of the MA Policy and Professional Studies programme) (1997) Guilty in whose eyes? University students' perception of cheating and plagiarism, *Studies in Higher Education*, 22: 187–203.

Badley, G. (2000) Towards a pragmatic scholarship of academic development, paper presented at the 3rd International Conference of the International Consortium for Educational Development, Bielefeld, Germany.

Badley, G. (2001) Towards a pragmatic scholarship of academic development, *Quality Assurance in Education*, 9(3): 162–70.

Bain, K. (1999) What the Best Teachers Do. Unpublished manuscript. New York: NYU.

Ballantyne, R., Bain, J.D. and Packer, J. (1999) Researching university teaching in Australia: themes and issues in academic's reflections, *Studies in Higher Education*, 24: 237–57.

Barnett, R. (1990) *The Idea of Higher Education*. Buckingham: SRHE and Open University Press.

Barnett, R. (1994) *The Limits of Competence*. Buckingham: SRHE and Open University Press.

Barnett, R. (1997) *Higher Education: A Critical Business*. Buckingham: SRHE and Open University Press.

Barnett, R. (2000) *Realizing the University: in an age of supercomplexity*. Buckingham: SRHE and Open University Press.

Barnett, R. and Griffin, A. (1997) (eds) *The End of Knowledge in Higher Education.* London: Cassell.

Barrie, S., Brew, A. and McCulloch, M. (1999) Qualitatively Different Conceptions of Assessment Criteria. Paper presented at the AARE–NZARE Conference on Research in Education.

Bass, R. (1998) The scholarship of teaching: what's the problem?, *Inventio,* 1998–99, online journal at www.doiiit.gmu.edu/archives/feb98/randybass.htm.

Baume, D. and Baume, C. (1994) Staff and educational development: a discussion paper, *SEDA Newsletter,* 2 (March): 6–9.

Baume, D. (1996) Editorial, *International Journal for Academic Development,* 1(1): 3–5.

Beard, R. and Hartley, J. (1984) *Teaching and Learning in Higher Education,* 4th edn. London: Harper & Row.

Beaty, E., France, L. and Gardiner, P. (1997) Consultancy style action research: a constructive triangle, *International Journal for Academic Development,* 2(2): 83–8.

Beaty, L. (1995) Staff development across the hierarchy, in A. Brew (ed.), *Approaches to Staff Development in Higher Education.* Buckingham: SRHE and Open University Press.

Becher, T. (1989) *Academic Tribes and Territories: Intellectual enquiry and the cultures of disciplines.* Buckingham: SRHE and Open University Press.

Becher, T. and Trowler, P.R. (2001) *Academic Tribes and Territories,* 2nd edn. Buckingham: SRHE and Open University Press.

Bennett, J.B. (1998) *Collegial Professionalism: The Academy, Individualism, and the Common Good.* Arizona: Oryx Press.

Berkeley, G. (1734) A Treatise Concerning the Principles of Human Knowledge, in *Philosophical Works* (1975). London: Dent.

Biggs, J. (1999) *Teaching for Quality Learning at University: What the Student Does.* Buckingham: SRHE and Open University Press.

Bligh, D. (1998) *What's the Use of Lectures?,* 5th edn. Exeter: Intellect.

Booth, C. (1998) *Accreditation and Teaching in Higher Education.* London: Committee of Vice-Chancellors and Principals of the Universities of the United Kingdom.

Boud, D. (1999) Situating academic development in professional work: using peer learning, *International Journal of Academic Development,* 4(1): 3–10.

Bourner, T., O'Hara, S. and France, L. (2000) Practitioner-centred research, in T. Bourner, T. Katz and D. Watson (eds), *New Directions in Professional Higher Education.* Buckingham: SRHE and Open University Press.

Bowden, J. and Marton, F. (1998) *The University of Learning: Beyond Quality and Competence in Higher Education.* London: Kogan Page.

Boyer Commission (1998) *Reinventing Undergraduate Education: A Blueprint for America's Research Universities.* Stoneybrook: State University of New York.

Boyer, E.L. (1990a) *Scholarship Reconsidered: Priorities of the Professorate.* San Francisco: The Carnegie Foundation for the Advancement of Teaching, Jossey-Bass.

Boyer, E.L. (1990b) *Scholarship Revisited.* Princeton, N.J.: Carnegie Foundation for the Advancement of Teaching.

Boyer, E. (1994) Scholarship reconsidered: priorities for a new century, in G. Rigby (ed.), *Universities in the Twenty-First Century,* pp. 110–24. London: National Commission on Education.

Brew, A. (1993) Unlearning through experience, in D. Boud, R. Cohen and D. Walker, *Using Experience for Learning*, pp. 87–98. Buckingham: SRHE and Open University Press.

Brew, A. (ed.) (1995) *Directions in Staff Development*. Buckingham: SRHE and Open University Press.

Brew, A. (2001) *The Nature of Research: Inquiry in Academic Contexts*. London: RoutledgeFalmer.

Briggs, D., Parker-Jenkins, M. and Taylor-Basil, V. (2000) A whole department gets involved in research at Derby, *Research Intelligence*, 72 (June): 18–19.

Brown, J.S. (2000) Growing up digital – how the web changes work, education and the ways people learn, *Change*, 32: 11–47.

Browne, M. and Freeman, K. (2000) Distinguishing features of critical thinking classrooms, *Teaching in Higher Education*, 5(3): 301–10.

Bruner, J.S. (1986) *Actual Minds, Possible Worlds*. Cambridge, MA: Harvard University Press.

Bruner, J. (1996) *The Culture of Education*. London: Harvard University Press.

Camblin, L.D. and Steger, J.A. (2000) Rethinking faculty development, *Higher Education*, 39: 1–18.

Cambridge, B. (1999) The scholarship of teaching and learning: questions and answers from the field, *American Association of Higher Education*, 52: 7–10.

Candy, P. (1996) Promoting lifelong learning: academic developers and the university as a learning organisation, *International Journal for Academic Development*, 1(1): 7–19.

Caplan, N. (1974) *Social Sciences Knowledge Utilization by Federal Executives*. Houghton, MI: University of Michigan.

Carr, W. and Kemmis, S. (1983) *Becoming Critical: Knowing Through Action Research*. Victoria: Deakin University Press.

Carr, W. and Kemmis, S. (1986) *Becoming Critical: Education, Knowledge and Action Research*. London and Philadelphia: The Falmer Press.

Castells, M. (2001) The New Global Economy, in J. Muller, N. Cloete and S. Badat (eds), *Challenges of Globalization*. Cape Town: Maskew Miller Longman.

Chaiklin, S. and Lave, J. (eds) (1993) *Understanding Practice: Perspectives on Activity and Context*. Cambridge: Cambridge University Press.

Chelimsky, E. (1995) Politics, policy and research synthesis, *Evaluation*, 1: 97–104.

Clark, B.R. (1997) The modern integration of research activities with teaching and learning, *Journal of Higher Education*, 21(1): 31–42.

Clark, G., Healey, M., Jenkins, A., *et al.* (2002) Developing new lectures: the case of a discipline-based workshop, *Active Learning in Higher Education*, 3(2): 128–44.

Coffey, M. and Gibbs, G. (2000a) Can academics benefit from training: some preliminary findings, *Teaching in Higher Education*, 5(3): 385–9.

Coffey, M. and Gibbs, G. (2000b) The evaluation of the Student Evaluation of Educational Quality Questionnaire (SEEQ) in UK higher education, *Assessment and Evaluation in Higher Education*, 26(1): 89–93.

Coffey, M. and Gibbs, G. (2001) The strategic goals of training of university teachers, in C. Rust (ed.), *Improving Student Learning Strategically*. Oxford: Oxford Centre for Staff and Learning Development.

Coffey, M. and Gibbs, G. (under review) Measuring teachers' repertoire of teaching methods, *Assessment and Evaluation in Higher Education*.

Cousin, G. (2000) Strengthening action-research for educational development, *Educational Developments*, 1.3 August: 5–7.

Coventry University (1997) *Towards a Teaching and Learning Strategy*, Internal committee paper.

Cronbach, L.J., Ambron, S.A., Dornbusch, S.A. *et al.* (1980) *Towards Reform of Program Evaluation.* San Francisco and London: Jossey-Bass.

D'Andrea, V. and Gosling, D. (2001) Joining the dots: reconceptualizing educational development, *Active Learning in Higher Education*, 2(1): 64–80.

Dalgaard, K.A. (1982) Some effects of training on teaching effectiveness of untrained university teaching assistants, *Research in Higher Education*, 17(1): 39–50.

Dearing, R. (1997) Higher Education in the Learning Society, Main Report. The National Committee of Inquiry into Higher Education. London: The Stationery Office.

Derrida, J. (1978) *Writing and Difference* (tr. A. Bass). London and Henley: Routledge & Kegan Paul.

Dickens, L. and Watkins, K. (1999) Action research: rethinking Lewin, *Management Learning*, 30(2): 127–40.

Donald, J.G. (2002) *Learning to Think: Disciplinary Perspectives.* San Francisco: Jossey-Bass.

Elliott, J. (1987) Teachers as Researchers, in J. Dunkin (ed.), *The International Encyclopedia of Teaching and Teacher Training.* Sydney: Pergamon.

Elton, L. (1993) *Managing Change in Universities.* London: Committee of Vice-Chancellors and Principals.

Elton, L. (1995) Effect of Funding Council policies on teaching quality, in B. Smith and S. Brown (eds), *Research, Teaching and Learning in Higher Education*, pp. 40–8. London: Kogan Page.

Elton, L. (2001) Research and Teaching: Conditions for a positive link, *Teaching in Higher Education*, 6: 43–56.

Entwistle, N. (1992) *The Impact of Teaching on Learning Outcomes in Higher Education: A Literature Review.* Sheffield: Committee of Vice-Chancellors and Principals of the Universities of the United Kingdom, Universities' and Colleges' Staff Development Unit.

Entwistle, N. (1997) Contrasting Perspectives on Learning, in F. Marton, D. Hounsell and N. Entwistle (eds), *The Experience of Learning.* Edinburgh: Scottish Academic Press.

Eraut, M. (1995) Outcomes and Professional Knowledge, in J. Burke (ed.), *Outcomes, Learning and the Curriculum*, pp. 260–72. London: Falmer Press.

Feyerabend, P.K. (1970) Against method: outline of an anarchistic theory of knowledge, in M. Radner and S. Winokur (eds), *Minnesota Studies in the Philosophy of Science*, Vol. 4. Minnesota: University of Minnesota Press.

Flowers, S., O'Hara, S. and Reeve, S. (1997) The Impact of 'Hi-fidelity' Case Work on Organisational Learning. Published conference proceedings: *Universities as Learning Organisations*, Nottingham Trent University/Higher Education for Capability, February 1997.

Foucault, M. (1970) *The Order of Things: An Archaeology of the Human Sciences*, translation Alan Sheridan. New York: Vintage.

Foucault, M. (1979) *Discipline and Punish: the Birth of the Prison.* Harmondsworth, UK: Peregrine Books.

Franklyn-Stokes, A. and Newstead, S.E. (1995) Cheating: Who does what and why?, *Studies in Higher Education*, 20: 159–72.

Fraser, K. (2001) Australasian academic developers' conceptions of the profession, *International Journal of Academic Development*, 6: 54–64.

Freire, P. (1972) *The Pedagogy of the Oppressed*. Harmondsworth: Penguin.
Fullan, M. (1993) *Changing Force: Probing the Depths of Educational Reform*. London: Falmer Press.
Fuller, A., Jones, L., Maguire, M. and Pugh, V. (1994) *Dissemination of Best Practice with Regard to Effective Learning*, CLMS Report for the Employment Department, University of Leicester.
Furlong, J. (2000) Intuition and the crisis in teacher professionalism, in T. Atkinson and G. Claxton (2000) (eds), *The Intuitive Practitioner – On the Value of Not Always Knowing What One is Doing*. Buckingham: Open University Press.
Gibbons, M. (1999) Changing research practices, in J. Brennan *et al.* (eds), *What Kind of University? International Perspectives on Knowledge, Participation and Governance*. Buckingham: SRHE and Open University Press.
Gibbons, M., *et al.* (1994) *The New Production of Knowledge: The Dynamics of Science and Research in Contemporary Societies*. London: Sage.
Gibbons, M., Limoges, C., Nowotny, H. *et al.* (1994) *The New Production of Knowledge: The Dynamics of Science and Research in Contemporary Societies*. London: Sage.
Gibbs, G. (1999) *Institutional Learning and Teaching Strategies: A Guide to Good Practice* (Report 99/55). Bristol: HEFCE.
Gibbs, G. (2000) Are the pedagogies of the discipline really different?, in C. Rust (ed.), *Proceedings of the 1999 7th International Symposium Improving Student Learning: Improving Student Learning Through the Disciplines*, pp. 41–51. Oxford: Oxford Centre for Staff and Learning Development, Oxford Brookes University.
Gibbs, G. (2001) *Improving university teaching*. Inaugural Lecture. The Open University, October.
Gibbs, G. and Coffey, M. (2001) The impact of training on university teachers' approaches to teaching and on the way their students learn. Paper presented at the 9th Conference of the *European Association for Research in Learning and Instruction*, Fribourg, September.
Gibbs, G. and Coffey, M. (in press) New teachers' approaches to teaching and the utility of the ATI, *Higher Education Research and Development*.
Gibbs, G., Habeshaw, T. and Habeshaw, S. (1984–1988) *53 Interesting Things . . . Series*. Bristol: Technical and Educational Services.
Gibbs, G., Habeshaw, T. and Yorke, M. (2000) Institutional learning and teaching strategies in English higher education, *Higher Education*, 40: 351–72.
Gibson, S. and Dembo, M. (1984) Teacher efficacy: A construct validation, *Journal of Educational Psychology*, 76: 569–82.
Giertz, B. (1996) Long-term effects of a programme for teacher training, *International Journal for Academic Development*, 1(2): 67–72.
Gilbert, A. and Gibbs, G. (1999) A proposal for an international collaborative research programme to identify the impact of initial training on university teachers, *Research and Development in Higher Education*, 21: 131–43.
Glassick, C.E., Huber, M.T. and Maeroff, G.L. (1997) *Scholarship Assessed: Evaluation of the Professoriate*. San Francisco: Jossey-Bass Publishers.
Goldman, C.A., Gates, S.M. and Brewer, D.J. (2001) *In Pursuit of Prestige: Strategy and Competition in U.S. Higher Education*. Somerset, NJ: Transaction Publishers.
Gosling, D. (1997) Educational Development and Institutional Change in Higher Education, in K. Moti Gokulsing and C. DaCosta (eds), *Usable Knowledges as the Goal of University Education*. London: Edwin Mellen Press.
Gosling, D. (2000a) Using Habermas to evaluate two approaches to negotiated assessment, *Assessment and Evaluation in Higher Education*, 25(3): 293–304.

Gosling, D. W. (2000b) Conceptual issues in higher education, in C. Rust (ed.), *Improving Student Learning Through the Disciplines*. Oxford: Oxford Brookes University.

Gosling, D. (2001) Educational development units in the UK – what are they doing five years on? *International Journal for Academic Development*, 6(1): 74–90.

Gravestock, P. and Healey, M. (1998) *Guides to Good Teaching, Learning and Assessment in Geography*. Cheltenham: Cheltenham and Gloucester College of Higher Education, Geography Discipline Network.

Gravestock, P. and Healey, M. (2000) *Guides to Key Skills in Geography in Higher Education*. Cheltenham: Cheltenham and Gloucester College of Higher Education, Geography Discipline Network.

Gravestock, P. and Healey, M. (2001) *Guides to Providing Learning Support for Disabled Students Undertaking Fieldwork and Related Activities*. Cheltenham: Cheltenham and Gloucester College of Higher Education, Geography Discipline Network. http://www.chelt.ac.uk/gdn/disabil/.

Guba, E.G. and Lincoln, Y.S. (1994) Competing paradigms in qualitative research, in N.K. Denzin and Y.S. Lincoln, *Handbook of Qualitative Research*, pp. 105–17. California: Sage Publications.

Habermas, J. (1971) *Knowledge and Human Interests*. Boston: Beacon Press.

Habermas, J. (1984) *The Theory of Communicative Action*, Vol. 1, (tr. T. McCarthy). London: Heinemann.

Handy, C. (1989) *The Age of Unreason*. London: Business Books Ltd.

Hart, E. and Bond, M. (1995) *Action-Research for Health and Social Care: A Guide to Practice*. Buckingham: Open University Press.

Hativa, N. and Marincovich, M. (eds) (1995) *Disciplinary Differences in Teaching and Learning: Implications for Practice*. San Francisco: Jossey-Bass.

Hawkins, P. and Winter, J. (1997) *Mastering Change*. London: DfEE.

Healey, M. (1998) Developing and disseminating good educational practice: lessons from geography in higher education. http://www.chelt.ac.uk/gdn/confpubl/iced.htm

Healey, M. (2000) Developing the scholarship of teaching in higher education: a discipline-based approach, *Higher Education Research and Development*, 19(2): 169–87.

Healey, M. (2001) Developing learning partnerships through the disciplines, *Research and Development in Higher Education*, 24: 42–50. http://www.chelt.ac.uk/gdn/confpubl/herdsa_01.htm.

Healey, M. (2002) The scholarship of teaching: issues around an evolving concept, *Journal on Excellence in College Teaching* (in press).

Healey, M., Jenkins, A. and Kneale, P. (2000) Small worlds on an interconnected planet: teaching and learning geography in higher education, in C. Rust (ed.), *Proceedings of the 1999 7th International Symposium Improving Student Learning: Improving Student Learning Through the Disciplines* (125–34). Oxford: Oxford Centre for Staff and Learning Development, Oxford Brookes University.

HEFCE (1995) *Fund for the Development of Teaching and Learning* [Circular 29/95]. Bristol: Higher Education Funding Council for England.

HEFCE (1998) *Learning and Teaching: Strategy and Funding Proposals*, Consultation 98/40.

HEFCE (1999) *Learning and Teaching: Strategy and Funding* (Report 99/26). Bristol: Higher Education Funding Council for England.

HEFCE (2000a) *Performance Indicators in Higher Education, 1997–98, 1998–99* (Report 00/40). Bristol: Higher Education Funding Council for England.

HEFCE (2000b) *Review of Research* (Report 00/37). Bristol: Higher Education Funding Council for England.

HEFCE (2000c) *Review of Research 00/37.* Bristol: HEFCE.

HEFCE (2001a) *Strategies for Learning and Teaching in Higher Education* (Report 01/37). Bristol: Higher Education Funding Council for England.

HEFCE (2001b) *Analysis of Strategies for Learning and Teaching* (Report 01/37a). Bristol: Higher Education Funding Council for England.

HEFCE (2001c) *Invitation to Bid for Funds under Phase Four of the Fund for the Development of Teaching and Learning* (Invitation 01/60). Bristol: HEFCE.

Heidegger, M. (1962) *Being and Time.* Oxford: Basil Blackwell.

Heller, F. (1986a) Conclusions, in F. Heller (ed.), *The Use and Abuse of Social Science.* London: Sage Publications.

Heller, F. (1986b) Introduction and overview, in F. Heller (ed.), *The Use and Abuse of Social Science.* London: Sage Publications.

Hillage, J., Pearson, R., Anderson, A. and Tamkin, P. (1998) *Excellence in research on schools* (DfEE Research Report RR74). Norwich: The Stationery Office.

Hirst, P. (1996) The demands of professional practice and preparation for teaching, in J. Furlong and R. Smith (eds), *The Role of Higher Education in Initial Teacher Training.* London: Kogan Page.

Ho, A. (1998a) Changing teachers' conceptions of teaching as an approach to enhancing teaching and learning in tertiary education. Unpublished PhD thesis, The University of Hong Kong.

Ho, A. (1998b) An example of a conceptual change approach to staff development. Supporting Educational, Faculty and TA Development within Departments and Disciplines, International Consortium for Educational Development in Higher Education Conference, Austin, Texas, USA.

Ho, A.S.P. (2000) A conceptual change approach to staff development: a model for programme design, *International Journal of Academic Development,* 5: 30–41.

Ho, A., Watkins, D. and Kelly, M. (2001) The conceptual change approach to improving teaching and learning: An evaluation of a Hong Kong staff development programme, *Higher Education,* 42: 143–69.

Hollis, M. (1994) *The Philosophy of Social Science – An Introduction.* Cambridge: Cambridge University Press.

Hounsell, D. (1994) Educational Development, in J. Bocock and D. Watson (eds), *Managing the University Curriculum: making common cause,* pp. 89–102. Buckingham: SRHE and Open University Press.

Huber, M.T. (2000) Disciplinary styles in the scholarship of teaching: reflections on The Carnegie Academy for Scholarship of Teaching and Learning, in C. Rust (ed.), *Proceedings of the 1999 7th International Symposium Improving Student Learning: Improving Student Learning Through the Disciplines,* pp. 20–31. Oxford: Oxford Centre for Staff and Learning Development, Oxford Brookes University.

Huber, M.T. (2001) Balancing acts: designing careers around the scholarship of teaching, *Change,* July–August: 21–9.

Huber, M.T. and Moreale, S.P. (eds) (2002) *Disciplinary Styles in the Scholarship of Teaching and Learning: Exploring Common Ground.* Washington, DC: The American Association for Higher Education.

Hume, D. (1739) *A Treatise of Human Nature.* Selby Bigge, L.A. (1949): Oxford University Press.

Husserl, E. (1931) *Ideas: General introduction to pure phenomenology*. London: Allen & Unwin.

Husserl, E. (1970) *The Crisis of European Sciences and Transcendental Phenomenology*. Evanston: Northwestern University Press.

Hussey, J. and Hussey, R. (1997) *Business Research: A Practical Guide for Undergraduate and Postgraduate Students*. Basingstoke: Macmillan.

Hutchings, P. and Shulman, L. (1999) The Scholarship of Teaching: new elaborations, new developments, *Change*, 31(5): 11–15.

Hutchings, P. and Shulman, L.S. (2000) The scholarship of teaching: new elaborations, new developments, in D. DeZure (ed.), *Learning from Change: Landmarks in Teaching and Learning in Higher Education from CHANGE Magazine 1969–1999*, pp. 423–37. Sterling, VA: Stylus Publishing, LLC, in association with AAHE.

Hutchins, E. (1993) Learning to navigate, in S. Chaiklin and J. Lave (1993) (eds), *Understanding Practice: Perspectives on Activity and Context*, pp. 35–63. Cambridge: Cambridge University Press.

Ilott, I. and Murphy, R. (1999) *Success and Failure in Professional Education*. London: Whurr Publications.

ILT (Institute for Learning and Teaching in Higher Education) (2001) *Accreditation of members: core knowledge*. http://www.ilt.ac.uk/accreditation/appendix1.html (accessed 1 September 2001).

Innovations Fund Project Briefing (2000) Dissemination Briefing No. 2 Prepared by the Innovations Team, Centre for Higher Education Practice, The Open University.

Isaacs, G. and Parker, R. (1996) Short courses, beyond and beside: what do newly appointed university teachers want? International Consortium for Educational Development Conference: *Preparing University Teachers*, Vasa, Finland.

Jenkins, A. (1995) The Research Assessment Exercise, funding and teaching quality, *Quality Assurance in Education*, 3: 4–12.

Jenkins, A. (1996) Discipline-based educational development, *The International Journal for Academic Development*, 1(1): 50–62.

Jenkins, A. (1997) Twenty-one volumes on: Is teaching valued in geography in higher education?, *Journal of Geography in Higher Education*, 21(1): 5–14.

Jenkins, A. (1998) *Curriculum Design in Geography*. Cheltenham: Cheltenham and Gloucester College of Higher Education, Geography Discipline Network.

Jenkins, A. (2001) Moving with the times: an oral history of a geography department, *Journal of Geography in Higher Education*, 25(2): 191–208.

Jenkins, A., Breen, R., Lindsay, R. and Brew, A. (2002) *Reshaping Teaching in Higher Education: Linking Teaching and Research*. London: Kogan Page and the Staff and Educational Development Association.

Jenkins, D., Cousin, G. and Bhanot, R. (2000) The literal and the metaphorical: some recent factual and figural accounts of Educational Development Units in british universities, *Educational Developments*, 1,4 (November).

JM Consulting Ltd, Centre for Higher Education Studies, Commonwealth Higher Education Management Service and Higher Education Consulting Group (2000) *Interactions Between Research, Teaching, and Other Academic Activities* (Final Report to the Higher Education Funding Council for England as part of the Fundamental Review of Research Policy and Funding). www.hefce.ac.uk/Research/review/sub/teach.pdf

Kember, D. (1997) A reconceptualisation of the research into university academics' conceptions of teaching, *Learning and Instruction*, 7: 255–75.

Kemmis, S. and McTaggart, R. (1988) *The Action Research Planner.* Victoria: Deakin University Press.

Kemmis, S. (1988) *The Action Research Reader.* Victoria: Deakin University Press.

Kolb, D.A. (1984) *Experiential Learning: Experience as the Source of Learning and Development.* Englewood Cliffs, N.J.: Prentice-Hall.

Krell, T.C. and Dobson, J.J. (1999) The use of magic in teaching organizational behaviour, *Journal of Management Education,* 23(1): 44–52.

Kugel, P. (1993) How professors develop as teachers, *Studies in Higher Education,* 18(3): 315–28.

Kuhn, T. (1970a) *The Structure of Scientific Revolutions,* International Encyclopedia of Unified Science, 2(2). Chicago: The University of Chicago Press.

Kuhn, T.S. (1970b) *Postscript to the Second Edition of The Structure of Scientific Revolutions,* pp. 174–210. Chicago: University of Chicago Press.

Land, R. (2001) Agency, context and change in academic development, *International Journal for Academic Development,* 6(1): 4–20.

Lave, J. and Wenger, E. (1991) *Situated learning: Legitimate peripheral participation.* Cambridge: Cambridge University Press.

Lave, J. and Wenger, E. (1993) *Situated Learning: Legitimate Peripheral Participation.* Cambridge: Cambridge University Press.

Lévy-Levoyer, C. (1986) Applying psychology or applied psychology, in F. Heller (ed.), *The Use and Abuse of Social Science.* London: Sage Publications.

Light, G. and Cox, R. (2001) *Learning and Teaching in Higher Education: The Reflective Professional.* London: Paul Chapman Publishing.

Lyotard, J.F. (1984) *The Postmodern Condition: A Report on Knowledge.* Manchester: Manchester University Press.

Macdonald, R. (2002) Educational development: research, evaluation and changing practice in higher education, in R. Macdonald and J. Wisdom (eds), *Academic and Educational Development: Research, evaluation and changing practice in Higher Education.* London: Kogan Page.

Malcolm, J. and Zukas, M. (2000) Becoming an educator: communities of practice in higher education, in I. McNay (ed.), *Higher Education and its Communities,* pp. 51–64. Buckingham: SRHE and Open University Press.

Mann, S.J. (1987) On knowing ourselves as learners and researcher, in J.T.E. Richardson, M.W. Eysenck and D. Warren Piper (eds), *Student Learning – Research in Education and Cognitive Psychology.* Milton Keynes: SRHE and Open University Press.

Marsh, H.W. (1982) SEEQ: a reliable, valid, and useful instrument for collecting students' evaluations of university teaching, *British Journal of Educational Psychology,* 52: 77–95.

Marsh, H.W. (1987) Students' evaluations of teaching: Research findings, methodological issues and directions for future research, *International Journal of Educational Research,* 11(3): 253–388.

Martin, E. (1999) *Changing Academic Work.* Buckingham: SRHE and Open University Press.

Martin, E. and Ramsden, P. (2000) Introduction. Special issue: scholarship of teaching, *Higher Education Research and Development,* 24(2): 163–77.

Martin, E., Benjamin, J., Prosser, M. and Trigwell, K. (1999) Scholarship of teaching: a study of the approaches of academic staff, in C. Rust (ed.), *Proceedings of the 1998 6th International Symposium Improving Student Learning: Improving Student Learning Outcomes,* pp. 326–31. Oxford: Oxford Centre for Staff and Learning Development, Oxford Brookes University.

Martin, E., Prosser, M., Trigwell, K., Ramsden, P. and Benjamin, J. (2000) What university teachers teach and how they teach it, *Instructional Science*, 28: 387–412.

Marton, F. (1975) What does it take to learn?, in N.J. Entwistle and D. Hounsell (eds), *How Students Learn*, pp. 125–38. Lancaster: Institute for Post-Compulsory Education.

Marton, F. (1981) Phenomenography: describing conceptions of the world around us, *Instructional Science*, 10: 177–200.

Marton, F. (1994) Phenomenography, in T. Husen and T.N. Postlethwaite (eds), *International Encyclopedia of Education*, Vol. 8, 2nd edn. London: Pergamon.

Marton, F. (1999) *Variatio est mater studiorum*, Opening address, 8th Conference for Research on Learning and Instruction (EARLI), Gothenburg, Sweden, August 24.

Marton, F., Beaty, E. and Dall'alba, G. (1993) Conceptions of Learning, *International Journal of Educational Research*, 19: 277–300.

Marton, F. and Booth, S. (1997) *Learning and Awareness*. New Jersey: Lawrence Erlbaum Associates.

Marton, F., Hounsell, D.J. and Entwistle, N.J. (1997) (eds) *The Experience of Learning*, 2nd edn. Edinburgh: Scottish Academic Press.

Marton, F. and Säljö, R. (1976) On qualitative differences in learning. I – Outcome and process, *British Journal of Educational Psychology*, 46: 4–11.

Marton, F. and Säljö, R. (1997) Approaches to learning, in F. Marton, D. Hounsell and N. Entwistle (eds), *The Experience of Learning: Implications for Teaching and Studying in Higher Education*, pp. 39–58. Edinburgh: Scottish Academic Press.

Marton, F. and Trigwell, K. (2000) Variatio est mater studorium, *Higher Education Research and Development*, 19: 381–95.

McDonald, B. and Walker, R. (1976) *Changing the Curriculum*. London: Open Books.

McGill, I. and Beaty, E. (2001) *Action Learning: A Guide for Management, Professional and Educational Development*, Revised 2nd edn. London: Kogan Page.

McKenzie, J. (2001) Variation in university teachers' accounts of changing teaching. Paper presented at the 9th European Conference of the European Association for Research in Learning and Instruction, Fribourg, Switzerland, September.

McNay, I. (1997) *The impact of the 1992 RAE on institutional and individual behaviour in English higher education: the evidence from a research project* (Report M 5/97). Bristol: HEFCE.

McNiff, J. (1988) *Action Research: Principles and Practice*. London: Routledge.

McNiff, J. (1993) *Teaching as Learning: An Action Research Approach*. London: Routledge.

Merleau-Ponty, M. (1962) *Phenomenology of Perception*. London: Routledge and Kegan Paul.

Mezirow, J. (1991) *Transformative Dimensions of Adult Learning*. San Fransisco: Jossey-Bass.

Mezirow, J. (1995) Transformation Theory in Adult Learning, in M.R. Welton, *In Defense of the Lifeworld: Critical Perspectives on Adult Learning*. New York: State University of New York Press.

Millar, R., Prosser, M. and Sefton, I. (1989) Relationship between approach and development in student learning, *Research and Development in Higher Education*, 11: 49–53.

Mollas-Gullart, J., Tang, P., Sinclair, T., Morrow, S. and Martin, B. (2000) *Assessing Research Impact on Non-Academic Audiences* SPRU. Report to the ESRC.

Mourad, R.P.J. (1997) *Postmodern Philosophical Critique and the Pursuit of Knowledge in Higher Education*. Westport, Conn.: Bergin & Garvey.

Murphy, R. (1996) Like a bridge over troubled water: realising the potential of educational research, *British Educational Research Journal*, 22: 3–15.

Murphy, R. (1998) Selecting and Supporting Effective Development Projects: A review of the 1997 HEED Development Prospectus Processes. Report to DfEE, Moorfoot.

Murray, H.G. (1983) Low inference classroom teaching behaviours and student ratings of college teaching effectiveness, *Journal of Educational Psychology*, 71: 856–65.

Murray, K. and Macdonald, R. (1997) The disjunction between lecturers' conceptions of teaching and their claimed educational practice. *Higher Education*, 33: 331–49.

Nasr, A., Gillett, M. and Booth, E. (1996) The relationship between university lecturers' qualifications in teaching and student ratings of their teaching performance. Paper presented at *ICED Preparing University Teachers Conference*, Vasa, Finland.

NCIHE (1997) *Higher education in the learning society* (Report of the National Committee of Inquiry into Higher Education). Norwich: The Stationery Office.

NERF (2000) *Research and Development for Education: A national strategy consultation paper*. London: National Educational Research Forum.

Neumann, R. (2001) Disciplinary differences and university teaching, *Studies in Higher Education*, 26: 135–46.

Nisbet, J. and Broadfoot, P. (1980) *The Impact of Research on Policy and Practice in Education*. Aberdeen: Aberdeen University Press.

Nowotny, H., Scott, P. and Gibbons, M. (2001) *Re-thinking Science: Knowledge and the Public in an Age of Uncertainty*. Cambridge: Polity Press.

Nyquist, J.D. and Wulff, D.H. (1996) *Working Effectively with Graduate Assistants*. Thousand Oaks, C.A.: Sage.

Nyquist, J.D. and Wulff, D.H. (1998) Disciplinary differences in preparing future college/university professors. Supporting Educational, Faculty and TA Development within Departments and Disciplines, International Consortium for Educational Development in Higher Education Conference, Austin, Texas, USA.

Otter, S. (1982) *Learning Outcomes in Higher Education: a development project report*. London: UDACE.

Outhwaite, W. (1987) *New Philosophies of Social Science – Realism, Hermeneutics and Critical Theory*. London: Macmillan Education.

Perkins, D. and Wilson, D. (forthcoming) Knowledge directions, *The Journal of the Institute for Knowledge Management*.

Phipps, A. (2001) Measuring performance: some alternative indicators, in M. Walker (ed.), *Reconstructing Professionalism in University Teaching*. Buckingham: SRHE and Open University Press.

Piccinin, S., Cristi, C. and McCoy, M. (1999) The impact of individual consultation on student ratings of teaching, *International Journal for Academic Development*, 4(2): 75–88.

Polkinghorne, D. (1983) *Methodology for the human sciences*. Albany: State University of New York Press.

Potter, J. and Wetherell, M. (1987) *Discourse and Social Psychology: Beyond Attitudes and Behaviour*. London: Sage.

Powell, J. (1980) The impact of research, *SCRE Research in Education Bulletin*, 25: 1–2.

Prosser, M. and Trigwell, K. (1997a) Perceptions of the teaching environment and its relationship to approaches to teaching, *British Journal of Educational Psychology*, 67: 25–35.

Prosser, M. and Trigwell, K. (1997b) Using phenomenography in the design of programs for teachers in higher education, *Higher Education Research and Development*, 16: 41–54.

Prosser, M. and Trigwell, K. (1998) Teaching in higher education, in B. Dart and G. Boulton-Lewis (eds), *Teaching and Learning in Higher Education*, pp. 250–68. Melbourne: Australian Council for Educational Research.

Prosser, M. and Trigwell, K. (1999) *Understanding Learning and Teaching: The Experience in Higher Education.* Buckingham: SRHE and Open University Press.

Quinlan, K.M. and Åkerlind, G.S. (2000) Factors affecting departmental peer collaboration for faculty development: Two cases in context, *Higher Education*, 40: 23–52.

Raelin, J.A. (1999) Preface to the Special Issue 'The Action Dimension in Management: Diverse Approaches to Research, Teaching and Development', *Management Learning*, 30(2): 115–25.

Ramsden, P. (1991) A performance indicator of teaching quality in higher education: the course experience questionnaire, *Studies in Higher Education*, 16: 129–50.

Ramsden, P. (1992) *Learning to Teach in Higher Education.* London: Routledge.

Ramsden, P. (1998) *Learning to Lead in Higher Education.* London: Routledge.

Rawls, J. (1972) *A Theory of Justice.* London: Oxford University Press.

Reichenbach, H. (1938) *Experience and Prediction.* Chicago: University of Chicago Press.

Revans, R. (1998) *ABC of Action Learning.* London: Lemos and Crane.

Revans, R.W. (1984) *The Sequence of Managerial Achievement.* Bradford: MCB University Press.

Rice, R.E. (1992) Towards a Broader Conception of Scholarship: The American context, in T.G. Whiston and R.L. Geiger (eds), *Research and Higher Education.* Buckingham: SRHE and Open University Press.

Robbins, H. and Finley, M. (1997) *Why Change Doesn't Work.* Princeton, NJ: Orion Business Books.

Roberts, D.M. and Toombs, R. (1993) A scale to assess perceptions of cheating in examination-related situations, *Educational and Psychological Measurement*, 53: 755–62.

Rogers, J. (2001) Personal communication.

Rorty, R. (1980) *Philosophy and the Mirror of Nature.* Oxford: Blackwell.

Rorty, R. (1982) *Contingency, Irony and Solidarity.* Cambridge: Cambridge University Press.

Rowland, S. (2000) *The Enquiring University Teacher.* Buckingham: SRHE and Open University Press.

Rowland, S. (2001) Surface learning about teaching in higher education: The need for more critical conversations, *International Journal of Academic Development*, 6(2): 162–7.

Rowland, S., Byron, C., Furedi, F., Padfield, N. and Smyth, T. (1998) Turning academics into teachers? *Teaching in Higher Education*, 3(2): 133–41.

Rudduck, J. and McIntyre, D. (eds) (1998) *Challenges for Educational Research.* London: Paul Chapman.

Runesson, U. and Marton, F. (in press) The space of learning, in F. Marton and A.B.M. Tsui (eds), *Classroom Discourse and the Space of Learning.*

Rust, C. (1999) The impact of educational development workshops on teachers' practice, *International Journal for Academic Development*, 3(1): 72–80.

Rust, C. (2000a) Do initial training courses have an impact on university teaching? The evidence from two evaluative studies of one course. International Consortium for Educational Development Conference, Bielefeld.

Rust, C. (ed.) (2000b) *Improving Student Learning Through the Disciplines: Proceedings of the 7th International Symposium.* Oxford: Oxford Centre for Staff and Learning Development, Oxford Brookes University.

Ryan, B. (2001) Letter to *The Times Higher Education Supplement,* No. 1502 (31 August): 15.

Ryle, G. (1967) *The Concept of Mind.* Harmondsworth: Penguin.

Schön, D. (1983a) *The Reflective Practitioner.* New York: Basic Books.

Schön, D.A. (1983b) *The Reflective Practitioner – How Professionals Think in Action.* London: Temple Smith.

Schreurs, M-L. (1998) The improvements of students' skills in a problem-based curriculum, in C. Rust (ed.), *Improving Students as Learners.* Oxford: Oxford Centre for Staff and Learning Development.

Scott, P. (1997) Changes in knowledge production and dissemination in the context of globalisation, in N. Cloete, J. Muller, M.W. Makgoba and D. Ekong, *Knowledge, Identity and Curriculum Transformation in Africa.* Cape Town: Maskew Miller Longman.

Scott, D. and Usher, R. (1999) *Research Education: Data, Methods and Theory in Educational Enquiry.* London: Cassell.

Seymour, E. and Hewitt, N.M. (1997) *Talking about Leaving: Why Undergraduates Leave the Sciences.* Oxford: Westview Press.

Shulman, L.S. (1993) Teaching as community property, *Change,* November/December: 6–7.

Shulman, L. (1998) 'Introduction' of *The Course Portfolio: How Faculty Can Examine Their Teaching to Advance Practice and Improve Student Learning,* Pat Hutchings (ed.), Washington, DC: American Association for Higher Education.

Shulman, L. (2000) Conclusion: Inventing the future, in P. Hutchings (ed.), *Opening Lines: Approaches to the Scholarship of Teaching and Learning.* San Francisco: The Carnegie Foundation for the Advancement of Teaching, Jossey-Bass Publishers.

Smart, J.C., Feldman, K.A. and Ethington, C.A. (2000) *Academic Disciplines: Holland's Theory and the Study of College Students and Faculty.* Nashville: Vanderbilt University Press.

Stark, J.S. and Lattuca, J.S. (1996) *Shaping the College Curriculum: Academic Plans in Action.* Boston: Allyn and Brown.

Stenhouse, L. (1979) 'Research as a basis for teaching', inaugural lecture, University of East Anglia, in L. Stenhouse (1983), *Authority, Education and Emancipation.* London: Heinemann Educational Books.

Stones, R. (1991) Strategic context analysis: a new research strategy for structuration theory, *Sociology,* 25(3): 673–95.

Stones, R. (1996) *Sociological Reasoning: Towards a Past-modern Sociology.* London: Macmillan.

Strauss, A. and Corbin, J. (1990) *Basics of Qualitative Research: Grounded Theory Procedures and Techniques.* Newbury Park, CA: Sage.

Task Group on Education Research (1999) *Report of the work of the RAE 2001 Task Group on Education Research.* www.niss.ac.uk/education/hefc/rae2001/edtaskgrp.html

Tooley, J. with Darby, D. (1998) *Educational Research: A Critique.* London: Office for Standards in Education.

Trigwell, K. (1995) Increasing faculty understanding of teaching, in A.W. Wright (ed.), *Successful Faculty Development Strategies*. Bolton: Anker Publishing Co.

Trigwell, K. (2002) Approaches to teaching design subjects: a quantitative analysis, *Journal of Art, Design and Communication in Higher Education*, 1.

Trigwell, K. and Prosser, M. (1996a) Congruence between intention and strategy in university science teachers' approaches to teaching, *Higher Education*, 32: 77–87.

Trigwell, K. and Prosser, M. (1996b) Changing approach to teaching: A relational perspective, *Studies in Higher Education*, 21: 275–84.

Trigwell, K., Prosser, M., Martin, E. and Ramsden, P. (2000) Discipline differences in relations between learning, teaching and ways of leading teaching departments, in C. Rust (ed.), *Improving Student Learning: Improving Student Learning Through the Disciplines*. Oxford: Oxford Centre for Staff Development, 502–1509.

Trigwell, K., Prosser, M., Ramsden, P. and Martin, E. (1999) Improving student learning through a focus on the teaching context, in C. Rust (ed.), *Improving Student Learning*, pp. 97–103. Oxford: Oxford Centre for Staff Development.

Trigwell, K., Prosser, M. and Taylor, P. (1994) Qualitative differences in approaches to teaching first year university science, *Higher Education*, 27: 75–84.

Trigwell, K., Prosser, M. and Waterhouse, F. (1999) Relations between teachers' approaches to teaching and students' approaches to learning, *Higher Education*, 37: 57–70.

Uljens, M. (1992) *Phenomenological Features of Phenomenography*. Goteborg: Department of Education and Educational Research, University of Goteborg.

Usher, R. and Edwards, R. (1994) *Postmodernism and Education*. London: Routledge.

van Manen, M. (1990) *Researching Lived Experience. Human Science for an Action Sensitive Pedagogy*. Albany: State University of New York Press.

van Rossum, E.J. and Schenk, S.M. (1984) The relationship between learning conception, study strategy and learning outcome, *British Journal of Educational Psychology*, 54: 73–83.

Watkins, C. and Mortimore, P. (1999) Pedagogy: What do we Know?, in P. Mortimore (ed.), *Understanding Pedagogy and its Impact on Learning*. London: Paul Chapman Publishing.

Webb, G. (1993) Announcing the death of development, again, in G. Ryan, P. Little and I. Dunn (eds), *Research and Development in Higher Education 16*, pp. 99–104. Higher Education Research and Development Society of Australasia, Campbelltown, NSW.

Webb, G. (1996a) *Understanding Staff Development*. Buckingham: SRHE and Open University Press.

Webb, G. (1996b) Theories of staff development: development and understanding, *International Journal for Academic Development*, 1(1): 63–9.

Webb, G. (1996c) Theories of staff development: progress and power, *International Journal for Academic Development*, 1(2): 59–66.

Webber, T. and O'Hara, S. (1997) Forming action learning sets in management education programs, *Action Learning and Action Research Journal*, 2(3): 21–33.

Weick, K.E. (1995) *Sensemaking in Organisations*. Thousand Oaks, CA: Sage Publications.

Weimer, M. and Lenze, L.F. (1997) Instructional interventions: a review of the literature on efforts to improve instruction, in R.P. Perry and J.C. Smart (eds), *Effective Teaching In Higher Education: Research and Practice*. New York: Agathon Press.

Weimer, M. (1993) The disciplinary journals of pedagogy, *Change*, November/December: 44–51.

Welton, M.R. (1995) In defense of the lifeworld: A Habermassian approach to adult learning, in M.R. Welton, *Defense of the Lifeworld: Critical Perspectives on Adult Learning.* New York: State University of New York Press.

Wenger, E. (1998) *Communities of Practice: Learning, Meaning and Identity.* Cambridge: Cambridge University Press.

Wright, A. and Miller, J.F. (2000) The Educational Developer's Portfolio, *International Journal for Academic Development,* 5(1): 20–9.

Yorke, M. (1999) *Leaving Early: Non-completion in Higher Education.* London: Falmer.

Yorke, M. (2000) A cloistered virtue? Pedagogical research and policy in UK higher education, *Higher Education Quarterly,* 54: 106–26.

Zamorski, B. (2000) Research-led teaching and learning in higher education, University of East Anglia, Norwich, UK.

Zuber-Skerrit, O. (1992a) *Professional Development in Higher Education: A Theoretical Framework for Action Research.* London: Kogan Page.

Zuber-Skerritt, O. (1992b) *Action Research in Higher Education: Examples and Reflections.* London: Kogan Page.

Index

The Society for Research into Higher Education

The Society for Research into Higher Education (SRHE) an international body, exists to stimulate and coordinate research into all aspects of higher education. It aims to improve the quality of higher education through the encouragement of debate and publication on issues of policy, on the organization and management of higher education institutions, and on the curriculum, teaching and learning methods.

The Society is entirely independent and receives no subsidies, although individual events often receive sponsorship from business or industry. The Society is financed through corporate and individual subscriptions and has members from many parts of the world. It is an NGO of UNESCO.

Under the imprint *SRHE & Open University Press*, the Society is a specialist publisher of research, having over 80 titles in print. In addition to *SRHE News*, the Society's newsletter, the Society publishes three journals: *Studies in Higher Education* (three issues a year), *Higher Education Quarterly* and *Research into Higher Education Abstracts* (three issues a year).

The Society runs frequent conferences, consultations, seminars and other events. The annual conference in December is organized at and with a higher education institution. There are a growing number of networks which focus on particular areas of interest, including:

Access
Assessment
Consultants
Curriculum Development
Eastern European
Educational Development Research
FE/HE
Funding
Graduate Employment
Learning Environment
Legal Education
Managing Innovation
New Technology for Learning
Postgraduate Issues
Quantitative Studies
Student Development
Qualifications Vocational

Benefits to members

Individual

- The opportunity to participate in the Society's networks
- Reduced rates for the annual conferences
- Free copies of *Research into Higher Education Abstracts*

- Reduced rates for *Studies in Higher Education*
- Reduced rates for *Higher Education Quarterly*
- Free copy of *Register of Members' Research Interests* – includes valuable reference material on research being pursued by the Society's members
- Free copy of occasional in-house publications, e.g. *The Thirtieth Anniversary Seminars Presented by the Vice-Presidents*
- Free copies of *SRHE News* which informs members of the Society's activities and provides a calendar of events, with additional material provided in regular mailings
- A 35 per cent discount on all SRHE/Open University Press books
- The opportunity for you to apply for the annual research grants
- Inclusion of your research in the *Register of Members' Research Interests*

Corporate

- Reduced rates for the annual conferences
- The opportunity for members of the Institution to attend SRHE's network events at reduced rates
- Free copies of *Research into Higher Education Abstracts*
- Free copies of *Studies in Higher Education*
- Free copies of *Register of Members' Research Interests* – includes valuable reference material on research being pursued by the Society's members
- Free copy of occasional in-house publications
- Free copies of *SRHE News*
- A 35 per cent discount on all SRHE/Open University Press books
- The opportunity for members of the Institution to submit applications for the Society's research grants
- The opportunity to work with the Society and co-host conferences
- The opportunity to include in the *Register of Members' Research Interests* your Institution's research into aspects of higher education

Membership details: SRHE, 76 Portland Place, London W1B 1NT, UK Tel: 020 7637 2766. Fax: 020 7637 2781.
email: srhe@mailbox.ulcc.ac.uk
world wide web: http://www.srhe.ac.uk./srhe/
Catalogue: SRHE & Open University Press, Celtic Court, 22 Ballmoor, Buckingham MK18 1XW. Tel: 01280 823388. Fax: 01280 823233. email: enquiries@openup.co.uk

WOMEN AS LEADERS AND MANAGERS IN HIGHER EDUCATION

Heather Eggins (ed.)

There are very few women who hold senior management positions in universities worldwide. This volume, written entirely by women, examines the problem and suggests ways in which it might be remedied. It contextualizes the situation by discussing management styles, the ethics of leadership, and the influence of career trends outside academia; and then presents a series of fascinating case studies based on interviews with, and the experience of, senior academic women. Finally, it considers the benefits of support mechanisms such as networking, work-shadowing and equal opportunities policies, and what is being done in other countries to improve matters.

This book will appeal to all who wish to see women's talents used to their full capacity, and to those whose particular interests or activities lie in management and leadership, women's studies and career development. Women who want to get on in higher education will find it particularly stimulating.

Contents

The Contributors
Jocelyn Barrow, Jennifer Bone, Helen Brown, Heather Eggins, Ruth Gee, Christine King, Robin Middlehurst, Janet Powney, Yvonne Sarch, Andrea Spurling, Karen Doyle Walton.

160pp 0 335 19879 1 (Paperback) 0 335 19880 5 (Hardback)

THE ENQUIRING UNIVERSITY TEACHER

Stephen Rowland

The Enquiring University Teacher is an engaging account of an approach to professional development in which one's own teaching is an exciting field of enquiry. It emphasizes the intrinsic interest of learning about university teaching with colleagues who bring their insights from different subject backgrounds and thereby provide a richer understanding of teaching and learning processes. The book explores the nature of the university teacher's enquiry: a form of professional learning which is both collaborative and personally reflective. It involves questioning personal and intellectual values and placing these at the centre of university teaching.

The book is deeply thoughtful yet accessible to academics from all disciplines who may have no specialist educational background. While it is suitable for the relatively new, as well as the more experienced university teacher, it encompasses a view of teaching and learning that challenges many common conceptions about university teaching and its relationship to disciplinary research.

Contents

144pp 0 335 20507 0 (Paperback) 0 335 20508 9 (Hardback)